Bear Attacks

Bear Attacks
Their Causes and Avoidance

STEPHEN HERRERO

Lyons & Burford, Publishers

Printed in the United States of America

20 19 18 17 16 15 14

Illustrations by Chuck Blyth

Library of Congress Cataloging in Publication Data

Herrero, Stephen.
  Bear attacks.

  Includes index.
    1. Bear attacks. 2. Brown bear. 3. Black bear.
I. Title.
QL737.C27H48   1985   613.6'8   85-165
ISBN 0-941130-87-8 (cl.)
ISBN 0-941130-82-7 (pbk.)

Contents

To Blaine, Martha, David, and Robin for their help and love. With thanks to each of the hundreds of people and agencies who not only made my book possible but made it a pleasure to write. Special thanks to those who reviewed and made editorial suggestions concerning the draft manuscript: Peter Burford, Gray Campbell, Dr. Fred Dean, Bev Diamond, Dr. Richard Knight, Cliff Martinka, Martha McCallum, Wayne McCrory, Dr. Lynn Rogers, Richard Russell, Barney Smith, Linda Sutterlin, Dr. Dixon Thompson, and David and Robin Wensley-Hamer. I also thank the following agencies for financial support: Canadian National Sportsman's Fund; National Science and Engineering Research Council of Canada; Alberta Recreation, Parks and Wildlife Foundation; The University of Calgary; and the Killam Foundation.

Thanks to Alaska Northwest Publishing Company, Anchorage, for permission to quote extensively from Larry Kaniut's book, *Alaska Bear Tales*, 1983.

Introduction

IN June 1967, after finishing my Ph.D. at the University of California, Berkeley, I loaded my family into a Volkswagen bus and started traveling to a number of national parks. We visited Yosemite, Mount Rainier, Jasper, and Banff. Our next stop was to have been Glacier National Park, Montana. "There is no way we are going to Glacier Park," my wife stated firmly. She had a good reason: On August 13, 1967, two young women had been killed by different grizzly bears in separate parts of Glacier. We canceled our plans.

It seemed as though the grizzlies were on a rampage. Why? No one had been killed by a bear in Glacier National Park before these tragic deaths. The newspapers printed numerous theories to explain the deaths—dry weather and lightning storms had irritated the bears; the bears had been fed hallucinogenic drugs and had gone mad; one of the young women had been menstruating, and this had attracted the bear that killed her; grizzlies are always very dangerous and aggressive and this was "normal" for them. Many ideas, but were any true?

I was both horrified and puzzled by the Glacier Park deaths. Could the methods of science be used to reveal the causes of bear attacks? My Ph.D was in animal behavior, and so I thought that my parchment would probably help me get research money to investigate.

With these thoughts in my mind, our travels came to an end. We settled in Harvie Heights, a small, rural development adjacent to Banff National Park. We were surrounded by rugged limestone mountains and were close to bear country.

Grizzlies in subalpine meadow, Banff National Park.   *G.W. Vroom*

Thirteen years later, in September of 1980, I was autopsying a bear in Banff Park, searching for clues related to the cause of some of the most gruesome of the grizzly bear maulings I had studied since 1967. Before me and my co-worker, John Gunson, was the huge, dark, dead form of a 761-pound male grizzly bear, which we believed was responsible for the death of Ernest Cohoe, two serious injuries, and one minor injury.

These attacks had taken place over a period of eleven days on the outskirts of the town of Banff. The town's nearly five thousand residents, as well as tens of thousands of visitors, were living in fear as the attacks continued. As in 1967 in Glacier Park, the questions and speculations multiplied: Was this a bear on the rampage? What was it doing so close to Banff? Why did it attack? Would it attack again?

On Sunday afternoon, August 24, 1980, Cohoe and his friend Bob Muskett, accompanied by three boys, went fishing in some beaver ponds immediately north of Banff. After fishing, the party split into two groups, the boys returning to a train bridge by a game trail and the men aiming for the same place by cutting through dense brush in a bog.

At about 2:15 P.M., the men heard a crashing in the brush and then saw a bear very close and charging at them. The men shouted to the boys to run and then ran themselves. In their exictement each of the men ran in a different direction. The bear ran after Muskett, who only got about twenty feet before he fell down. The bear stopped, stood on its hind legs, looked at Muskett, but didn't injure him. The bear quickly dropped onto four legs and ran after and attacked Cohoe, who was still running. Within seconds the huge bear clasped its powerful jaws around Cohoe's face and bit. Cohoe screamed and within a minute or two the bear attacked twice more. Late the next morning an investigative team at the mauling site found fishing gear and the upper part of Cohoe's jaw and mouth with nine teeth, his nose, and a large piece of his cheek. About a week later Cohoe died from his injuries.

In this book I further describe the circumstances associated with the Banff and other maulings. My aim isn't to horrify, but to describe attacks sufficiently to characterize and explain them and to suggest how to minimize the chance of their occurrence.

After we captured and killed the grizzly, which we later positively linked to all attacks, we began looking for clues as to why the bear was so near Banff and why it attacked. In the park warden's garage, John Gunson and I began the autopsy. The grizzly had a healthy set of teeth and seemed to be a middle-aged bear (tooth sectioning later gave an age of ten). As we skinned the bear we were further impressed with its apparent health. Along the back and rump there was over four inches of fat. The autopsy and subsequent pathological work confirmed our impression. The bear was huge for its age (the largest bear on record at this age in either Banff or Jasper National Parks) and was in perfect health.

We were able to find important clues, however, that partially explained the reason for these maulings. Part of the reason was related to why I believe the two young women were attacked and killed by grizzly bears in Glacier National Park in 1967. The common thread binding these incidents was the history of feeding on garbage and people's foods by all three of these attacking bears. For some grizzly bears this is a specific circumstance that is related to attacks. In this book I describe how I think this relationship develops, and I also stress that this type of grizzly bear attack can be prevented.

There are seven living species of bears. This book deals with encounters in Canada and the United States between people and two of these species, the grizzly or brown bear (*Ursus arctos*), and the black bear (*Ursus americanus*). I use the term grizzly bear to refer not only to bears commonly known as grizzlies but also to bears usually called brown bears in portions of coastal Alaska. For clarity I have termed such bears "grizzly (brown)" bears in this book. (The common name of a bear does not necessarily refer to its color but rather serves to identify the species.) In Chapter 10 I describe different common names, coat colors, and other characteristics of grizzly and black bears.

It is important to be able to tell the species apart because the nature of encounters with each is different, as is what a person should do in response to aggression.

Throughout this book I've used the word *encounter* to refer to any aggressive meeting between people and bear. An encounter may or may not lead to injury. Often I refer to injurious encounters as attacks. Since 1967 I have tried to document and analyze all known encounters with accuracy. Only one major source of accurate records exists. These are the files of the national parks of Canada and of the United States where the bears live. I have had unrestricted access to these files.

The data on grizzly bear attacks in national parks include all recorded injuries between 1872, when the first national park, Yellowstone, was created, and 1980. During this period park personnel positively identified grizzly bears as being responsible for 111 incidents that resulted in 130 injuries. For various reasons this figure is a minimum estimate, but because park records are reasonably complete and accurate, I doubt that they underestimate the total by more than 25 percent. In this book I also discuss some incidents which have occurred between 1981 and 1984, but these were not included in my larger systematic data base.

In my research I've visited all, except one, of the national parks from Alaska to Wyoming that have grizzly bears. I've hiked thousands of miles of trails in grizzly country, examined mauling sites, and have talked with wardens, rangers, research biologists, and others about grizzly bear encounters. Whenever possible, I have interviewed victims of bear attacks. As my experience with bears grew and my research into the causes of injury became well known, I've been called on to investigate some maulings on site, to search for dangerous bears, and to sit on boards of inquiry to determine the circumstances associated with bear-inflicted deaths and major injuries. I've also served as an expert witness in trials where injured persons have tried to sue for damages.

In conducting further studies of grizzly bear attacks, I wrote to every non-national-park agency in North America that has management jurisdiction over grizzly bears. From these agencies I collected detailed information on attacks that occurred between 1960 and 1980. To a limited extent I supplemented these records with descriptions of attacks in books or articles for which I had cross-checks on the accuracy of the encounter descriptions. This yielded records of thirty-three incidents and thirty-five injuries inflicted by grizzly bears outside the national parks. Because of incomplete record keeping, these represent only a sample of these incidents.

Besides studying attacks by grizzly bears, I also analyzed 135 records of encounters in which neither a person nor a bear was injured. All but twelve of these cases occurred in national parks. All told, I analyzed 279 records of injurious and noninjurious encounters with grizzly bears.

Black bear encounters I treated differently. National park data only covered the period from 1960 to 1980. Over this twenty-year period, at least five hundred people were injured by black bears in the national parks, but most injuries were minor, requiring less than twenty-four hours of hospitalization. These injuries were easily understood from summary statistics kept by national parks and my knowledge of black bears. Therefore I relied on the national park analyses and entered only selected incidents into my data base. There were only three records of major injuries inflicted by black bears in three incidents in the national parks. Records related to black bear attacks outside national parks were collected for the period between 1960 and 1980 in the same manner as were records of grizzly bear attacks. I usually kept detailed records, however, only on black bear attacks that resulted in major injury or that revealed something new about black bears. Accurate records of deaths inflicted by black bears were recorded and analyzed as far back as 1900. All together I found and analyzed records of thirty-two major injuries (including deaths) inflicted by black bears outside national parks. A few attacks resulting in death occurred between 1980 and 1984. These weren't analyzed with my data, but are discussed.

I ended up with a total of 414 detailed records of interactions between people and grizzly or black bears through 1980. Of these, 357 incidents involved injury or aggression. In the rest the bear either ignored people, acted curiously, avoided people, or the behavior couldn't be classified. To analyze this number of incidents I put them into a standard format (though the amount of information often varied considerably from one incident to the next) and entered the data into a computer. The computer helped me to analyze the data and to pick out common circumstances associated with encounters.

Throughout this book I illustrate these circumstances by discussing specific incidents. They weren't picked without bias. I chose certain ones because they illustrated a point. Often I describe incidents that I investigated myself or in which I knew the persons involved and I believe that the details are accurate. I stress incidents that resulted in major injury or death because this is what people most want to avoid— and such cases may be remembered better than statistics.

When I began studying encounters with bears, I recognized that statistics left important questions unanswered. To achieve a better understanding of the behavior of bears in aggressive interactions with people, I realized that I would also have to study how they interacted with each other and with their environment. A seminal study of these issues was going on in Yellowstone Park, where Frank and John Craighead were finishing a long-term project on grizzly bear ecology.

I visited the Craighead research project in July 1968. One evening, at the Trout Creek Dump, I saw twenty-two grizzlies compressed into a feeding aggregation that occasionally erupted into bouts of roaring and flashes of teeth and claws. There was no doubt that this animal could be dangerous. John Craighead told me that they often saw as many as fifty grizzlies together at this dump. On some evenings up to seventy grizzlies would come to feed. Scarring and wounding was obvious, especially on the males. One bear had a J-shaped scar covering half its face. What if this power were focused on a person? I had new motivation for my work.

I was shocked by this large aggregation of bears. Weren't grizzlies normally supposed to be solitary, except for females with cubs? Why were all these grizzlies congregating, up to their ankles in garbage? Why were burned marshmallows and stale hot-dog buns so attractive to them? Couldn't we dispose of our garbage better? The grizzly is usually a part of the wilderness. What was going on in Yellowstone?

My research later showed that before 1970, over half of all grizzly bear-inflicted injuries to people in national parks occurred in Yellowstone.[1] Here grizzly bears not only routinely fed on garbage at open pit dumps but also foraged for garbage and people's foods in campgrounds. Many Yellowstone grizzlies had lost their natural wariness of people but retained their aggressive nature—a dangerous combination.

I knew this situation first hand because during 1968 and 1970 my family and I had camped in Yellowstone. While we were there grizzly bears prowled at night among tents and trailers searching for garbage or improperly stored food. If I had known then what I know now, we would have packed and left.

However, our home was Canada and while Yellowstone and Glacier Parks had grizzly bear problems that made headlines it looked to me as if we had the same potentially dangerous conditions in our Rocky Mountain national parks. I looked for an opportunity to study grizzly bear ecology in Canada to complement my continuing research on causes of human injuries.

In 1968 I proposed to study grizzly bear behavior and ecology in Banff National Park. My research proposal was politely turned down by the Canadian National Parks Branch (now Parks Canada) and the Canadian Wildlife Service. I was told that I did not have enough field experience with bears and that such work could be dangerous. In a few years, as I learned more about bear attacks, I came to appreciate the wisdom of their decision.

Research on grizzly bears can be dangerous. In 1973, Wilf Etherington, a Canadian Wildlife Service biologist, was involved in a grizzly bear study in Banff Park. Etherington was killed by a grizzly bear when he approached too close while filming.[2] Later, in 1977, Dr. Barrie Gilbert, a colleague of mine, was beginning a grizzly bear study in Yellowstone Park. During the first week of work Barrie and his assistant, Bruce Hastings, may have intercepted the travel route of a female grizzly with cubs, and Barrie subsequently confronted her at close range. Barrie's wounds required about a thousand stitches.[3] I was deeply saddened by each of these incidents, but they further motivated me to continue my research into causes of attacks and the nature of bears.

Despite these incidents I believed then, as I do today, that one's chances of being injured by a grizzly are small if proper precautions are taken. Examination of the circumstances of Etherington's mauling revealed that he made a serious mistake that led to his death. Barrie Gilbert knew that behavioral work with grizzly bears put him at risk.

After my research proposal to study grizzlies in Banff was rejected, I began field studies on black bears. This close relative of the grizzly is normally smaller and less aggressive. Important questions needed answering: why should one species be less aggressive than another? Should a person act differently if attacked by a black bear instead of a grizzly bear?

During the summer of 1968 John Courtney and I began a study of black bears in Jasper Park. We observed and analyzed 131 encounters between black bears, and every day we saw encounters between black bears and people, yet not one injury resulted.[4] These observations confirmed that the black bear was, for the most part, a tolerant animal capable of adjusting to human beings. Still, I discovered through other research that there were specific and rare circumstances in which black bears killed human beings. Why did these attacks occur and how did they fit with the image of the black bear as a moderately aggressive species?

The black bear work, and a subsequent study in the early 1970s of the fewer than one hundred European brown bears in Italy, gave me the experience I needed to undertake the grizzly bear study that I had first proposed in 1968.

In 1976 I and my graduate student David Hamer became project leaders for a study of grizzly bear ecology and behavior in Banff Park.[5] This work continued until 1980. We focused on how the grizzlies used their environment. Where did they feed and when? Why did they

Trapping and tagging grizzly bears, Banff National Park.   *Stephen Herrero*

choose certain foods over others? Where did grizzlies den? When and where did they mate? Our objective was to take this ecological information about Banff's grizzly bears and apply it in minimizing conflicts between grizzlies and people. We concluded that trails and campsites could be located so that chances of confronting a grizzly were decreased. Once grizzly bear habitat and its specific seasonal use was accurately described, this information could be used to reroute or periodically close certain trails or campsites to allow grizzlies to feed undisturbed and to decrease chances of encounters.

Requests for this type of research have increased. In 1980 we began a similar project in Kananaskis Country, Alberta,[6] and in 1981 in Waterton Lakes National Park, Alberta.[7] Today, locating hiking trails and campsites in grizzly country is one of my specialties.

During my research I have been fortunate not only to study bear maulings and ecology but also to live near bears. In the summer, when not involved with wildlife research, I live with my family on a small farm surrounded by mountains and woods in British Columbia. While writing this book, I have sometimes watched black bears out of our window or from our front porch. The subalpine meadow outside our kitchen window is called Grizzly Meadow because a grizzly bear sometimes is seen there. Through life at our summer home, I have come to know bears not just as a research scientist but also as a small-scale agriculturalist trying to protect my crops and animals from predation and as a parent who takes his family camping, hiking, fishing, and berry picking in bear country.

This book is the result of my seventeen years of studying black and grizzly bears and encounters between them and people. The first nine chapters describe encounters, suggest what to do if they happen, and how to minimize the chance of their happening. In order to do this you need to understand not only encounters but also bears and their management. Therefore Chapters 10 through 15 are about bears—their characteristics, what they eat, where they are most likely to be found, what field sign they leave, and how they behave. In Chapters 16 and 17, I discuss bear and people interactions in rural and remote areas and how to manage bears with human and bear safety in mind. I could have written several volumes on these topics but I have tried to include mainly information relevant to safety.

This book is for people who live, hike, camp, or work near bears, as well as those who are just curious about them. I write knowing that many people fear bears without understanding the danger. I can't allay all fears; I can reduce them and base them on reality.

I have written this book because I love bears and the wildlands where they live. Bears have fascinated me, scared me till my heart pounded, and inspired me to see my way to writing this book. They have helped me to learn about the diversity of life on earth and how nature works. Few biologists can study bears without seeing in them traits that are distinctly human. Such traits make people feel a strong attachment toward bears. Needless killing of bears elicits compassion and anger in me. We know how to do things better, how to make bear country safer for both bears and people. This book tells some ways to do this.

Grizzly (brown) bear cub of the year rubs up against its mother. McNeil River Falls, Alaska.   *Derek Stonorov*

1

Grizzly Bear Attacks

"**K**ILLER Grizzly Strikes Again." "Men Mauled by Grizzly." When a grizzly bear kills or injures someone the story often makes headlines. Grizzly bear maulings are unusual. They awaken a fear of the unknown and images of huge, dark beasts with powerful jaws and protruding fangs rushing at us while we walk along previously serene trails. The grizzly bear and the polar bear are the most dangerous wild land mammals in North America except for Man.

Some of the most interesting encounters are historical and have been omitted from my analysis. The first white explorer to see grizzly bears and to mention them in his journal was also the first to write of their danger to people. On August 20, 1691, Henry Kelsey, writing from somewhere near The Pas of present-day Manitoba, mentioned seeing "a great sort of bear. . . ."[1] In the rhymed introduction to his journal of 1691, he makes further reference to the power and potential danger of the species:

> And then you have beast of severall kind
> Another is an outgrown bear wch, is good meat
> His skin to gett I have used all e, ways I can
> He is mans food & he makes food of man
> His hide they would not me it preserve
> But said it was a god & they should starve

Kelsey is also the first Caucasian thought to have killed grizzlies. One day he and an Indian were surprised by two grizzlies. The Indian climbed a tree, and Kelsey moved in amid some high willows. The bears made directly for the tree, and Kelsey fired at and killed one

10

of them. The other ran toward Kelsey after hearing the shot but stopped and returned to the tree where the Indian clung. Kelsey reloaded his flintlock and killed the second bear. His actions so impressed the Indians that they named him Miss-top-ashish—Little Giant.

The records of subsequent expeditions into western North America, such as the Lewis and Clark expedition and John Palliser's explorations, are punctuated with accounts of encounters with grizzly bears. Both of these expeditions' logs mention people being killed by a grizzly bear.[2] Lewis reported:

> The Indians give a very formidable account of the streng(t)h and ferocity of this animal; which they never dare to attack but in parties of six, eight or ten persons; and are even then frequently defeated with the loss of one or more of their party . . . two Minetaries were killed last winter in an attack on a white (grizzly) bear. . . .[3]

Indian tribes had coexisted with the great bear for thousands of years. Most tribes respected or feared the grizzly and seldom hunted it. This was true even for the aggressive and warring Blackfoot Indians, the recent "Raiders of the Northwest Plains."[4] For them the grizzly was sacred, possessing great supernatural and physical power. Occasionally an adventurous young man might hunt it for its claws, which, if he was fortunate, he would proudly display as a necklace. More often Indians and grizzlies kept their distance.

Lewis and Clark encountered many grizzly bears in their explorations along the Missouri River from the Yellowstone to the Marias tributaries, in what is today Montana. The Indians of this region regarded killing a grizzly bear an important act of heroism—as important as killing and scalping an enemy or leading a successful war party.[5] On April 29, 1805, Lewis compared grizzly bears to black bears and commented on the Indians' fear of grizzlies. He wrote:

> It is a much more furious and formidable anamal [than the black bear], and will frequently pursue the hunter when wounded. It is astonishing to see the wounds they will bear before they can be put to death. The Indians may well fear this anamal equipped as they generally are with their bows and arrows and indifferent fuzees, but in the hands of skillful riflemen they are by no means as formidable or dangerous as they have been represented.[6]

By May 11, 1805, after Lewis had more experience with grizzlies, his regard for them seems to have increased: "these bear being so hard to die reather intimedates us all; I must confess that I do not like the gentlemen and had reather fight two Indians than one bear. . . ."[7]

As long as the Indian and the grizzly coexisted alone, neither had a serious advantage over the other. With the coming of the repeating rifle, the balance of power between grizzly and people shifted. Indians and whites alike, but especially white settlers and hunters, attacked the grizzly with a greater margin of safety, although not without danger. Hunting grizzlies was the manly thing to do in California during the mid- to late-1800s as this flamboyant account suggests:

> The risk was great, to be sure. I knew of several gentlemen in California who had been horribly mutilated by these ferocious animals. One had the side of his face torn off; another had one of his arms "chawed up," as he expressed it; a fourth had received eighteen wounds in a fight with one bear; and I know of various cases in which men had been otherwise crippled for life or killed on the spot. Hence the peculiar charm of a fight with a grizzly! If you kill your bear, it is a triumph worth enjoying; if you get killed yourself, some of the newspapers will give you a friendly notice; if you get crippled for life, you carry about you a patent of courage which may be useful in case you go into politics. . . . Besides, it has its effect upon the ladies. A "chawed" man is very much admired all over the world.[8]

Large, spring-loaded bear trap used in Alberta, Canada, in the 1950s.
Glenbow Archives, Alberta

But grizzly hunting did not last long in California. At one time there may have been ten thousand grizzlies in the "golden state,"[9] but by 1924 a road crew had the last reported sighting of the California grizzly.[10] Today the grizzly bear is only an image on the state flag, a reminder of wilder days gone by.

The grizzly suffered a similar fate throughout most of the contiguous United States and in the developed portions of Canada. Before the arrival of the white man, the grizzly's range extended west to the Pacific Ocean, east to the Missouri River, north to the Arctic Ocean and across to Hudson's Bay, and south to Chihuahua and Sonora in Mexico.[11] Within this range grizzlies were found wherever suitable habitat existed. Today both range and numbers have contracted to a fragment of what they were before western Europeans arrived.

We have clearly demonstrated our ability to eliminate the grizzly. Today we are faced with a task more difficult: to coexist with it.

But how do we coexist with the grizzly, which is strong enough to move several hundred pounds of granite boulder to catch a marmot and which occasionally uses this strength in attacks on people? Fortunately grizzlies seldom attack people on sight, and the aggression of the grizzly has been exaggerated because of a few serious attacks. Research clearly demonstrates that the normal response of grizzly bears is to avoid people and not to act aggressively or to attack, even if a person suddenly appears nearby.[12] If grizzly bears readily attacked people, then there would be far more injuries and I, for one, wouldn't care to try to coexist with them. The challenge of continued coexistence, however, does require that we accept some small chance of injury, and even death.

It's worthwhile to consider some statistics of grizzly bear-inflicted injuries before examining specific incidents. My search for accurate records of injuries inflicted by grizzly bears turned up records of 165 injuries inflicted in 143 incidents. Most of these records came from national parks where reasonably accurate records exist. Table 1 (p. 15) shows the number of injuries recorded for each park through 1979. The total of 165 injuries that I documented both in and out of parks is probably less than half of the injuries that have occurred throughout North America from 1900 to 1980. More incidents from outside national parks were not included in my analysis because many incidents, especially those from Alaska, were often only recorded in magazine stories where the truth may have suffered in the telling.

In 88 percent of the incidents (126 out of 143), only one person was injured, while in 8 percent (12 out of 143), two people were injured, and in 3 percent (5 out of 143), three people were injured.

Approximate historic and present grizzly bear range. Squares or dots represent single specimens. Current population estimates appear below.

Grizzly bear population estimates

PLACE	POPULATION ESTIMATE	SOURCE
Alberta	1200	Prov. est. and Herrero for Nat'l. Parks—1981
British Columbia	6500	Prov. est.—1978
Northwest Territories	4000–5000	Pearson—1977
Yukon	5000–8000	Territ. est.—1982
Alaska	> 15,000	State est. ca. 1975–'76
Montana, Wyoming, Idaho	< 1000	Schneider—1977
	Total pop. est. approx. 35,000	

TABLE 1
Number of grizzly bear injuries inflicted in the National Parks*
NUMBER OF INJURIES PER DECADE

	1900-1909	1910-1919	1920-1929	1930-1939	1940-1949	1950-1959	1960-1969	1970-1979	TOTAL NUMBER OF INJURIES UP TO 1979
Denali (formerly Mt. McKinley)					2		1	7	10
Glacier (Mont.)				1		1	12	10	24
Katmai									0
Yellowstone	1	1		6	10	1	24	13	56
Banff						3	1	7	11
Glacier, (B.C.)							1	6	7
Jasper							7	6	13
Kluane									0
Kootenay									0
Revelstoke									0
Waterton								1	1
Yoho				2	2				4
	1	1		9	14	5	46	50	126

*Only injuries definitely or very probably inflicted by grizzly bears are included.

I found no records of four or more people being injured in an attack. In each of these incidents except one, a single grizzly inflicted the injury. This was true despite the fact that the attacking bear may have been part of a family group or a pair of bears prior to inflicting injury. A look at the incidents in which more than one person was injured shows a disproportionate involvement of grizzly bear females with cubs. They inflicted injury in 71 percent (12 out of 17) of all such cases.

Small parties of one or two people were injured more often than were larger parties. Caution is needed in interpreting this fact because, at least in backcountry areas, small parties are the most common.[13] I believe, however, that there is greater safety in large parties. There were no attacks on parties of six persons or more. Small parties generally make less noise to alert a grizzly of their presence at a distance, and small parties are less intimidating to a grizzly.

The extent of injury suffered by people attacked by grizzly bears tells a lot about the character of the animal, if it attacks. Fifty percent of the injuries (82 out of 165) could be classed as major, requiring hospitalization for more than twenty-four hours or resulting in death. These included nineteen deaths and many cases requiring extensive hospitalization. In addition to the nineteen grizzly bear-inflicted deaths for which I have accurate accounts, Sgt. Robert Brown of the Alaska Department of Public Safety and Larry Kaniut have cursory records of an additional twenty-two deaths in Alaska.[14] This brings the total to a minimum of forty-one through 1980. The extent of injury that characterizes grizzly bear attacks contrasts dramatically with the typical black bear-inflicted injury, which is minor and usually involves only a few scratches or light bites.

Most grizzly bear-inflicted injuries for which I have records occurred during July, August, and September. From this I conclude that most injuries occur when numbers of outdoor recreationalists are highest, this being mainly during summer for hikers and campers and during the fall for hunters. I do not think that there is a particular time of year when grizzly bears are more dangerous; rather I believe the chances of an encounter increase with the number of people traveling in grizzly habitat. More people in the backcountry mean more injuries.[15]

Some people have suggested that grizzly bears are particularly dangerous during the mating period in spring.[16] Adult males are aggressive during this time of year, but there is no evidence that human injuries increase. At least one attack can be attributed to a mating pair.[17]

We all accept some element of risk as a part of daily life. That risk is not appreciably higher in bear country. During the 1970s the grizzly bear-inflicted injury rates in the most heavily visited national parks in the United States where grizzlies live were one injury per 1.3 million visitors in Glacier Park, Montana,[18] and one injury per 1.5 million visitors in Yellowstone.[19] Injury rates to backcountry visitors are higher. During the early 1970s they ranged from approximately one injury per 2620 backcountry use days in Mt. Revelstoke and Glacier National Parks in Canada to one injury per 59,300 backcountry use days in Yellowstone National Park.[20] Public opinion polls have shown that these low injury rates are acceptable to most park visitors.[21]

A basic circumstance associated with grizzly bear-inflicted injury is people and grizzly bears getting close to one another. Poorly located trails and campgrounds, people hunting moose, elk, or deer and not thinking about bears, or people trying to photograph a grizzly—these bring people unnecessarily close to grizzlies. Other factors, such as improperly stored food or garbage, attract grizzlies to people, again unnecessarily. Whatever brings them close to one another, danger is the outcome. In the next five chapters I examine circumstances associated with grizzly bear-inflicted injuries, as well as circumstances that could have led to injury but didn't.

2

Sudden Encounters With Grizzlies

HIKERS, hunters, or other persons traveling on foot in bear country may suddenly confront a grizzly. If this happens, a grizzly may attack because it perceives a threat. It follows that in these situations one should do everything possible to signal to the bear that you are not threatening. In this chapter I describe sudden encounter incidents and recommend the best course of action should you be attacked as a result of a sudden encounter. In Chapter 4 I describe the other main set of circumstances associated with grizzly bear attacks—when a grizzly is seeking human food or garbage, or, rarely, humans as food. The course of action I recommend for someone attacked under these circumstances is different.

A tragic sudden encounter occurred on the morning of July 27, 1976. Barbara Chapman, age twenty-four, was hiking in Glacier National Park, Canada, with a friend, Andrew Stepniewski, age twenty-six.[1] They were on an old wagon road in the Cougar Valley, which the Parks Branch had allowed to revert to a trail. At the beginning of the trail there was a "Grizzly Bear" warning sign because there had been several sightings of grizzlies in the area that year, and it was known that the area had been frequented by grizzlies for years. Certainly Barbara knew this because of her work as a park naturalist. She had seen many black bears and a few grizzlies during the course of her work. Usually when she hiked she was careful to make some noise. On the morning of the attack they had been making noise repeatedly, especially by whistling.

They were about one-and-a-half miles up the trail with Andrew hiking in front. There was restricted visibility along several portions

Alert and agitated grizzly bear female with older cubs, Banff National Park.

G.W. Vroom

of the trail. They had just rounded a bend in the trail when they saw a grizzly bear, which was "huffing and puffing," charging toward them from less than fifty feet away. Andrew had only a second or two to notice that it was a grizzly, but not a big one, when the bear grabbed hold of him. He screamed, yelled, and resisted for a few seconds, and then realizing that resistance was futile, he relaxed and put his hands behind his head.

He thought that the attack on him lasted for only fifteen or twenty seconds and then the bear attacked Barbara. This attack lasted only a "few seconds." Andrew remembers Barbara kicking at the bear and briefly trying to resist, and then the attack was over.

Barbara Chapman was dead. Andrew Stepniewski was critically injured with head, facial, neck, and body wounds. Despite his injuries, he managed to hike out to the busy Trans-Canada Highway in an hour and a half.

Back at the site of the attack, the bear dragged Barbara's body about two-hundred feet down a steep bank into heavy alder undergrowth and began to eat it. Although it is possible that this was a predatory attack—that is, that the bear attacked to kill and eat—it is unlikely as it involved a female with cubs, encountered at close range, which abandoned Andrew once he played dead. I believe that the suddenness of the encounter triggered a defensive attack by the mother bear. Once dead, Barbara's inert body may have elicited scavenging by the bear.

Only a few hours after the attack, a grizzly bear female and her three cubs were killed by park wardens near the attack site. Evidence confirmed that the female was the bear involved in the attack. The subsequent investigation showed that the bear family had been digging for food at the side of the trail just before the attack.

Barbara Chapman is the only person who was hiking in a national park prior to being killed by a grizzly bear. In this incident I believe that, despite Barbara's whistling, the mother grizzly first became aware of Barbara and Andrew only when they were very close. I categorize this incident as a "sudden encounter" in which the bear was surprised to find people very near her and her cubs. The bear acted very aggressively, and the attack was probably triggered by the mother bear's instinct to defend her young.

We will never know if the bear heard Barbara's whistling before it attacked. I have watched grizzly bears that were so intent on feeding that they did not respond to my voice conveyed in a normal tone from 150 feet away (I was up in a tree at the time). Perhaps if Barbara and Andrew had been loudly making noise, such as by shouting or singing, the bear might have fled before they were too close. Once the attack occurred, both Barbara and Andrew seem to have actively resisted for a while. The data on what has happened during other similar attacks suggests that, if possible, both of them should have played dead when the attack began. Once Andrew did this, the bear left him and attacked Barbara. Whether or not passive resistance by Barbara might have prevented her death is unknown.

It is possible (although no specific evidence exists) that the bear that killed Barbara Chapman and injured Andrew Stepniewski was the same bear that injured three people in two separate incidents five years earlier, in 1971, on the Balu Pass Trail, only three miles away. The bear could have been involved in all three incidents because it was fourteen when autopsied in 1976. Grizzly bear adult females use the same home range year after year, and all of the attacks were probably within one adult female's home range. Consistent with this possibility was the highly aggressive nature of the female involved in one of the 1971 incidents and in the 1976 incident.

In my opinion the warden service was justified in killing the entire bear family. This may sound like an overreaction, but I consider it probable that aggressive behavior in bears has a significant degree of genetic predisposition. This bear could have attacked again, or her cubs might have grown up to have this tendency. Larry Kaniut, in *Alaska Bear Tales*, a book about bear attacks and bear lore in Alaska, suggests that once a bear has killed a person, it is likely to injure or kill other people.[2] Larry cites three grizzly (brown) bear-inflicted fatalities in which a bear that was thought to have killed one person subsequently went after others.

While only one attack preceded by a sudden encounter between people and a grizzly in a national park has led to death, many have resulted in major injuries. In the Introduction I mention an incident that occurred in June 1977 in which Dr. Barrie Gilbert was seriously injured by a grizzly bear in Yellowstone National Park.[3] Barrie, and his assistant, Bruce Hastings, had begun field work in early June on a study of grizzly bear behavior. The aim of the study was to understand grizzly bear behavior better and thus help prevent bear attacks.

The day before the attack occurred, Barrie and Bruce used binoculars to observe a single grizzly bear, thought to have been a male, and a female grizzly accompanied by three cubs of the year (i.e., cubs born the preceding winter). The bears were probably unaware of the researchers. The next morning they saw all of the bears again in a "grassy expanse" where they were feeding. At 6:15 in the morning, the bear thought to have been a male stood and looked toward the female and then ran off, apparently being chased by the female. Barrie and Bruce watched the female and cubs feed for two more hours. At about 8:30 A.M., the researchers left their base camp and tried to move along and behind a ridge to a knoll, which they hoped would be a good vantage point. They assumed that the grizzly bear family group would remain where it was, but at 10:30 they saw the bear, thought to be an adult male, back feeding in the area where he had been seen before. They did not see the mother or her cubs. Barrie and Bruce continued hiking along the ridge until, at about 10:45 A.M., Bruce dropped his pack and stayed behind for a few minutes. Barrie was about to use his binoculars to look at a distant meadow to see if the female and her cubs were there when he heard a low "woof" and saw a "ball of fur, low to the ground" coming his way.

Barrie told what happened next in a narrative he dictated about a week later in the hospital.[4]

(I) could not estimate distance or identify the bear. My first thought was that I had miscalculated our location and thus had stumbled onto the sow. Knowing that I could not bluff a sow I felt the only solution was to give her as much room as possible. I turned and ran toward a small tree with bushes around its base. The bear caught me before I got to the tree and I went down in the bushes. The bear started biting me on the back of the head, which felt like a pick-axe scraping along my skull bones. In defense I turned over to kick and push the bear off but then she/he bit my face. I recall a deep bite which crushed the bones under my left eye—which was also lost. The face biting continued. . . . I cried out during the attack . . . but the bear kept biting. I lifted my legs up to try to kick him away but was unsuccessful. This was the time I got bitten on the leg. . . ."

When the attack on Barrie began, Bruce heard sounds that "weren't right" but also were not clearly identifiable because high winds were rushing through the branches. Bruce stepped back to his pack and about fifty feet ahead he could see the grizzly bear. Although he could not see Barrie he realized that the bear must be mauling him. Bruce stepped toward a shrubby clump of trees and emitted a loud and low "Ha!" The bear lifted its head and bolted off. Although neither man saw any cubs, both felt that it was probably the female that had attacked.

Bruce went to Barrie's side, where he could see that he had suffered severe injuries. Bleeding was extensive. Barrie told Bruce to take the VHF radio and call for a helicopter. Bruce administered first aid. Both men kept calm.

A helicopter soon arrived with paramedics. They did an excellent job, but Barrie remembers one of them saying something like, "If it will make you feel any better the park killed dozens of bears in the last ten years." Barrie replied that he did not want the bear killed because it had been an accident.

It took over 1440 hours in the hospital and more than a year, as well as many bouts of plastic surgery, for Barrie to be repaired. His strength came back fast, and within three weeks of release from the hospital he was riding his bicycle to Utah State University where he worked. The trauma of the attack and a missing left eye will be with Barrie all his life.

It appears probable that the bear that attacked Barrie was the grizzly bear mother with three cubs of the year. If it was the mother bear, then the earlier interaction that she had with the other single grizzly bear may have left her agitated or at least left her alert to potential threats to her family.

Barrie first became aware of the attacking bear when it was very close and was "woofing" and running toward him. Because Barrie and Bruce were hiking quietly in the high wind on the ridge, this suggests that the bear may have suddenly discovered Barrie nearby, felt threatened, and charged, probably leaving her cubs behind. If he and Bruce had been making loud noise, this might have alerted the bear to them when they were still distant. However, Barrie said the wind was so strong on the ridge top that he felt sound wouldn't carry.

It was probably a mistake for Barrie to try to run from the bear and to fight back once he was attacked.

The bear's fleeing in response to Bruce's emitting of a low pitched, loud sound during the attack was unusual. I know of no other attack where this sound has been tried to repel a bear. Loud shouting has occurred during several incidents, but this usually has served to redirect an attack to the person shouting.

The Chapman and Gilbert incidents are typical of sudden injurious encounters between grizzly bears and hikers. Hiking prior to being attacked was the most common circumstance associated with injury (50 percent, or 68 out of 135 incidents in which the party's activity prior to injury was known). In injurious encounters preceded by hiking, the persons injured were seldom aware of the bear until within fifty-five yards or less (83 percent, or 29 out of 35 incidents in which data exist regarding the distance at which a person first became aware of the bear that injured them). I assume that the surprise was mutual in most of these cases since grizzlies normally flee, or at least avoid contact, when a person approaches.[5] Therefore, I describe these incidents as being "sudden encounters," although it is possible that in some of these incidents the bear had either stalked the person injured or heard the person coming from a distance and waited or approached.

In only 15 percent of the injurious incidents (10 out of 68) preceded by hiking did a party report making noise prior to being attacked. Evidence suggests that making noise may help to alert grizzly bears to your travel, therefore lessening the chances of sudden encounters (see pp. 126–128). This idea should be tested experimentally before being accepted. Rarely did a traveling grizzly appear to have blundered onto a person who was resting or camping, apparently not becoming aware of the person until at close range.

Sudden encounters leading to human injury usually did not last long. Good data on the duration of such attacks were only available for thirteen incidents. All of these ended in less than ten minutes, and 54 percent (7 out of 13) were over in less than two minutes. The short duration of these encounters is consistent with my view that grizzlies attacking under these circumstances are responding to a perceived threat and, when they have dealt with it, they leave.

Grizzly bear mothers were responsible for 74 percent (20 out of 27) of all incidents that I regarded as sudden encounters and where records existed of the age/sex class of the bear. I regard this as a minimum figure because sometimes cubs remain hidden and a female with young is mistaken to be a single bear. Older cubs may charge people with their mothers, but it is the mothers that injure people. Mother grizzlies that injure people who suddenly confront them appear to be acting to protect their cubs in a sort of "defense reaction."[6] Grizzly bear females with cubs of the year are probably more dangerous than are mothers with cubs more than a year old, although data adequate to test this contention weren't available.

The defense reaction is so much a part of some mother grizzlies that they have been known to charge small groups of people and even trucks: I well remember a mother grizzly running flat out toward David Hamer and me while we, protected within my panel truck, sped up and swerved to avoid being caught. She had good reason to charge us; we had one of her cubs in a trap.

Hikers who find themselves close to a grizzly bear may discern some signs of the bear's intentions. A grizzly bear rearing onto its hind legs, a common stance, is trying to sense what is happening. Normally this is not an aggressive posture. On its hind legs the bear sniffs, listens and looks, trying to discover what kind of animal stands before it. Standing on its four legs a grizzly may show agitation by swaying its head from side to side, making huffing noises, or by opening and closing its mouth and making clacking noises with its teeth. Running and circling, usually to get downwind, may follow to get into a better position to sense (especially smell) the strange object. If the bear feels threatened, fleeing or a charge may follow. The seriousness of a grizzly's charge is usually indicated by the position of its ears. Like wolves and dogs, grizzly and black bears use the position of their ears as an indication of aggressive intent. Generally speaking, the farther back the ears are, and the more they are flattened to the neck, the more the grizzly is aroused.[7] In combination with this, the hair may be raised on the back of the neck and on the front portions of the back.

In encounters where grizzly bears act aggressively for several minutes, but haven't attacked a person, I think that attack can usually be avoided by proper response. In Chapter 6 I give detailed recommendations regarding what a person should do during encounters with a grizzly.

Case histories of hiker-bear injurious encounters suggest that there are few aggressive displays preceding an attack and that contact most often occurs during the first charge. Available information is inadequate to test this impression scientifically.

There are data documenting that a loud growl or deep gurgling was the noise that most often accompanied charges that led to injury. People injured by a grizzly bear described this sound in fifteen incidents. In nine incidents the attacking bear was reported to have made an explosive sound such as a snort or a woof. During aggressive encounters that did not lead to injury, the relative frequency of these two sounds was reversed. In these incidents, grizzlies were reported to have growled or gurgled only ten times and to have snorted or woofed twenty-three times.

Because of the difficulties in getting accurate records about sounds emitted during encounters I would only tentatively suggest that, during aggressive encounters between people and grizzly bears, the growl is more likely to be associated with injury than is the snort. The snort may serve more as a warning sound. This seems to be the case in encounters between bears. Some sudden encounters between grizzlies and people that resulted in major injury were not preceded by any sound.

If you are attacked while hiking in the backcountry, or if, during the day, a female grizzly with cubs wanders into your camp, discovers you, and charges, you can assume that the bear is responding to the sudden encounter. Such attacks usually occur when there is sufficient daylight for a person to see. They are normally preceded by a charge, not by slow approaches or by walking later followed by a charge.

If you are attacked by a grizzly bear following a sudden encounter, I recommend that you passively resist by playing dead. I have chosen two of many similar incidents to illustrate this point.

June 4, 1976, was clear and crisp in the treeless alpine zone of Spatsizi Wilderness Park in northern British Columbia. An acquaintance of mine, Judith Donaldson, a wildlife biologist, and her companion, Mike Sather, also a wildlife biologist, were traversing a sidehill as part of their work.[8] Neither Judy nor Mike was making any noise and neither was specifically watching for bears. At 4:00 P.M. Mike said to Judy, "Don't move." Above and upwind from them, Mike noticed a blond grizzly bear accompanied by two older blond cubs. The bears were close together in a small depression on the hillside, about fifty feet from Mike and eighty feet from Judy. The cubs noticed the biologists first and then the mother bear saw them. The adult bear waited about two seconds and then charged, roaring as she came at Mike and Judy. Mike stood and faced the female until she was about ten feet away. He then dropped to his knees, face to the ground, hands behind his head. The grizzly mother attacked Mike first. She straddled him and began biting and "batting him around like a Ping-Pong ball." Mike did not fight back and remained curled up as best he could.

As soon as Mike saw the bears and spoke to Judy she continued walking down the hill, away from the bears. A cub ran toward her and continued on down the hill. Judy stopped and watched the cub as he ran. She saw that the mother bear was mauling Mike. The attack on Mike seemed to have lasted about fifteen seconds when the bear looked up and noticed Judy, who turned and continued walking down the hill. The mother bear waited another two seconds and then charged Judy.

As Judy wrote to me:

> She got me (standing) from behind, knocked my snugly fitting hat off and my light nylon day pack, and bit me. The upper teeth entered my right shoulder, the lower teeth my ribs about ten inches lower. . . . She knocked me about eight feet down the hill. I hit the ground, curled into the same position as Mike, hands behind my neck, arms protecting my head, but on my right side facing into the hill. She could not have bitten me once I hit the ground, as my only wounds were on my right side on which I was lying. I did not lift my head or move until Mike called saying the bear had gone. We both had remained silent throughout the encounter.

Mike's injuries kept him hospitalized for a day. They included a cracked shoulder blade, puncture wounds from bites, and a C-shaped cut on his head, which required twelve stitches. Judy, who had torn puncture wounds on her shoulder and back, was treated at the hospital emergency room and released.

Given the circumstances of suddenly confronting an aggressive grizzly bear mother with her cubs, both biologists received relatively minor injuries. The attack on Mike lasted only about fifteen seconds, and the attack on Judy was probably briefer. Had either biologist actively resisted by fighting or screaming, I suspect that the attack would have lasted longer and would have resulted in more severe injuries.

This encounter could possibly have been prevented if Mike and Judy had spotted the bears sooner and had not approached the family. Since the biologists were hiking into a brisk wind, the bears probably didn't get the biologists scent and were probably completely unaware of them until they spotted Mike only fifty feet away from the family group. Had Mike and Judy made loud noises while hiking, the bears might have been given advance notice, and the mother bear might have chosen to flee rather than attack. Such a choice by a bear is dependent on many factors such as the personality of the bear, its' family status, and the specific circumstances of the encounter.

In late June 1960 Dr. Ian Stirling and a companion were working in the Verendrye Creek Basin of Kootenay National Park, British Columbia. Ian, a research biologist with the Canadian Wildlife Service who is well known for his research on polar bears, showed significant calm and carefully thought-out action during a very frightening encounter.[9]

At the time of the incident, Ian was a summer student working for the warden service of Kootenay Park. He and his partner's job for the day was to clear deadfall from the trail in Verendrye Creek Basin. Ian was a short distance off the trail and was standing by the roots of a large spruce tree that had fallen over. He heard "sporadic puffing" coming from the direction of the trail. He peered through a hole in the roots and saw a grizzly bear. He next saw the bear "lift its nose, test the wind," and then it came running toward him. Ian and the bear next did two-and-a-half laps around the roots of the tree with Ian staying ahead of the bear. Ian saw an opportunity to sneak away to a big tree that he wanted to climb. Ian's letter to me tells what happened next.

I had only moved maybe twenty feet when she [Ian states elsewhere that he never was sure of the sex] saw me, let out a most electrifying vocalization that I could only call a "roar," and she bolted after me. I can still see her clearing the log in as much detail as if it were yesterday. I began to run for the heavy timber but, after a few steps, realized it was futile. The choice was then to get knocked down or lie down myself and play dead. I dove head first into the edge of a thick clump of alders so that my head and neck and part of my shoulders were in between some of the thin trunks. I was lying on my stomach, [and I] crossed my heels and clasped my fingers together over the back of my neck. I lay absolutely still. At the time, I fully expected to be mauled or at the least bitten a couple of times. I also knew quite well I might be killed. I was terrified at my circumstance but calm in that I knew what I was trying to do. The difficulty was going to be to carry it out if things started to get painful. I was concentrating as hard as I could on trying to be motionless and to endure whatever happened next to the best of my ability. . . . I can still remember rather clearly how annoyed I was with my heart. Here was I, trying to lie still and be quiet while my heart seemed to be thumping like the pistons of a locomotive. It felt as if it was bouncing me off the ground and it seemed the bear could surely hear it.

The bear ran up and stopped by my left leg and stood there for a moment. Then it nosed my left leg and I tried to brace myself mentally for the begining of a mauling. Nothing happened. It nosed me a second time, not hard but about like you might tap someone's shoulder to get their attention. Then it stood still beside me. There was no sound in the basin except for the heavy breathing of the bear. I could hear the saliva bubbling in his mouth as he breathed. I lay still, face down, eyes closed, while my heart threatened to leap out of my rib cage.

I don't know how long the bear stood there, probably only a few minutes although it seemed like an eternity. Then I heard it move and readied myself mentally again but suddenly realized it was moving slowly away. . . .

The bear left without further incident. When Ian tried to stand, his knees were so shaky that he fell to the ground. He soon regained his coordination and walked to the trail, where he met his partner who was up a tree during Ian's encounter with the grizzly. Ian's partner casually said something like, "Hey! Did you see the bear?"

Not everyone would have the mental toughness to play dead under such circumstances. Given the choices of running, getting ready to fight the bear, and playing dead, I feel that Ian did the right thing. Although he could have been mauled, he played the odds and won.

Table 2 presents the data on which I base my recommendation regarding what to do if attacked during a sudden encounter. Passively resisting the attack by remaining as motionless and soundless as possible—playing dead—seems to have decreased the intensity of injury in this type of incident. This is a probability statement, which means that usually, but not always, playing dead decreases the intensity of such attacks. Trying to fight an attacking grizzly during a sudden encounter can't be ruled out as a strategy based on the data in Table 2. Because of the difficulty in quantifying these situations I have not used statistics to test for significance. My recommendation for playing dead under such circumstances is therefore based mainly

TABLE 2
Response of attacking grizzly bear* to a person playing dead or fighting back

Intensity of Attack

	INCREASE	DECREASE	NO CHANGE
PLAY DEAD/ PASSIVELY RESIST	2	16	8
FIGHT BACK/ ACTIVELY RESIST	3	7	3

*The circumstance precipitating attack was in all cases judged to be defense of young, responding to sudden surprise, or responding to harassment.

on my impressions from examining similar incidents, and my understanding of bear behavior.

After being attacked in a sudden encounter, or perhaps when a charging grizzly is just about to contact you, a person should assume a position that will minimize exposure of vital areas and parts of the body where such attacks normally focus. I recommend the position of hands behind the neck, fingers interlocked, with the forearms and elbows protecting the face as best as possible. A bear's bite can break or crush the face or neck, but its jaws won't open wide enough to crush the skull of an adult. The knees should be drawn up to the face—the fetal position. Hands interlocked around the knees with the face, especially the eyes, buried in the knees, would also be a good position except that this doesn't protect the neck. Lying flat on the ground, face down, with your hands locked behind your neck is another possibility. Leave your pack on if you have one and didn't drop it to distract the bear. The pack should help to protect your body.

During sudden encounter attacks, the face and skull commonly receive injury. I noted this in my data, and Kaniut also mentions many

Possible positions for playing dead

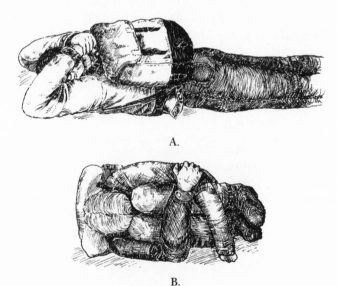

A.

B.

A. Lying flat on the ground, face down, with hands locked behind neck and arms protecting face and side of head.

B. Foetal position: curled into a ball, lying on side, head buried into knees and arms around legs with wrists locked together.

cases of facial and skull or scalp injuries.[10] Attacks are usually directed to the head probably because during aggressive encounters between grizzly bears they frequently bite each other's faces and heads, trying to grab the opponent's jaws in order to disable their primary weapon.

Historical records also suggest playing dead during sudden encounters. On July 14, 1806, Simon Fraser, an explorer in western Canada, wrote of an Indian and his wife who were walking along a riverbank and surprised a large grizzly with two cubs. The Indian fired at the mother bear and wounded her. In return she attacked his wife, "and she instantly laid down flat upon the ground and did not stir, in consequence of (which) the bear deserted (her) and ran after her husband. . . ."[11] The same response to sudden encounters with a grizzly was also recommended by a California pioneer: "If the man lies still, with his face down, the bear will usually content himself with biting . . . for a while about the arms and legs, and will then go off a few steps and watch . . . the bear will believe him dead, and will soon . . . go away. But let the man move, and the bear is upon him again; let him fight, and he will be in imminent danger of being torn to pieces."[12]

You should not play dead before you are attacked unless a charging grizzly is extremely close and you feel certain that attack is imminent. While standing, you have options such as dodging to avoid attack. I know of several cases in which people have successfully dodged attack by dropping an object, such as a camera, to distract the bear and give themselves time to climb a tree, or by using clothing to redirect the attack away from the body, or by keeping trees between themselves and an attacking bear.

The active person in a group typically draws the brunt of an attack after a sudden encounter. This suggests that if a companion were being severely mauled you might shout or wave your arms to draw the attack to yourself, and then play dead after being attacked. This tactic frequently has worked.

A few minutes after an attack, or after playing dead, you should cautiously raise your head to see if the bear or bear family is still around. Normally a grizzly will leave within a few minutes after a sudden encounter. If it has not left, continue to be passive. Once the bear has left, determine the extent of injury to yourself or others and begin first aid. As soon as the victim is stable and the bear seems to have left, leave for help. Remember the location of the victim. If the bear attacks again (which is very rare), then play dead again.

Instead of playing dead after a sudden encounter, some people have chosen to try to fight a bear using fists, knives, or whatever weapon they might have. In exceptional cases people have stunned such attacking grizzly bears by hitting them with a club, or just their fists or knees, or by sticking their fingers in a grizzly's large nostrils, and the bear has left. Because grizzlies are stronger and have superior natural weapons, it is usually the human being who takes the worst punishment in a fight with an attacking bear.

I do not want to leave the impression that suddenly meeting a grizzly bear just about guarantees injury. Such is not the case. In the first place, most grizzlies are tolerant of people. Each year hundreds of thousands of people visit grizzly country and few injuries occur. Even when suddenly confronted at close range, most grizzlies flee without any aggressive action.

Dick Knight, who has been studying grizzly bears in the Yellowstone ecosystem for more than ten years, describes the behavior of twenty-nine radio-instrumented grizzly bears that he knew were in close proximity to people at one time or another.[13] Only five of the twenty-nine grizzlies were ever reported to have acted aggressively toward people, and none had ever injured a person. As part of his research he deliberately approached a number of grizzlies, usually to distances of less than three-hundred feet, before they sensed his presence. He noted eight instances of bears fleeing in response to such provocation and four instances in which the grizzly acted aggressively, usually charging a short distance before fleeing.

In Waterton Lakes National Park, Canada, David Hamer, Keith Brady, and I recorded thirteen instances during 1981 in which a radio-collared female grizzly with two cubs of the year was located 110 yards or less from people.[14] This grizzly bear mother did not act aggressively

Grizzly bear female and young, Banff National Park.   *Chris Shank*

in any of these instances. In two cases she slowly approached people, causing them to slowly retreat; seven times she appeared to ignore people; and four times she moved away.

Research shows that most grizzly bears are normally tolerant of people under a great variety of circumstances. However, one of the most common situations that sometimes leads to a breakdown of this tolerance is when a person suddenly gets too close to a grizzly.

One of the most dangerous situations in which to come nose to nose with a grizzly is when it is feeding on or is near a carcass. Any grizzly bear near a carcass is potential dynamite that may explode in the direction of any animal that the bear thinks is competing with it for the food. Crows, ravens, magpies, jays, and other scavenging birds often dart in and out trying to get their share. A grizzly bear will swat and bite at these competitors. Other bears, wolves, coyotes, foxes, wolverines, and other scavenging mammals often try to approach as well. A grizzly will usually be aggressive toward such animals. To avoid having parts of a carcass taken, grizzlies will sometimes completely cover a carcass with vegetation and dirt and then sleep on top or nearby. Prudent people do everything possible to avoid suddenly confronting a grizzly bear that is near a carcass.

On Sunday morning, September 18, 1983, Trevor and Patricia Janz, both in their twenties, were backpacking on the Crypt Lake trail, in Waterton Lakes National Park, Canada.[15] They were returning from camping overnight and it was snowing lightly, but not enough to obscure their vision. Patricia remembers the wind blowing into their faces before they were attacked by a grizzly bear. Trevor was 100 to 130 feet ahead of Patricia and was singing softly when he suddenly saw the head of a bear below the trail about fifty feet to his left. He had no way of knowing that eighty feet away there was a partly consumed bighorn sheep carcass on which the bear, a female grizzly, and her two yearling cubs had been feeding.

Later in the hospital, Trevor told me, "It was coming toward me when I saw it." He recalls that the bear ran faster as it came closer, but he does not think that it made any noise. The bear grabbed Trevor by the front of the leg and he fell to the ground. Trevor had on a large pack containing his gear and part of Patricia's gear, and when he fell to the ground the pack covered his back, neck, and the back of his head. The pack and his heavy clothing seem to have helped protect him. Trevor's face was toward the ground, and his hands were underneath his body. He stressed that he did not fight the bear but tried to keep his head down. He thinks he was mauled this time for approximately one to one-and-a-half minutes. He remembers grunting and low growling sounds between the bites. Although he was injured more severely during a second attack, Trevor thinks that his jaw was broken on the right side during the first attack.

Just before the bear left, it nosed the ground around Trevor and made low growling sounds for about fifteen seconds. Trevor thinks he then lay there for about ten minutes, during which time he heard Patricia scream twice.

Patricia had seen the bear charging Trevor until they both disappeared behind some trees. She was spared a clear view of Trevor's mauling. She was, however, aware that Trevor was being mauled and took two steps back on the trail. Then she took her pack off almost automatically, having recalled that this was a good diversion for a bear, and she picked out and began climbing a tree. She was part way up the tree (her hands were about sixteen feet above the ground according to measurements I and the park wardens made) when she paused momentarily from what seemed like a firm stance in the tree. She looked down the trail and made eye contact with the bear, which was about eighty feet away. The bear immediately charged her or may have already been charging her when she made eye contact. The bear continued the charge without hesitation up the tree, and at the ten-foot level it broke a branch that formed one of Patricia's footholds. This caused Patricia to fall out of the tree, and she remembers screaming "No!"

While she was on the ground being attacked by the bear, Patricia held her hands on the side of her head and tried to keep her head down on the trail. Patricia was uncertain but she thought that the bear had tried to turn her over. The attack continued, still violently, despite the fact that Patricia offered little if any resistance. At one point Patricia got mad, and seeing the bear's nose she "tweaked" it. The bear snorted and jumped back as though surprised. It made a few woofs and then left.

Patricia felt that "her head was in pieces." She stated, "I tried to find out if I was dead or alive." She last saw the bear about twenty-five to thirty-five feet away "just kind of standing there woofing." Sometime after this, the bear returned to maul Trevor a second time.

Meanwhile, Trevor, being a medical student, tried to assess his condition. He counted his heart rate to figure his blood loss. He later stated that he was not thinking too well and got up, loosened his pack straps, and started to climb a tree, getting about five feet off the ground. The bear returned and pulled Trevor to the ground. This time the pack did not cover his entire back and head but was across his body, exposing his neck, head, and face. This time he felt that the bear inflicted worse injuries, especially to his face. He stated in retrospect that he "was happy there was just crunching and not crunching and ripping." He thought that his heavy, layered clothing helped to protect him in the arm and shoulder regions. During the second mauling he stated that he wasn't protecting his head as well as the first time because he was weaker and generally less focused. He said he thought about dying quickly. He had impressions of "the smell of blood, bear, and of his bones cracking."

Finally the bear left Trevor, and within about eight to ten minutes two hikers arrived. The hikers took Trevor and Patricia down the trail, and they were soon rushed to a hospital where their conditions were stabilized but still critical. A short while later they were moved to major medical facilities in Calgary, Alberta.

Both Trevor and Patricia had only seen one bear during the attack. They didn't know that the bear that had attacked them was a mother with cubs and that a carcass had been involved. Because these details were unknown at the time, the incident sounded to park wardens as though it might have been an unprovoked attack. Because of this, the wardens went to the mauling site hours after the attack and set snares to catch the bear. Darkness fell before they searched the area thoroughly, and they still didn't know that a female with young and a carcass were involved.

The next morning four armed wardens and I approached the mauling site. We checked the snares, discovering that one of them had been sprung. Tracks in the snow showed that at least three grizzlies were around. During the initial check of the trap site one of the wardens heard snorting noises from a bear estimated to be about 110 yards above the trail. Nothing further happened then.

We continued searching the mauling site and the surrounding area for clues that might further explain the attack. Just below the trail, we found a sheep carcass on which the grizzly bear family had recently fed. We remained cautious even though we assumed that the bears had accepted our presence because we had been near the carcass for the better part of five hours.

We left the carcass and returned to the mauling site. We radioed our findings back to Max Winkler, the chief warden, and Bernie Lieff, the park superintendent, and awaited their instructions. Because a female with young and a carcass were involved, we considered pulling the snares and closing the area for the rest of the season. The mother bear had acted very aggressively, but defensively.

We were walking from the tree that Patricia had climbed toward the site where Trevor was mauled when Keith Brady, the lead warden, saw the bear family approaching the carcass only 150 feet away. Keith quickly told two of the other wardens to back up and moved back about three feet himself. The mother bear charged almost as soon as she saw us. Keith shouted at her to warn and deter her, but she didn't break stride as she charged through the trees. Keith thought to himself, "Oh my God, no," when he was aware she probably wouldn't stop. I was about a hundred feet or so behind Keith and two other wardens, and I stood my ground and glanced at a tree that looked good to climb if the situation allowed. I also thought of playing dead if I was among the first to be attacked.

Keith had his rifle at his shoulder as the bear lurched toward us, dodging around trees. Here was a man, mature and experienced with bears and firearms, who hated to kill any bear but had cautioned other wardens in the event of necessity to wait, never take their eyes off a charging bear, and make the first shot count. Keith shot her when she was only eight or nine paces away. The first shot from his .338 Magnum hit her in the neck and shoulder region and stopped her. Several more shots killed her. At the distance she was shot, she could have reached Keith in less than half a second. The whole incident, from when we first saw her to when she was first shot, had taken three or four seconds.

The bear lay still. Her cubs had run off, never charging. In the silence after the shots I could hear my heart pounding. In examining the situation after we calmed down, we judged that Keith was standing within about ten feet of where Trevor Janz was mauled. Given the personality of this bear and the circumstances, it seemed unlikely that she would have stopped her charge without attacking us.

Both Trevor and Patricia had extensive hiking and general mountain experience before the attack. After the incident Trevor told me that "we usually avoid areas that have posted bear warnings" and that "we usually keep our heads up and watch around corners . . . and usually make noise." Sometimes such encounters at carcasses can be anticipated and avoided, but this time there were no good clues to suggest the possibility of a carcass or an attack. Fortunately such incidents are very rare. My records had ten similar cases. There were a few things that Trevor and Patricia might have done differently. They could have been making more noise prior to the attack, which might have warned the bears of their presence at a greater distance and caused them to retreat. In this particular circumstance I doubt that this would have occurred. Patricia, when she began climbing the tree, should not have stopped until she was at least thirty-three feet off of the ground. (The highest a grizzly is known to have climbed during an attack is slightly less than thirty-three feet.) The tree was a good one to climb, but whether she could have made it this far or whether the bear could have climbed higher than the ten-foot height where Patricia fell from the tree, is unknown. (Tree climbing to avoid aggressive grizzly bears is discussed on p. 86.) Autopsy suggested that the female grizzly was physically normal and healthy. Tooth sectioning put her age at fifteen or sixteen years. She probably lived for most of this time, and raised several litters, having hikers within her home range. But on September 18, 1983, a combination of circumstances— a dead bighorn sheep nearby a trail, the presence of cubs, and approaching hikers, led to attack and injury for the Janz's and the death of the bear.

Carcasses which have been claimed by a grizzly may lead to encounters if people suddenly come upon them. A carcass left overnight by hunters may also be claimed by a grizzly. Both black and grizzly bears are efficient scavengers with an acute sense of smell. Hunters should try to hoist a carcass high into the air using ropes and pulleys. This will probably save the meat, but will disperse the odor, which may attract a bear to the area. If a carcass must be left on the ground, it should be put in an open area where a scavenging bear could be seen at a distance. Many grizzly bears have been shot unnecessarily and at least six hunters have been injured as a result of approaches to carcasses left overnight.

If a carcass is left overnight in grizzly country, it should be approached the next day with the assumption that a grizzly has discovered it. Come in on horseback or by vehicle if possible. Make lots of noise from a safe distance before approaching. A grizzly may have dragged the carcass a short distance or buried it. The bear will probably be close by. If the situation looks suspicious, it is safest to abandon the kill.

I investigated one such carcass-related incident that had occurred near Grand Cache, Alberta, in mid-September 1968.[16] Mr. Kelly Joakim, a guide, and his two American clients had been moose hunting. The day before the incident occurred, the party had shot two moose, gutted them, and dragged them to a nearby seismic line. The moose were left together on top of a small hill.

Kelly, an Indian, had lived in grizzly country most of his life. When I interviewed him in the Hinton hospital, he said that he had shot one grizzly bear before at close range, but then he had his dogs with him, which helped to keep the bear at bay. He said that his grandfather had shot and killed grizzlies by hitting them in the ear with .22 long rifle bullets.

On the day of the mauling Kelly was unarmed as he and the

hunters approached the moose carcasses at about eight o'clock in the morning without thinking about grizzly bears. They were at the bottom of the hill where the carcasses lay when they saw a grizzly charging from about thirty-five feet away.

When he first saw the grizzly, Kelly was about ten feet in front of the hunters. As the bear charged, Kelly immediately turned and ran. In the interval, the hunters shot the bear twice but it still caught the fleeing Kelly. He felt the grizzly sink its teeth into the back of his thigh as the bear stood on top of him, biting and pinning him to the ground. The hunters waited for opportunities to shoot the bear without wounding Kelly. Four more shots from their .307 Magnums and the bear was dead. Kelly told me that each time the bear was shot it bit yet harder on his leg.

Examination of the moose carcasses revealed that both had been partly dismembered and buried with sticks, earth, grass, and detritus. Obviously, the bear had been scavenging. Had the hunting party taken precautions, this attack—and Kelly's injuries—could have been avoided.

Another carcass-related incident, described by Larry Kaniut,[17] suggests that under these circumstances fighting without weapons is usually futile and most likely increases the severity of an attack. In September 1955, Forest H. Young, Jr., and his partner, Marty Cordes, had killed a moose on the Chilkat River, Alaska, and over several days packed most of the meat to camp. All that was left at the kill site were the gut piles and the hide. Forest decided to make a last trip for the hide.

> When he arrived, weaponless, at the kill site, Young found that bears had taken over—they had covered the remaining gut piles with sticks and moss. Forest went to the tree and began to retrieve the hide when he noticed two bears a hundred yards away. He figured they were grizzlies but wasn't concerned, his bear experience convinced him they wouldn't bother him.
>
> Instantly one of the animals charged him. Still unalarmed, he waved his arms and shouted, normal procedures in such a situation. But this bear wasn't going to be bluffed. Forest jumped for a low branch on a tree and had hardly climbed half a dozen feet when the grizzly cleared the brush and clamped down on his right leg, ripping him from the tree.
>
> When he landed, the bear held him down with one paw and chomped on his thigh with its teeth, ripping out a mass of flesh. Forest pounded the brute in the face with his fists—tantamount to a mouse chasing a cat. Their faces were only a foot apart as the bear ripped flesh and clothing. Forest broke his hand pounding on the bear's face, and the beast continued to shred his lower limbs.

Young determined to play dead and fell to his side. The bear stopped immediately and may have left, but Forest groaned in spite of himself. The bear bit him in the side exposing his bladder.

The pain was excruciating; but Forest did not move. The bear took a few more bites, ripping three ribs loose from the spine and opening up the chest cavity. Forest remained silent and motionless. The bear left.

Young tried to relax and tell himself the bear was gone, but the bear roared back two or three times to inspect his victim. The ground trembled under him, and he lay there expecting the bear to rip him apart any moment. After a while it became necessary for the man to turn his face to facilitate breathing and to allow fluids to drain.

It was too much to hope for. Here came the bear again! He must have sensed the man's different position because he lit into Forest anew, spanning his buttocks with its jaws and biting to the bone, picking him up and shaking him. Forest thought his head would pop off, and he feared his spine would snap. The bear then dropped him and left.

It was some time later that Marty called from a distance. He was aghast when he discovered his partner. Marty wanted to carry Forest back to camp, but the pain was unbearable for the injured man. Marty went to camp to retrieve a sleeping bag, air mattress, some food, water, gas lantern, a shotgun and shells. He took them back to Young, made him comfortable and then headed for Haines and help.

During the next 14 1/2 hours Forest hung on to the thin thread of life. The bear returned a few more times and was frightened away by shotgun blasts. Late that night Marty returned with help, but the brute was reluctant to give up his victim for he followed them all the way back to the cabin, roaring in the distance.

The next morning a helicopter picked Forest up and took him to Juneau where Dr. Cass Carter worked on him. Young suffered a severe mauling, which included having a rib ripped out by the bear. The extent of his injuries was so critical that Dr. Carter gave little hope of survival unless the victim had received medical attention within six hours. But Forest Young, Jr., did survive.

I want to bring grizzly bear-inflicted injuries back into perspective. During the five years of our research on grizzly bears in Banff Park, I was more concerned about accidents while driving to and from the park or during my occasional helicopter flights than I was about bear attack, even though I spent far more time in the grizzly's home than on the highway or in the air. My second main concern was the crossings that we had to make across a river that even in midsummer is cold enough to numb legs and feet within seconds. Only third was I concerned about grizzlies.

My colleagues and I faced all three hazards without injury. We put in more than ten thousand hours working with the densest population of grizzly bears in Banff National Park. Eighty percent of the time we were on foot, visiting areas where grizzly bears had recently been active. We worked unarmed except when visiting carcasses where grizzlies might be nearby or when checking traps set for grizzlies. If grizzlies wanted to attack us they had ample opportunity.

The Craighead brothers reported the same absence of injury during their research on grizzly bears in Yellowstone Park. This was despite the fact that they individually color-marked 256 grizzlies and handled 524 during an eleven-year period of study. They instrumented forty-eight grizzlies with radio transmitters and tracked these animals in the backcountry for over 29,000 hours. They estimated that they hiked about 162,000 miles during the course of their work.[18]

Another perspective on the danger posed by grizzly bears is to compare all known sources of death in a national park such as Glacier Park, Montana, which has had more grizzly bear-inflicted deaths than any other park. Even here only six of the 150 fatalities (4 percent) in the park through 1980 were caused by grizzly bears.[19] Most deaths resulted from falls, automobile accidents, drownings, and hypothermia. Grizzly bears also kill far fewer people in the United States (two deaths in 1976, none in 1977) than does lightning (81 deaths in 1976; 116 in 1977) or the bites or stings of venomous animals (53 deaths in 1976; 55 in 1977).[20] Grizzly attacks occur infrequently enough that most people, including even the injured, support maintaining grizzlies in the national parks and wilderness areas where they are still found. Land and wildlife managers throughout North America must take all possible steps to help people avoid injury—but should stop short of destroying the grizzly.

3

Provoked Attacks

ONLY in a very few of the maulings that I examined had the attacking grizzly been obviously provoked, such as when a hunter shot or otherwise harassed a bear, a photographer approached a grizzly to take a picture, a dog attacked a grizzly, or a bear was drugged or captured and then injured a person soon after its release.

Other books discuss grizzly bear maulings related to hunting in greater detail than I do here.[1] Part of the grizzly's reputation for being "ferocious" has come from the ability of a few of them to keep coming at a hunter despite serious wounds. Alaska is where most of the injured hunters have been attacked by grizzly bears.[2] The following account illustrates this type of incident. It was given to Larry Kaniut by Creig Sharp, a hunter who was mauled at Karluk Lake, Kodiak Island, Alaska, during April 1977.[3] The incident shows the astonishing amount of damage from rifle fire a grizzly (brown) bear can take and still have the strength to attack. Creig Sharp was hunting with a companion, Gary Grindle, when they saw a big, cinnamon-colored grizzly (brown) only eighty yards away. Creig described the situation as follows:

I had a .340 caliber Weatherby Magnum with a 3x9 Redfield wide-field scope on 6-power. The rifle was sighted in dead at 200 yards, and I was using 250-grain Nosler factory-loaded ammunition. I had a left front, almost broadside shot, and aimed a little low into the shoulder. When I fired, the bullet hit and knocked the bear up over on his back with all four feet sticking up in the air. As I tried to get another round into him my rifle jammed! The bolt extractor had slipped over the spent casing which was still in the chamber. I pushed the ammo down into the magazine and shoved the bolt closed and opened it again.

The case came part of the way out this time so I grabbed it and threw it to the ground. I chambered another round as the bear sat up. Just as I readied to fire again, he rolled back over on his back; and when he came up, he had done a complete tumble and started to tumble down the mountain. I fired another shot, which was later found to have hit within five inches of the first shot.

The bear was hit hard twice and fell down over a 200-foot embankment into an alder patch. Gary and I ran for the edge of the cliff to look for him, but couldn't see him anywhere. We skirted down the hill through the snow leaving a wide berth between us and the alders in case the bear decided to come out for us. After circling the alder patch, we crossed a blood trail two and a half to three feet wide.

Gary and I stopped for a 10-minute rest and figured we would have to track down the bear through the alders. We started after him, following a trail of blood for a distance of about two and a half to three miles. He went up over hills and down through alders that were so thick we had to crawl on our hands and knees to get through them at times. The blood trail was so heavy, it was on the bushes as well as the snow. We found two spots where he had stopped and rooted out the alders, just breaking them off and leaving pools of blood.

I shot the bear at about 7:15 P.M., and it was now about 9:15 P.M. We had tracked him for two hours. We stopped on a steep descent facing down the mountain. The alder patch was so thick that visibility was about 10 feet in any direction except toward the lake where we could see the water through the branches. Ahead of us was a trail of broken branches and blood leading toward the lake. We knew the bear had gone down that way.

After discussing what to do next, we decided to get the raft, go back to the cabin and finish tracking the bear the next morning. It was getting dark and a slight drizzle of rain had started.

I turned to go down the trail and had taken only 8 to 10 steps when I heard a big roar and a rushing sound from behind my left shoulder. As I turned and looked back, I saw the bear charging at me full speed. He was only six or seven yards away. I tried to fire but couldn't turn completely around as my right foot was caught in some alders. I turned back to my right just as the bear hit me.

He was coming so fast I had the impression that he was going to overshoot me. He started to skid, stiffened up his front legs and just kinda bounced up to me. He grabbed my upper left thigh for a moment as I was turning and then released his grip. I rolled into a ball on the ground and he bit the back part of my left thigh twice, picked me up and flipped me over. I covered my face and neck with my arms and had my rifle in my hands. He tried to bite me in the face and I shoved my rifle into his mouth. He bit it and broke the stock. Then as he was letting go, he tore the sling off. He sheared the sling swivels right off the rifle.

Gary was about 8 or 10 feet up the trail from me while the bear was on top of me. He stood there and fired three shots into the bear, hitting him in the lung area, shoulder and neck. One of the bullets passed through my ankle up my leg—the bullet shattered all bones in the ankle and fractured the two large bones in my lower leg. The bullet hole was nine inches deep from the bottom of my foot.

After the third shot, my partner accidentally hit the floor plate release lever on his rifle, and the other three rounds fell out just as the bear dropped me. Looking up, the bear headed for Gary, changed his mind, turned back down the hill and ran over me as he left. The force tumbled me up to a sitting position facing downhill. I raised my rifle and fired, hitting the bear in the left rump cheek as he retreated. The shot knocked him down in the alders about 100 yards away where we couldn't see him but could hear his bellering.

Gary came over to survey my injuries. I told him I thought my right leg was broken, and I had been bit a couple of times on the left thigh (at that time we didn't know I'd been shot).

Barney Smith, the Yukon Territorial Game Biologist in charge of bear management, has examined many cases of hunters shooting grizzly bears. He believes that wounded grizzlies normally don't charge hunters; rather, the wounded bear runs for some cover, such as dense brush. Barney further states that most Yukon guides "do not carry backup rifles when accompanying hunters." Barney also added in a note to me that he usually does carry a rifle in any potentially dangerous situation around a grizzly, as do guides in Alaska.

Photographers can easily provoke grizzlies because they normally must get close to one. Photographers who specialize in grizzlies know that the safest way to approach for a picture is to let the bear sense them when they are still far away before beginning a slow, deliberate, and obvious approach. Approaching in this way avoids surprising the bear, but it places the photographer dangerously close. The records show that eight people were injured while trying to photograph grizzlies. Robert Hahn, a schoolteacher, was one such person. He visited

Glacier National Park, Montana, during the spring of 1968. While photographing a grizzly bear family at close range, he was attacked by the mother. His wounds required twenty-nine stitches. Despite his moderate injury, he acknowledged that his actions precipitated the incident:

> The thing that makes me very unhappy about the whole incident is my fear that this will only add fuel to the fire for those people who advocate the destruction of the grizzly to make our national parks safe. There is no reason, in the name of civilized progress, to kill an animal for doing what is natural. I feel no malice toward the bear. It was my fault in sticking my neck out too far—the bear was only protecting her young and her territory.
>
> I certainly don't recommend my experience to anyone. Yet, I will photograph bears again and I will hike alone again—which is also not recommended. The only thing that will prevent me from hiking in the wilderness again is the eventual destruction of that wilderness itself and when anyone advocates the destruction of grizzlies they are in essence advocating the destruction of true wilderness.[4]

The grizzly bear mother that injured Hahn was neither destroyed nor captured and moved. Cliff Martinka, Chief Research Biologist for Glacier Park, Montana, stated that this bear seems to have lived without incident for many years after the mauling.[5]

Some photographers have made grizzly bear photography into a dangerous but sophisticated pastime. Among the best are John Crawford, and Andy Russell and his sons, Dick and Charlie,[6] who have spent years observing the moods and behavior of grizzlies. They begin their photographic sessions in the wild by letting the bear know of their presence from fairly far away. Then they maneuver into picture-taking position while watching the reactions of the bear. Sometimes they wait out charges while still photographing, protected only by their intuitive sense of what the bear will do next. When a bear appears too aggressive, they readily abandon their stalk. None of them normally carries firearms when photographing because they feel they might try to push their luck and have to shoot a bear. Crawford sums up their outlook by saying, "the change in attitude that occurs with the half-aggressive, half-fearful feeling of an armed individual [comes from] projecting the thought, 'if he tries to get tough with me I'll bust him.' "

I do not recommend that anyone try to take grizzly bear photographs at closer than one thousand feet, and even this distance can be dangerous under certain circumstances. I personally do not like to photograph grizzlies—not only because of the danger but also because to get photographs one has to harass the bear.

On September 11, 1973, Al Johnson, a game biologist with the state of Alaska, cautiously approached a grizzly bear mother with three cubs in Mt. McKinley National Park.[7] He went to the park to photograph moose, but the chance to photograph the bear family seemed too good to pass by. For about three hours he photographed the bears, never coming closer than one hundred yards. He was downwind of them and quiet, and so he felt sure that they were unaware of his presence. By late afternoon the light began to fade, and he concluded that his 1000mm lens wouldn't get good pictures. Also, the bears were moving away from him and into an area where there were no good trees to climb. At this point Johnson climbed what he thought was a safe, sturdy tree. He took his 105mm and 300mm lenses with him, hoping for close-ups. From about ten to fifteen feet up the tree he began making squeaking sounds like a rabbit in order to draw the bears closer. At first only the cubs were interested, but after about five minutes of squeaking the mother bear looked up and headed in an arc toward the tree. Johnson described what happened next in an interview given to Larry Kaniut:[8]

I stopped calling and started taking pictures. At about 50 yards distant I yelled at her, hoping to impress upon her that I was man. My yelling didn't cause any visible reaction. Some 30 to 40 yards out she looked back to the cubs. If there were any vocal signals, I never heard them; but the cubs then held back and followed the sow in some 30 yards behind her.

When she was about 20 yards out, she had increased her speed to a slow gallop; and at that point I recorded a blurred image on film. Either because things started happening so fast or because of my state of mind, my images of some events aren't real sharp.

Because of the lower limbs I could only hear the sow when she arrived at the tree base. She hit my pack and continued on beyond the tree another 10 to 15 yards before she stopped and looked back towards the cubs, which by this time were stopped a similar distance from the tree but on the opposite side from her and in full view of me.

When I glanced at the sow, I realized she was confused— wanting to run but not wanting to leave the cubs. Like a young, dedicated, foolish photographer, I was trying to focus on the three standing cubs. I remember thinking, "What a fantastic photo!"

Unfortunately, I never pushed the shutter button for about then a cub let out a bawl which instantly sent the sow for my tree.

I felt the tree shake violently. When I looked down, I saw her head and shoulders. The next thing I knew, I was being pulled from the tree. Evidently she had enough momentum and claw power to carry her up to my boot, for that is what she got hold of. I got the impression that had I been up the tree another foot or had I held fast to the tree, she would not have gotten me. The tree diameter at the butt was close to eight inches, and I was roughly 15 feet up; but until I return to measure, I'll never know for sure. . . .

I had held both arms in front of my face for protection. I pushed once with one leg but decided it was fruitless and I'd best not get her mad. She bit each arm three or four times and made a few lacerations in my scalp with her claws. Fortunately she had the safety of the cubs on her mind and wasn't a hundred percent bent on getting me.

After I pushed with one leg, I had my eyes closed except once when I looked up and saw her standing with mouth agape, arms open with claws exposed—just like a "live mount" one sees in a museum with the exception that she was looking to one side.

After she bit into my right elbow a good one, she grabbed my right shoulder and raised me off the ground a couple of feet. When she let go, I turned a little and came down on my stomach (just after I got on my stomach I remember thinking, "I hope she hurries and gets it over with").

I then pulled my head in and clasped the back of my neck with my hands to give some protection to my head and neck. Earlier I was reluctant to roll to my stomach since I knew that would expose my head. I knew that bears have a tendency to go for the head.

Though she worked me over only a short while, it seemed like ages.

She next bit the small of my back but couldn't get much of a bite because of my heavy clothing and because of the concave surface. She then stepped forward and bit my head.

I remember hearing what sounded like the crushing of bone and wondered why I did not die or at least pass out. Come to find out she had only removed a strip of scalp, and it was the scraping of her teeth against my skull and not the crushing of bone that I had heard. As I said earlier, I don't remember any pain.

She evidently figured I wouldn't give her any more problem for I heard her leave in the direction I vaguely remember the cubs moving. Right away I got up and headed towards the road, which was roughly 300 yards distant. I turned and looked back once, but I couldn't see much.

My right eye was swollen shut and I could only see out of my left by holding my head higher than normal. I pulled my coat hood over my head and held my right arm tight against my body to reduce bleeding. I lay down twice to rest before I made the road. Fortunately I lay on the road less than a minute before two vehicles came along.

Help did arrive soon, including a paramedic who bandaged Johnson's wounds. Johnson was airlifted to Fairbanks:

The nurses told me that I was a bloody mess and that they spent over three hours in the emergency room cutting my hair and clothes, and cleaning me for surgery.

Two doctors worked me over, transplanted some skin from my thigh to my head, patched the torn main artery in my right shoulder and sewed shut some cuts on my head. The puncture wounds on my arms were left open to drain and heal.

One doctor told me that the paramedic from Healy probably saved my life by stopping the flow of blood—they put four pints of blood into me before I went to surgery.

After two weeks in the hospital and some fine treatment by the nurses, doctors, my girlfriend, who is now my wife, and friends, I recovered almost to prior condition.

The grizzly bear family was not shot or held to blame for the incident. The bears were known to be in the area of the encounter for about a week prior to the mauling, but no other aggressive incidents had occurred.

In another incident involving picture-taking, one of the photographers was killed by the grizzly bear being photographed.[9] Late in the afternoon of September 25, 1973, Wilf Etherington, a biologist with the Canadian Wildlife Service, and Bill Schmaltz, a photographer working for Parks Canada, were helping to relocate a troublesome grizzly. The bear was a 527-pound male with a known history of feeding on human foods and garbage. The bear had been trapped twice previously in connection with break-ins at a bungalow camp. On September 23, the bear was trapped after breaking into Baker Creek bungalows, which had been broken into previously by a bear when they were poorly boarded up and food had been left inside. The bear was held in the trap over the weekend and then was lightly sedated with Sernylan so that it would recover quickly for filming.

Schmaltz intended to photograph the grizzly for a film he was making for Parks Canada about people and grizzly bears in the Canadian national parks. Etherington was engaged in a study of grizzly bear management problems, especially those related to garbage. He was also an amateur photographer and chose to get some footage of his own that day.

The bear and the men were flown by helicopter to the summit of the alpine pass over Totem Creek in the remote northern part of Banff Park. After a short while, the bear began to recover from the effects of the drug, but both men continued to photograph it and to move even closer. The helicopter pilot, Jim Davies, who had extensive experience in relocating grizzly bears, was concerned enough about the photographers that he took off and flew low over the bear to check if it was still under the effect of the drug. The bear charged the helicopter, and as he circled the bear a second time, the bear charged again, showing very good mobility. Etherington took movie film of the bear charging the helicopter. Because the bear had moved upslope and away from the photographers, Jim Davies landed and shut down the helicopter.

This was Etherington's first experience in observing a bear recovering from drugging at a release point. Perhaps because of his inexperience he and Schmaltz decided to approach closer to the grizzly, in spite of the agility and aggression the bear had just shown. They moved to between 90 and 140 feet for closer filming.

Davies, who was still concerned about the situation, left his helicopter and moved to about sixty feet from the photographers. He was there for only a moment before the bear moved rapidly toward Schmaltz and Etherington. They moved away from the bear, walking fast at first and then running. Etherington was slightly behind Schmaltz as both men moved uphill. Davies yelled to Etherington, who was closest to the bear, to drop his pack, which he did. The bear ignored it and soon caught up with Etherington. Davies ran back to his helicopter and just as he got there he could hear Etherington screaming, "No, no." Schmaltz could see the bear standing over Etherington and biting his head. Schmaltz threw three large rocks at the bear but missed. The bear ignored Schmaltz. By this time Jim Davies had taken off in the helicopter and, by flying only ten feet above the bear, he managed to draw the bear off Etherington and down the valley about 450 feet.

Schmaltz and Davies reached Etherington but his face was mostly gone and it was obvious that he was dead. Fearing another attack by the bear both men left in the helicopter for help. When they returned with armed wardens about half an hour later, the body had not been disturbed.

A short while later the bear, still nearby, was spotted from the helicopter. It was in a brush pile and, as the helicopter approached and circled, he ran in circles and jumped, apparently trying to attack the helicopter. The bear, still trying to get at the helicopter, was shot three times and killed.

The major cause of this tragic incident was the willingness of Etherington and Schmaltz to move close to the bear after it was clear that the bear was aggressive toward the helicopter. The extent to which the drugs used on the bear might have contributed to the bear's aggression is unknown, but other evidence suggests that drugs currently being used do not increase a bear's aggressiveness toward people after the period of recovery from the drugs.[10]

Sernylan, the drug used on the bear that killed Etherington, is also known as "angel dust." It is a "street" as well as a research drug (one reason why it is seldom used on bears any more), which is said to make some human users unusually aggressive. Since the bear was just recovering from the drug when it killed Etherington, this could have been a contributing factor. It is much less likely that longer-term effects of Sernylan will create aggressive bears. Thousands of black, grizzly, and polar bears have been handled using Sernylan, and only two (possibly three) attacks can be attributed to these bears. The evidence from the other known case suggests it was unlikely that Sernylan influenced the attack (see p. 71).

One of two really close calls that I have had with a grizzly bear occurred as we were releasing a large male grizzly from a trap. In August 1977 an ignorant person left a horse carcass outside the fenced Cascade Sanitary Landfill in Banff National Park, and the dead horse attracted several grizzly bears. After the park wardens discovered the carcass, it was moved into the fenced landfill. A large, aggressive male grizzly bear bent two-inch steel fence posts and tore cyclone fencing to get at the carcass. This bear was trapped while inside the landfill.

On the morning of August 19, Andy Anderson, the chief warden, asked me if I would help in the relocation and also if I would photograph the bear after it was released. The wardens had decided not to drug the bear before releasing it, and so it would not be marked and photographs might be useful in identifying it. I too did a foolish thing during the episode, partly to get photographs.

I knew that a grizzly coming out of a trap might try to attack people nearby. I vividly remember the grizzly's huge, black head banging against the bars of the trap as I approached. Between his eyes there was a raw spot from where he had hit his head on the trap. As I came near, he did it again while swatting the bars with his paws and making loud, blowing noises. The trap shook violently with his motions. My field notes state: "He looks like he could be trouble on the move. . . ."

Four of us, in two trucks, set off to relocate the bear in the backcountry. After a long, bouncing ride over a dirt road we set up for the release. The truck with the bear in the trap was in front with its engine running and we had a remote release for the trap door. Facing the other way, and one hundred feet distant in the second truck, was warden Jack Willman with a .308 rifle, biologist Luigi Morgantini, and myself. Both Luigi and I had cameras to get pictures of the bear as he left the trap.

Luigi had never seen a wild grizzly bear before, and so I warned him about the potential danger. I left our engine running as a further precaution. Luigi and I hung just outside the half-opened doors with our cameras. Jack sat in the middle seat with the rifle. I was on the driver's side.

We were ready, or so we thought. The guillotine gate of the bear trap was raised, and we waited. Nothing happened. Johnny Nyland, who was driving the other truck, jerked the trap back and forth. Still no response from the bear. Johnny threw his Stetson hat in a neat arc that ended with the hat sailing in front of the trap door. The bear didn't move.

We closed the trap door and decided to try to lure the bear out by building a "straw man" in the road in front of the bear. We propped a broom up with rocks, draped a canvas over it, and put a hat on our man. We repositioned trucks and people as before. Not really expecting anything dramatic, Johnny raised the trap door.

The huge, black grizzly bounded out and in a fraction of a second hit our straw man, biting the broomstick in half and sending canvas flying in ripped pieces. All this delayed the bear no more than a second or two and he continued galloping toward our truck. I took no pictures and was inside and ready to go as the bear neared the truck. I glanced to my right and saw Luigi still hanging on his door taking pictures. I shouted at him to get inside. In the next instant, the bear hit the fender on my side with his paw and tried to climb onto the hood but slipped. For a long, frightening instant, I stared the grizzly in the eyes, fearing that he would come through the window. Luigi was inside and I hit the gas. The engine sputtered and then caught. The bear slid completely off the hood as we pulled away but ran alongside the door on my side for about a hundred feet. Then he dropped back, swerved off the road, and ran into the woods. We slowly regained our composure.

In organizing the release so as to get pictures of the bear for future identification, I had erred badly in getting our vehicle too close to the bear. At a full run I knew that it would take him only a few seconds to reach us, but I thought that we could be under way in that time.

Angry male grizzly leaves trap and charges and destroys straw man.

Luigi Morgantini

I had forgotten that Luigi was inexperienced with bears, and I expected things of him that I should not have.

Anyone involved in the capture and release or drugging of grizzly bears should be aware of the potential danger. Mine was not the only close call with grizzlies under these circumstances. People who play such dangerous games ought to play them well, and carefully, to avoid injury.

Provocation is also clearly present when a person's dog charges and barks at a grizzly prior to the person's being injured. My records include only one incident of this nature. A few days after the incident I interviewed Kevin Branner, the person involved.

On the morning of May 2, 1968, Branner, who worked at the Lake Louise Ski Area in Banff National Park, was out walking his bird dog. They were at the base of a chair lift when Branner noticed a grizzly bear female and cubs, "several hundred yards away," coming down the path of the lift. Shortly after Branner spotted the bears, his dog ran over and started barking at them. As the mother bear rushed at the dog it returned to its master, bringing the enraged bear with

Mother grizzly bear which injured Kevin Branner, May 1968, Banff National Park.
Stephen Herrero

it. On noticing Branner the bear focused its attack on him. Quick thinking along with agility saved Branner from serious injury: For several minutes the bear tried to attack but he dodged it by keeping trees between himself and the bear. Branner received a minor wound on one leg but was otherwise unhurt. The bear soon returned to its cubs.

A week later at the Lake Louise dump, and from the protection of a car, I photographed the bear that attacked Branner. Wally McPhee, the warden in charge of the Lake Louise District, had decided not to shoot or trap the bear because of the provocation involved in the incident.

4

The Dangers
Of Garbage
And Habituation

A new noise, sight or smell usually catches an animal's attention and it responds in some way. But if the stimulus is presented repeatedly and nothing good or bad happens, then the animal becomes used to the stimulus, and attention and response wane. The animal has become habituated to the stimulus. If a bear regularly encounters quite a few people, but doesn't get food from them and isn't harmed, it simply gets used to people, will tolerate them at closer distances than before, and sometimes ignores them. Such a bear is habituated to people. Throughout this book, when I use the term "habituated" bears, I refer specifically to bears that have become used to people.

A habituated bear that also eats people's food or garbage behaves differently than a bear that is only habituated. Such a bear forms a simple association—"people" may be followed by "food." I refer to a bear with this expectation as being "food-conditioned." While habituation may occur without food conditioning, the food-conditioned bear is almost always somewhat habituated to the smell or sight of people.

Habituation combined with food conditioning has been associated with a large number of injuries. Inside the national parks it was probably the most frequent circumstance associated with injury.[1] Outside national parks, however, it is only rarely associated with injury. Outside parks, habituated, food-conditioned bears are usually shot and killed by hunters or poachers. Habituation by itself, without food conditioning, also can be dangerous, and it has been associated with at least one or two campers being killed by a grizzly bear (see pp. 69–70, 72).

How are habituation and food conditioning of grizzly bears, and their injuring people, related? One of the general rules of animal behavior is that animals are wary of strangers and are cautious regarding the unknown. Curiosity sometimes draws a grizzly into a person's camp, but grizzlies that are not accustomed to people normally avoid campgrounds and other areas of human activity.[2] If, however, these developments are located near regularly used grizzly bear habitat, then the unknown may become familiar. Grizzlies will explore such areas for all possible sources of food. If a campground offers them anything to eat, some grizzlies may begin regular nocturnal visits there in search of food.

Once a grizzly bear has learned that campground foraging seems to be all right, its close association with people may lead to confrontation or, more rarely, predation. However, even habituated and food-conditioned bears seldom injure people. The low rates of grizzly bear-inflicted injury in national parks are evidence of this. Most grizzly bears avoid direct contact with people and are much more interested in food than in trouble. Those bears that do injure people are usually trapped and killed.

My research showed that habituation and food conditioning of grizzly bears, and the consequent increased chances of injury, were most prevalent in major national park campgrounds that had motor vehicle access, especially when these campgrounds were near grizzly bear habitat. But the problem also occurs in backcountry areas where campers are careless with their garbage or storage of food.

Up to 1970, I calculated that inside the national parks, habituated, food-conditioned grizzlies were responsible for approximately two-thirds of all injuries inflicted on people.[3] About 90 percent of these injuries occurred in developed campgrounds in Yellowstone National Park.[4] Overall, Yellowstone has had more grizzly bear-inflicted injuries than any other park. Why? The answer to this question reveals the single most important thing that we have learned about situations leading to injury.

Prior to their suspension in 1941, grizzly and black bear "Feeding

Shows" were sanctioned by the National Park Service in Yellowstone. Park visitors seated in bleachers could watch bears eating freshly brought garbage, or even performing tricks to get choice tidbits (see p. 96). Open-pit garbage dumps, which grizzly bears regularly visited, were also used for many years in Yellowstone.[5] Many black bears were found along the roadsides, begging for handouts, although grizzly bears, always more shy of people, seldom did this.

Until the 1960s, garbage in Yellowstone Park was treated much like it was in other rural areas. Garbage cans were placed throughout the campgrounds. During the 1950s and 1960s, when most grizzly bear-inflicted injuries occurred in Yellowstone, grizzly bears regularly prowled several of the park campgrounds under cover of darkness, threading their way among campers sleeping inside tents. The hard-sided recreational vehicle was not common at campgrounds until the late 1960s. Edible garbage and casually stored human foods brought grizzly bears close to people, and the inevitable sometimes occurred. A camper on his way to the toilet in early morning might bump into a four-hundred pound grizzly bear; or a grizzly, smelling food in a tent, might rip into it and, when confronted with a person, attack.

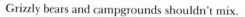

Grizzly bears and campgrounds shouldn't mix.

Yellowstone has recently led the way into a new era in which garbage, human foods, and grizzlies are more effectively separated. The abrupt closing of the garbage dumps inside the park in 1970, combined with enforcement of strict sanitation in the campgrounds and an effective bear-monitoring program, has reduced the number of grizzly bear injuries (see p. 15). Rangers at Yellowstone now have to trap only a few grizzlies each year for control actions. They do have a large trapping and radio-collaring program related to ongoing research.[6] Garbage and the availability of people's foods outside of the park continues to be a problem.

The problem of habituated, food-conditioned grizzly bears is not superficial. In the worst cases these circumstances have been associated with grizzly bear-inflicted deaths. Between 1967 and 1980, nine deaths occurred in Glacier, Yellowstone, and Banff National Parks. Eight of these deaths were caused by seven different grizzly bears, all of whom were habituated and food conditioned. The ninth incident was caused by a habituated grizzly bear that didn't have a known history of feeding on people's food or garbage (see pp. 69–70). These tragedies were probably avoidable.

Harry Walker and his friend Phillip Bradberry (nicknamed Crow) encountered a habituated and food-conditioned grizzly bear on the night of June 24, 1972.[7] Together they had hitchhiked into Yellowstone Park on June 22. A young woman, Vikki Schlicht, who worked as a chambermaid for the Old Faithful Inn, gave them a ride. Because she regularly entered and left the park, she did not receive the standard information handed out to visitors entering for the first time during a season. For this reason, Walker and Bradberry did not receive the warning literature about bears. Vikki Schlicht later testified, however, that she had warned the men about bears. Despite this warning, they chose to make an illegal campsite in the woods about a half-mile from the Old Faithful Visitor Center and sixteen miles from the nearest authorized campsite.

Walker and Bradberry stayed in the general area for two days. On the night of June 24, 1972, they visited with several young women, including Vikki Schlicht, at the Old Faithful Inn. At about midnight they were returning to their camp, talking quietly to one another. They started to walk into their campsite when Bradberry heard something in front of them and saw a bear coming at them fast. When he first saw that it was a bear, the animal was "approximately five feet away." Bradberry dove to his left and rolled down an embankment. At about the same time Walker shone his flashlight toward the bear. Bradberry got to his feet and ran. Walker ran also, but the bear soon caught him. Bradberry heard his friend cry out, "Help me, Crow, help me," and then there was silence. Bradberry heard more ruffling and reported that it sounded like the bear was coming toward him. He ran all the way to the Inn where he fell to the floor shouting, "Bear! Bear! Has my friend."

A search party found the campsite and Walker's body at about 5:00 A.M. A careful description and photographs of the site were made, Walker's body was removed, and snares were set to capture the bear. At 7:45 the next morning, a grizzly bear was trapped at the campsite. It was subsequently killed. Upon autopsy, human hairs, identified to be those of Walker, were found in its digestive system.

Michael Weinblatt, a park ranger for the Old Faithful District, investigated the site where the attack occurred. He called it "the dirtiest I have ever seen." He found a pot of "rice stew combination" in the crotch of a tree about "eleven feet from the tent at a level of about five feet off the ground." Weinblatt described the smell as "putrid." He also noted "cooked food in the fire pit, which was directly in front of the tent." Next to the tent there was also cooked food in pots and pans, and there were also other stored foods.

The bear that killed Walker was an old female, about twenty years, without cubs. She had broken and worn canine teeth, and her molar teeth had been flattened by wear. She weighed 232 pounds and was normally fat considering the time of year. Rabies was not detected. This bear had a previous documented history of garbage feeding and had been trapped in the garbage-holding area behind the Old Faithful Inn almost two years before, on October 14, 1970. At that time she was given tag number 1792 and was transplanted eighteen miles to Gibbon Meadows.

My interpretation of the facts related to Walker's death is that the grizzly bear was attracted to the camp by the odors of the foods left around it. The bear probably had little reluctance to enter such a place, despite human odors being mixed with food odors, because this bear had previous experience with eating human food and garbage. When the men suddenly confronted the bear at close range, she responded as if she were defending a food supply, much the same as if she had been defending a carcass.

Walker died of apparent suffocation caused by extensive damage to his trachea. Had he curled up on the ground when attacked and put his face between his knees and his hands behind his neck, he might have been spared the fatal injuries.

Clearly the major culprits in the death of Harry Walker were ignorance of the ways of bears, resulting in negligence by the men, their choice of an illegal campsite, and the long history of garbage and human-food feeding by many of Yellowstone's grizzly bears.

In nearby Glacier National Park, Montana, grizzly bears killed six people between 1967 and 1980. Before 1967 there had been no recorded fatalities, and there had also been relatively few visitors, small volumes of garbage, and most travel was by horse rather than on foot. Before 1941 only one person had been injured there by a grizzly bear.[8] Montana had had only two other recorded bear-inflicted fatalities since the days of the Lewis and Clark expedition.

Glacier Park is unique in the lower forty-eight states because it has the most hiking and camping in backcountry areas that are also the home of grizzly bears. A number of Glacier Park bears have had some experience feeding on human foods or garbage. However, the food-garbage-bear problem at Glacier has never been as extensive as it was in Yellowstone. Subsequent to the two grizzly bear fatalities in 1967, Glacier has generally managed food and edible garbage well. But only a few problems with garbage can lead to tragedy.

The first clues that something was wrong in Glacier Park came on August 13, 1967, when two young women were killed by different grizzly bears on the same night. A male companion of one of the young women was serious injured. Both of these incidents are mentioned in the Introduction and have been described in narrative form in Jack Olsen's book, *Night of the Grizzlies*. A Park Service report on them also exists.[9]

Granite Park Chalet is a backcountry lodge approximately four miles from the nearest road, high in the subalpine meadow-forest zone of the park. The area's scenic beauty had for many years attracted parties on horseback, but by the late 1960s the clientele had mainly shifted to hikers. Most overnight visitors stayed in the quaint chalet. Less than a quarter-mile from the chalet, the Park Service had established a campgound.

Julie Hegelson and her companion, Roy Ducat, were both summer concessionaire employees at East Glacier Lodge, which was run by Glacier Park Incorporated. On their days off in mid-August 1967, they hiked to Granite Park Chalet and eventually set their sleeping bags out in the campground. They did not have a tent. Just before going to bed, Ducat cached a couple of leftover sandwiches under a big log about two hundred yards away. He left his pack, which contained two candy bars and two packs of chewing gum, near their sleeping bags.

At about 12:45 A.M., screams were heard by guests staying at the Chalet. The Glacier National Park report on the incident describes what occurred:

While in a sound sleep he [Roy Ducat] remembered being awakened by Julie who was nearby. She told him to pretend he was dead. Roy stated that he and Julie were suddenly knocked about five feet outside of their sleeping bags by a blow. He recalled being on his stomach facing down. Julie was about two feet away. The bear "gnawed" into his right shoulder. Roy made every effort to remain still and kept his eyes closed. The bear then went to Julie and chewed on her, but soon returned and chewed on Roy's left arm and the back of both legs near his buttocks but he did not once utter a sound. The bear again returned to Julie and chewed on her. Roy recalled hearing her say, "It hurts," on two occasions. She then yelled, "Someone help us." She started to scream. Roy then heard the bear dragging her away rapidly down the hill. All the time she continued to scream. Her voice faded away as though the bear were dragging her a long distance away.

The attack left Julie Hegelson near death. Although the bear later abandoned her, she died shortly after she was found early the next morning. Roy Ducat's wounds were serious, but he recovered after hospitalization and surgery.

The country around Granite Park Chalet attracts grizzly bears during summer and early fall. They come to eat the abundant huckleberries and to dig the corms of glacier lilies. While they must have done this for thousands of years, a major change in their food supply occurred with the construction and operation of the Chalet. As the Chalet became popular and attracted more and more tourists, garbage overflowed. An incinerator was installed during the mid-1960s but it was inadequate to handle the volume of garbage. During 1967 there was a table-scrap pile only two hundred feet from the Chalet. Six grizzly bears, including one female with cubs, were known to feed on the garbage. In the past, but apparently not during 1967, grizzly bears had been hand-fed by tourists standing on the upper balcony of the Chalet. Park naturalists complained in writing that this practice could lead to human injury.[10]

After Julie Hegelson was killed, two adult grizzlies returned the next night to feed on the garbage. These bears, possible suspects, were killed. The next night the female with cubs appeared. She was known to be an old and experienced garbage feeder. She too was killed. Strong circumstantial evidence linked her to the attacks. When autopsied she was negative for rabies but did have a deep laceration on one hind foot. I doubt that this cut would have led to the attack. Aside from the cut the bear appeared to be healthy, though old. She weighed 265 pounds, which is normal during August for adult female grizzly bears in this area.

Why did the attack occur? Because the bear was a female with cubs, the Park Service report suggested that she may have been protecting her young. But this is inconsistent with the nature of the attack and with its continuance despite the fact that both Ducat and Hegelson played dead for quite a while. Furthermore, mother grizzlies defending their young seldom drag off a live person.[11] Julie Hegelson was dragged 342 feet from where she was attacked.

Other theories suggested that the attack was related to hot, dry weather and numerous lighting strikes and fires that were occurring at the time. These theories couldn't be rejected since on the same night another girl, elsewhere in the park, was killed by another grizzly. Odor was also suggested as causing the attack on Julie Hegelson and Roy Ducat. The couple had in their immediate possession lipstick, toothpaste, insect repellent, and Chapstick, although whether they used these was unknown. The young woman carried two tampons with her, suggesting that her period was about to begin.

While the cause of the attack must remain speculative I believe that the most probable contributing circumstance was the relationship between this particular grizzly and her experience with garbage feeding and people. It is likely that this bear fed on garbage at the Chalet for a number of years. She apparently had learned that, under certain circumstances, people could be approached. When she entered the camp she apparently ignored the candy bars and chewing gum, although their odors may have helped to attract her, as may some of the other odors I mentioned. Once in camp, the bear's evolutionary design as an opportunistic feeder, combined with her learned association of the smell of people, garbage, and nothing bad happening to her, led her to the point at which she treated Julie Hegelson and Roy Ducat as possible prey. The attack, however, was probably not focused on killing because, if it had been, death would have come quickly. The nature of the attack suggests that Ducat and Hegelson were first explored as possible prey. The bear may have abandoned Hegelson's body as a result of a conflict between having prey and the fear of being in a campsite occupied by people.

The absence of a tent to separate the campers from the grizzly probably contributed to Julie's death and at least four of the other six deaths in Glacier Park. Although a flimsy physical barrier, a tent may be enough of a psychological barrier to prevent the early stages of an incident, when a grizzly explores a person as something to eat. However, grizzlies have ripped tents and dragged people out and killed them. A tent only offers some protection.

Playing dead was the wrong strategy for Ducat and Hegelson.

Grizzly bears entering camp at night and methodically starting to chew on people, in contrast to grizzlies who charge and attack, are most likely acting as predators. The best resort in this case is to flee or fight back, depending on the circumstances.

The most likely predisposing factor related to the attack on Julie Hegelson and Roy Ducat was garbage feeding and habituation. An even stronger confirmation of the role of garbage, human-food feeding, and habituation, however, is found in the death of Michele Koons.

On the same night of the attack at Granite Park Chalet, a group of five other young employees of Glacier Park Incorporated were having a harrowing night.

Trout Lake in Glacier Park is only 4.6 miles from a paved road, but it is a stiff uphill hike over a steep ridge to get there. During the sunny and warm weather of 1967, many visitors came for the good fishing for cutthroat trout. Some of Michele Koons' party fished, catching at least one, but she did not, nor is she known to have handled any fish. Fish odors were no doubt prevalent in camp since a fish was cooked that night, and people had regularly cooked fish at this camp throughout the summer. Several fishermen had surrendered strings of fish to an aggressive grizzly during the summer, very probably the same one involved in the August 13 attack on Michele Koons.

The day before the attack, an aggressive grizzly treed a father and his son while on the trail above Trout Lake. The son, when confronted by an aggressive grizzly on the trail, dropped his pack and climbed a nearby tree. The bear tore the pack open and remained in the area for two hours while the father and son remained up separate trees.

This bear was by then well known to the Park Service. It was even better known at nearby Kelly's Camp, which is a private piece of land just inside the park. Here, the bear had been seen about fifteen times from mid-June to August 1.[12] It was involved in several break-ins and aggressive confrontations. It had fed on garbage and human food repeatedly, and it was sufficiently unafraid of people that it was aggressive in getting these items and in confronting people. Residents at Kelly's Camp wanted to shoot it, as did the Park Service, although the Service was slow to act.

When Michele Koons and her friends set up camp at Trout Lake, they knew nothing about the troublesome grizzly. They arrived around 5:00 P.M. and fished until 8:00 P.M. They then cooked a fish and some hot dogs. Soon Michele saw a bear approaching the camp. The campers fled down to the beach where they soon built a fire, hoping to keep the bear away. The grizzly rummaged through their camp and ate their dinner food. It took a pack and tore it apart.

When the bear left, they returned to the site, got their camping gear, and moved to the beach where they had their fire. They took only cookies and Cheezits to their new camp.

They arranged their sleeping bags in a ring around the fire. At about 2:00 A.M. the grizzly returned, going to their old camp and then the new one where it grabbed the cookies from under a log. It left and returned several times, each time prowling through the campsites. At 4:30 A.M. it was back, sniffing the campers as they lay in their sleeping bags on the ground. It bit Paul Dunn's sleeping bag and tore the back off his sweatshirt. Prior to this, Dunn had remained perfectly still but he now jumped and ran for a tree. The bear backed off and then followed. Several of the party started shouting and running for trees to climb. Michele Koons either made no effort to get out of her sleeping bag or her zipper was stuck. The bear bit her bag and started dragging her away. The Park Service report provided details on what happened next.[13]

> While in a tree Paul stated that he yelled to Michele to unzip her bag. She answered back that the bear had the zipper in his mouth. Paul remembered hearing Michele saying, "He's got my arm off," and "Oh, God, I'm dead," which is the last time he heard any sound from her. The bear dragged her up the hill and out of sight.

Her companions remained in the trees until dawn, when they climbed down and hiked to the road and McDonald Ranger Station.

A day later, August 15, an old grizzly bear female, matching the description of the attacking animal, was shot by park rangers two-and-a-half miles up the valley from the attack site. The autopsy confirmed that this bear had human hair in its stomach.

There were several factors that may have contributed to the attack. The hot, dry weather and lightning strikes may have agitated the bear. The party slept in the open without even the modest protection of a tent. Michele Koons was a fairly heavy user of cosmetics, and odors associated with this may have had some role in attracting the bear to her. Fish and hot dog or cookie odors may have also brought the bear into camp in the first place. Michele was menstruating and using external pads, which held the odor of menstrual blood. At least as important as any of these factors was Michele's inability to flee when the others did. She thus became the easiest prey.

In a broader perspective, the bear's personality combined with its garbage and human-food foraging experience predisposed it to attack. It was an aggressive individual encouraged to be so by the outcomes of its many interactions with people and their garbage and food. As with the bear that killed Julie Hegelson, this bear's long experience in getting food and garbage from people led it to decide to treat a person as prey. Michele Koons's body was partly devoured after having been dragged 107 feet from camp.

After the bear first entered their camp, the entire party should have left for the road despite the darkness. Habituated, aggressive grizzly bears such as this one are too dangerous to gamble with. A large party such as this *might*, had they acted together, have been able to chase the attacking bear from Michele by using noise and throwing objects at the bear. Given the circumstances and their lack of knowledge about bears, however, they certainly were justified in climbing trees. There is little doubt that the Park Service should have previously killed this bear and forced the cleanup of the backcountry campsites and Kelly's camp. Today these circumstances would not be allowed to develop.

That Julie Hegelson and Michele Koons were killed on the same night, in the same park, by different bears suggested the possibility of a common environmental trigger for the deaths. These were the first grizzly bear-inflicted deaths in the history of the park. Recent dry lightning storms, fire, sonic boom, cosmetics, and the odors of menstruation and premenstruation were all mentioned as possible triggers. We simply do not know. In my opinion any one of these may have contributed to the attacks, either by leaving the bears agitated or by influencing each bear's choice of a victim.

Despite the improbability of both attacks occurring on the same night without a common environmental trigger, I still believe that the most important factor influencing both attacks was the prior experience of both bears with human foods and garbage and that this made both bears willing to enter campgrounds. Both bears had lost most of their natural fear of people. The bear that killed Michele Koons was rewarded with food as a result of aggressive action on many previous occasions. The bear that killed Julie Hegelson was apparently one of six bears that regularly visited Granite Park Lodge to feed on garbage. The odors and activities of people were well known to each bear. When the opportunity presented itself in the form of unsheltered campers, each bear acted like a predator. Avoidable deaths and tragedy were the outcome.

It was nine years before the next grizzly bear-inflicted fatality occurred in Glacier Park. On September 23, 1976, Mary Pat Mahoney, a woman in her early twenties, and four female companions of about the same age were camped in two two-person tents at the Many Glacier Campground on the eastern side of Glacier Park. This is a drive-in campground, and at the time eight other campsites were occupied. All of the women were experienced campers and hikers. They were concerned about bears. They had a clean camp, no food was in their tents, they had no deodorants, perfumes, or odorous materials on them, and none of them was menstruating. They had even left their unlocked car ten feet from their tent as a refuge in case a bear did bother them. The board of inquiry that investigated the case concluded that they had "followed or exceeded the precautions one would take in avoiding conflict with bears."[14]

Despite their precautions, at around seven on the morning of September 23, Mary Pat Mahoney was dragged from her tent, killed, and partly devoured by a grizzly bear. One-and-a-half hours later two young grizzly bear siblings, both male, were killed. One of them had human blood between its front claws. Strong circumstantial evidence, including the similarity of the distance between puncture marks on Mahoney's body and the distance between both bears' canine teeth, suggested that one of these bears killed her.

Both bears had a known, but brief, history of feeding on human food or garbage and harassing people. On September 14 and 15, the two had come to an illegal camp at nearby Iceberg Lake. Six people were camped there with two horses. The campers had taken no precautions concerning food. Two bears ate some of the campers' food. This was the first report of the bears being in the area. Their experience with people and food seems to have quickly increased. On September 17, two grizzlies, thought to have been this sibling pair, encountered two hikers on the trail near Ptarmigan Lake. The hikers dropped their packs and left the trail. The bears fed on the food in their packs for about an hour and a half. On September 19, two grizzly bears moved through the Many Glacier campground, getting some garbage from one can. Later in the day, at nearby Fisherman Lake, two bears approached two fishermen. One bear had earlier approached a sunbather. Both of the fishermen ran and one, or both, bears trotted after them. One man climbed a tree and the other went into the water. One bear went into the water and shook the man's toe. The man yelled; the bear let go and left to climb up after the man in the tree. This man descended and also entered the water. Both men swam to the middle of the lake, and the bears did not follow. Three days later, on September 23, two campers made camp near Redrock Falls in an area closed to camping because of grizzlies.

The two men were discovered and charged with violating park regulations. During the afternoon the men returned to their campsite to collect their gear when two grizzlies, again thought to be the siblings, came into the camp and tore it up. The campers were kept at bay until the bears left.

This pair of grizzly bears seems to have had a history of only one week of feeding on human food and garbage, coupled with aggressive behavior toward people. This history began with their finding food carelessly left at an illegal camp on September 14 or 15. They next encountered hikers who fled and left their packs for the bears. Soon they got garbage at the Many Glacier campground. By September 19 they began to be aggressive around people, presumably because they had learned to associate humans with food. By September 23, one of the two bears, both of which were now well habituated to people, apparently treated Mary Pat Mahoney as prey. The excellent precautions taken by the five women did little to deter the bear. Its prior experience had taught it that approaching people could lead to a meal.

It is easy to say that once the bears showed aggressive behavior they should have been destroyed, but at the time nine years had elapsed since the death of Michele Koons. Today it is also known that young grizzly bears, after they have been weaned but before adulthood, can be a particular challenge in parks. These bears, especially males, have not yet established their home range and have no predictable sources of food or retreat. They still have youthful curiosity, and they explore and test a lot. Unfortunately they are also strong and therefore dangerous to people. Such a young male grizzly carried off three-year-old Brendan Harrop from a picnic area in Banff National Park on July 21, 1982.[15] Prompt aggressive action toward the bear by the child's mother and family prevented serious injury to the boy.

Current bear-management policy in Glacier Park, Montana, dictates that such bears be killed or captured and removed from the park after one aggressive incident. Such action is probably necessary to give an acceptable level of safety. But this new toughness toward grizzly bears must come in conjunction with a similar toughness toward ignorant and careless park visitors, whose food or garbage starts a grizzly off on such a path.

In late July 1980, I was at our farm in British Columbia, beginning this book, when I heard that a young woman and man, Jane Ammerman and Kim Eberlee, had been killed by a grizzly bear in Glacier Park, Montana, near St. Mary. The next day, Phillip Iversen, then the park superintendent, called me and asked if I would serve on the board of inquiry that was being convened to determine and interpret the facts about the deaths.

Jane and Kim worked at Lake McDonald Lodge in Glacier Park. In late July they decided to go hiking and camping. They ended up at the small resort area at St. Mary. Here was a developed campground catering mostly to people with truck campers, trailers, or other mobile homes. The teenagers chose not to stay in the campground and made an illegal camp between the campground and the development at St. Mary.

The details surrounding their deaths had to be inferred from circumstantial evidence because there were no witnesses. They camped alongside a stream that cuts through a very bushy area. The shallow stream, with its frequent meanders, appeared to our investigating team to offer a natural travel route for a bear moving through the bush. But why should a bear want to traverse this area, when most of its natural foods are found at higher elevations at this time of year?

About half a mile from their camp was a small garbage dump. The dump was on land that was a private inholding surrounded by the Blackfoot Indians. Years ago Glacier National Park had closed all refuse sites within the park because of bear problems. The Glacier Park officials had tried to get this dump closed, but the area was outside their jurisdiction. Because of the nature of the land holding— being surrounded by Indian land but not belonging to the Blackfoot— it was not clear if the county sanitary officer, normally responsible for supervising such operations, had jurisdiction over the site.

When our investigating team visited the dump we saw a horse carcass beginning to decay. Items such as this can attract bears from several miles away. Whether attracted by the dead horse or other garbage, the grizzly bear was probably heading to or from the dump in the early hours of July 24. Near his route of travel were the two teenagers, apparently sleeping on top of their tent because the night was warm and muggy. The bear had learned to accept the smell of humans from foraging at the dump. The bear might have approached the teenagers because of odors from sexual intercourse, but whether this was the case and what happened next are conjecture.[16]

One of the bodies was found by fishermen around noon of July 24. An investigating team of park rangers found the other body nearby. Both had been partly consumed. Early the following morning, Blackfoot Tribe members shot a grizzly bear near the site. Careful autopsy of the bear revealed identifiable remains of the victims still in the bear's digestive tract. Bite marks on the dead teenagers' bodies matched the dental pattern of the bear that was shot. The board of inquiry was unanimous in stating that the probability was very high that the "killer" grizzly had been located and killed.[17]

Because of the complexity of the jurisdictional issue, we were not sure how to prevent the problem from recurring. All of us were certain, however, that this and all similar refuse sites for edible garbage had to be removed from grizzly country. A bear scat collected at the death site contained, among other things, cellophane, Styrofoam, and cantaloupe rind, indicating that the bear had fed on garbage only a short time prior to killing Ammerman and Eberlee.

While Glacier National Park, Montana, has had the greatest number of grizzly bear-inflicted fatalities of any park in North America, deaths and serious injuries have happened in other national parks. In the late summer of 1980, shortly after I had returned from sitting on the board of inquiry that investigated the Ammerman-Eberlee deaths, I received a call from Andy Anderson, chief warden in Banff National Park. On August 24, there had been a serious bear mauling, referred to in the Introduction, in which the victim, Ernest Cohoe, had lost much of his face. Could I help in the investigation and the search for the bear? I offered my suggestions but couldn't help right away because I was scheduled to testify in a court case in Alaska regarding a grizzly bear mauling. When I returned, the situation seemed under control and a bear thought to be responsible had been shot. Then on September 1 a second incident occurred in the same area. This time two people were injured, raising the total to three within one week. It looked like a very dangerous bear was still loose. My phone rang and shortly afterward I left for Banff.

All three maulings took place in the Whiskey Creek area, less than half a mile from the town of Banff. Tense and armed, we visited the sites where the attacks took place and searched for clues to the bear's identity and the cause of the maulings. The maulings had all occurred in dense vegetation, and it appeared that the people had come very close to the bear before it rushed at them, attacked briefly but violently, and then left. The area where the attacks had occurred was surrounded by armed wardens, and we suspected that the bear was inside the ring.

We returned to the warden office and sat down to think. The area was completely closed to people and the perimeter was being patrolled twenty-four hours a day. We thought that this would prevent further injury to the public. Our planning session was interrupted by a radio message. We listened in disbelief and shock as the radio dispatcher described a man who had just staggered onto the Trans-

Canada Highway bleeding from numerous wounds. The bear had attacked again. Despite our precautions, a young man, possibly fleeing the police, had slipped into the closed area. The bear had a fourth victim.

Never before had I heard of a bear involved in so many incidents causing human injury. What was happening? Our first responsibility was to capture the bear. Dennis Weiser, a predator control officer with Alberta's Department of Fish and Wildlife, had come to help trap. He had extensive experience in capturing bears. He set several baited snares in the area, and we waited all night to see if we could either capture the bear or lure it to bait so that it could be shot.

The next morning, September 4, a large male grizzly bear was in one of the snares. Its almost jet black color suggested a black bear but its behavior and all other characteristics confirmed that it was a grizzly. It had felled trees and other vegetation in the area where it was snared. It charged violently when the wardens approached but was stopped by the steel cable of the snare. The wardens shot and killed it.

A few hours later, working with John Gunson, a Fish and Wildlife biologist, I began the preliminary autopsy on the bear. There were no significant wounds or injuries other than from the bullets that had just killed it. There was no apparent sign of disease; nor did subsequent lab work reveal any. The grizzly was huge, even for an adult male, weighing 761 pounds. This fact, combined with previous observations of the bear unknown to me at the time, provided clues that helped to explain the incidents.

A very important previous observation of the bear was reported about a week later. On the morning of the day of the first mauling, a reliable observer saw a large, black grizzly bear feeding on garbage in the refuse storage sites of a restaurant, less than half a mile from where the mauling subsequently occurred. The grizzly acted very agitated while feeding. It vocalized and swatted at the garbage bins. At one point the open gate of the compound swung shut and hit him in the rump. The bear wheeled and swatted the gate violently. The cause of the agitation seemed to be related to several black bears nearby in the bush. Until this bear arrived, they had been feeding regularly at the garbage bins for weeks. The grizzly periodically charged from the compound and into the bush. Several times the observer heard "bawling" much like a calf. He assumed that it came from one or several black bears that the grizzly had treed.

Our subsequent investigation of the site where the maulings occurred revealed that some natural foods for bears were present. However, the extensive bear trails leading into the woods from the restaurant

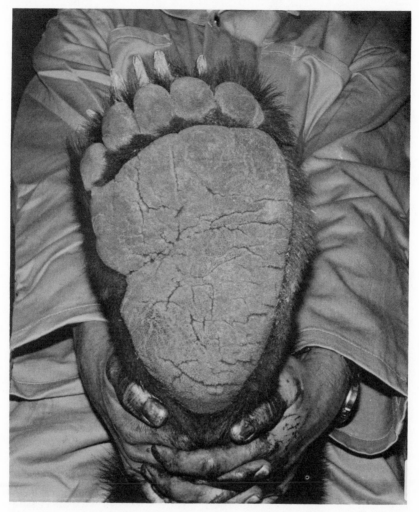

The author holds the hind foot of a 761-pound male grizzly which killed one man and injured three others, Banff National Park, 1980.   *Paul Kutzer*

garbage storage site made it clear that bears were in the area primarily to feed on garbage. We concluded that our bear had been attracted to the area to feed on garbage. Other evidence suggested that this bear had been feeding on garbage for many years. Tooth sectioning revealed that the bear was ten and a half years old when he was killed. Known growth rates of grizzly bears in nearby Jasper National Park showed that no male was ever known to attain this weight at this age without having fed on garbage.[18]

My explanation for the maulings (submitted to Parks Canada and accepted by a subsequent Superintendent's Review Team of which I was a member), was that the bear was attracted to the area by the ready availability of garbage. It was obviously a very aggressive individual, which, on the day of the first mauling, was additionally agitated by having interacted aggressively with black bears at the restaurant's garbage storage site. After feeding on garbage the bear apparently retreated into nearby dense shrub fields before returning again for garbage.

Unfortunately all of this occurred on the edge of Banff townsite, in an area frequented by hikers, fishermen, and tourists. While hiking in the bushes each of the injured people appeared to have come close to the bear, which charged and made a brief but violent attack. The attacks lasted only a few minutes each, and then the bear left. It did not appear that the grizzly intended to kill, or certainly each man would have been left dead because of the power and speed of this large bear. Instead, the bear acted as if it were responding to something that came too close.

The grizzly was willing to feed on garbage so close to Banff probably because it had a long history of having fed on it before, perhaps beginning in more remote sites. The attacks occurred because the victims repeatedly came too close to a bear that was habituated to people but was still very aggressive.

Habituation of grizzly bears can also occur without food conditioning, but this is a relatively recent phenomenon that has occurred mainly in Glacier National Park, Montana. In some portions of this park, grizzly bears are exposed to many hikers. Researcher Katherine McArthur found that this was associated with habituation of grizzly bears.[19] Grizzlies that seldom encounter people may act aggressively or flee when people are around. Neutral behavior, in which bears ignore people and go about their business, occurs with increasing frequency along trails where large numbers of hikers travel through grizzly bear habitat.

McArthur found that habituated grizzlies in Glacier Park not only act neutrally more often but they also approach people more often.[20] Approaching means slowly walking toward a person, in contrast to running toward him in a charge. McArthur has not found increased injury rates to hikers from grizzlies that approach people hiking on trails, despite the fact that in some areas of grizzly bear habitat that are popular with hikers, such as the Swiftcurrent trails near Many Glacier, one out of six hundred hikers was approached by a grizzly bear. McArthur believes that making people's activities predictable to grizzlies, such as by following regularly used trails and hiking during midday, helps keep bears from being startled and decreases the chance of injury to hikers.

My interpretation of her findings, however, is that habituated grizzly bears may be dangerous to campers. Once such a bear no longer avoids people the stage may be set for entering backcountry camps, especially if the bear has also learned to feed on people's foods.

One recent death, the sixth grizzly bear-inflicted death in Glacier Park, occurred on September 26 or 27, 1980, at Elizabeth Lake. The grizzly bear to which it was attributed was very habituated to hikers but was not known to have fed on people's food or garbage.[21] This attack on Lawrence Gordon took place at a campsite at the lower end of Elizabeth Lake, again in the eastern portion of the park. The victim's remains were discovered at this camp on October 3. The board of inquiry report concluded that there was a remote possibility the man was killed by another grizzly bear or he had died of other causes and that his body was then scavenged by a grizzly bear.

Lawrence Gordon was thirty-three years old and a former airline pilot. He secured a permit to camp and was twice warned by park staff that it was more dangerous to hike and camp alone than with a party. He did not, however, violate any park regulations and, except for storing his food quite close to his tent, his camp appeared to have been set up according to regulations. His camp was in disarray when found, and it was impossible to infer exactly what had happened. A sleeping bag, tent, and foam pad were scattered about along with several other items. Some of these were torn. There was no sign of a struggle.

Two days after Gordon's body was found, park rangers shot and killed a 379-pound male grizzly at nearby Helen Lake. The bear had tag number 201 in its left ear. Teeth marks in at least one book found in Lawrence Gordon's pack matched perfectly the dentition of bear number 201. The bear had been previously captured on August 8, 1978, in the Many Glacier area because it matched the general description of an aggressive bear. There were many subsequent probable sightings of bear 201 in the Glacier area, but he showed no further aggressive behavior. He seems to have tolerated the close presence of hikers and neither fled nor approached when they were nearby. Katherine McArthur, who was doing research in Glacier Park shortly before Gordon's death, wrote to me about her experience with 201:

I encountered him one day last summer as he was traveling on a trail. I called to make him aware of my presence, then moved off the trail and he passed by me only about ten to twelve feet away. After he had passed, I discreetly followed along behind him and watched as he encountered group after group of people (and horses). Yet he seemed to know exactly how to deal with them, moving slowly enough for them to be able to accommodate his presence. Once, he cut across the end of a switchback and stopped as a horse party and two hikers walked by, unaware of him. Then he moved onto the trail and continued on his way. . . .[22]

It is unknown how much experience this bear had with feeding on people's food or garbage, or if it did at all. There is no question, however, that bear 201 was thoroughly habituated to people and did not usually flee from them. Some of the thousands of hikers that each year walk the trails near Many Glacier had taught this bear that his instinctive urge to flee was inappropriate behavior when repeatedly confronted by hikers. Fleeing costs a bear energy and is a response that will wane unless a bear perceives that a threat exists.

Bear 201, thoroughly accustomed to people, probably entered Gordon's camp and, combining its past experience with people with a new urge, the bear attacked, killed, and partly devoured Lawrence Gordon.

Since 1980 two more people have been killed by two different grizzly bears in, or adjacent to, Yellowstone Park. Experience with peoples' food, garbage, and habituation to people, or possibly just habituation to people, were once again implicated as contributing circumstances. In each case the bear attacked during the night and treated its human victim as prey.

On the evening of June 24, 1983, Ted Moore and Roger May tent-camped out of their car at Rainbow Point Campground in Gallatin National Forest, adjacent to Yellowstone National Park.[23] A sign at the campground entrance recommended against tent camping, but there had been no bear encounters in 1983. On the evening of the 24th, Moore and May cooked a meal of steak and yams, cleaned up well, went to town for a few beers, returned and went to bed around 11 P.M. A board of inquiry report concluded that they had taken all recommended procedures for careful camping in bear country—their camp was clean, and food and garbage were stored in their vehicle. The clothes they cooked in were in the tent but not especially dirty.

At 2:30 A.M. on the 25th both men were awakened by their tent shaking. Moore later said it was like someone was playing a boy scout-type prank on them. Their tent poles were rattling, but they heard no other noise. Next Moore remembers the tent collapsing, and talking briefly with May. May then began screaming and was pulled through a hole torn in the roof of the tent. Moore exited by the same hole and in the full moonlight he could see a large bear, about ten feet away, standing over his screaming friend. When Moore stood up the bear grabbed May's ankle and ran, dragging May thirty feet. Moore bravely picked up a tent pole and, while yelling, charged the bear, finally throwing the tent pole at it. The bear backed away briefly. Moore approached no further but asked his friend, "Are you all right?" May replied, "I'm okay—but I'm not doing so good." Moore then quickly returned to the tent (thirty to forty feet from May) and tried to find his glasses, car keys, and a flashlight.

It took Moore several minutes to find these items. While searching he heard his friend scream again, then silence. Other people came and made noise, shone lights, and called for help.

The Sheriff arrived at about 3:20 A.M. The bear, still with his victim, was only 150–200 feet from the original attack site. A search party led by the Sheriff followed the blood trail toward the bear and May. The bear fled, again taking May's body. May was found at about 3:30 A.M. He was dead and approximately seventy pounds of him was consumed or lost as fluid.

Thirteen traps were set and less than twenty-four hours after the attack a grizzly bear was caught within ten feet of where May was killed. The successful trap was baited with garbage. Two other nearby traps which were ignored were baited with antelope. Lab tests confirmed the bear had eaten parts of Roger May.

The bear was a large adult male, identified as number 15. It had been studied for almost twelve years, including nine years of intermittent radio-tracking, by the Yellowstone Interagency Grizzly Bear Research team. Bear 15 was thoroughly habituated to people and had been observed a lot. Despite its extensive contact with people it wasn't known to have been aggressive toward people. All previous known human interactions resulted in the bear fleeing.

What caused bear 15 to attack and kill Roger May is speculative. Number 15 was captured twenty times previously and was drugged twelve times. Sernylan, "Angel dust," was used on six occasions, and another drug, M-99, was also used six times. Some people feel the Sernylan made number 15 irritable and aggressive before it killed May.

A more likely contributing circumstance was the bear's habituation to people and its history of garbage feeding. Its first known association with garbage and people was at Pelican Campground, Yellowstone Park, where it was captured in 1971. In 1974, number 15 was captured three times at West Yellowstone dump. Through the years it became so familiar with trap sets that it could get bait without always being caught. Up to 1982 it apparently only fed on garbage intermittently but during fall of that year garbage became increasingly important to it.[24] Just prior to the fatal attack on May "strong evidence" indicated the bear obtained garbage or dog-food within 200 yards of where May was killed. This food came from private residents who were not securing garbage properly.

Number 15 wasn't an overly aggressive bear. It was a bear who had learned over many years that people and garbage, or trap sites, yielded food. Number 15 had lost some of its fear of people. Under cover of dark, and in the quiet of a sleeping camp, this lack of fear combined with unknown other factors and Roger May was attacked and killed.

One action by Ted Moore was probably wrong. After he scared the bear from May, Moore returned to camp for glasses and a flashlight. At this point Moore probably could have gone to May and taken him to safety. But Moore acted bravely in chasing the bear off, and had he next gone to May he too might have been attacked.

On July 30, 1984, Brigitta Fredenhagen, of Basel, Switzerland, took out a back-country permit to hike the Astringent Creek trail and set up a backcountry camp in Yellowstone National Park.[25] She was warned by a park ranger about the hazards of backcountry travel and specifically about bears.

The area she was going to hike into was north of but near Pelican Valley, an area important to, and heavily used by, grizzly bears. Despite its importance to bears backcountry use in this scenic area has risen dramatically in the last six or so years.[26] Mary Meagher, a research biologist for the park, told me that at least four grizzlies in the area appeared to be habituated to people and to be reluctant to flee from them. This was probably the result of encountering too many people too often. Dr. Meagher also said that none of these bears was hooked on garbage.

Fredenhagen was concerned about bears and other wildlife. When she camped at White Lake, several miles short of her permitted site, she apparently boiled water for tea and ate precooked or cold food for dinner, and then cached her remaining food ninety feet from camp, suspended between two trees. When her camp was found two days later, on August 1, it was tidy and clean except for a fresh tear next to the front flap of her tent. Outside, six feet away, lay Fredenhagen's sleeping bag. Nearby was a piece of lip and scalp with hair still attached. The bear apparently pulled Fredenhagen out of the tent by her neck. The food cache had been torn out of the trees, apparently by a grizzly that climbed to a height of twelve feet. The food was eaten except for a granola bar. Fredenhagen's body was found 250 feet from the tent. Quite a bit of her soft tissue had been eaten.

Evidence strongly suggests that a grizzly bear pulled her out of the tent sometime after 10:30 P.M. on July 29. The bear involved was never identified or captured despite major efforts. Dr. Meagher used available evidence to conclude that the bear was probably a sub-adult grizzly (young grizzlies are more likely to climb trees), probably male, and apparently "not a naive bear relative to developed areas and human activities."[27]

Brigitta Fredenhagen did nothing to encourage the attack, in fact her cleanliness and neatness was said to be exceptional. Being by herself may have made her an easier victim. Another possible contributing circumstance was her camp location, adjacent to a hiking trail and in an area which was a cross-road for game travel. Fredenhagen wouldn't have known this, but the Park Service did. It is well known that in the Yellowstone region grizzly bears often travel hiking trails by night. Stormy weather present around the time of the attack was also proposed as possibly agitating the bear.[28]

In my opinion, the most obvious contributing circumstance was once again the prior conditions that allowed a grizzly bear to become used to people, and have little enough avoidance of them that it would enter camp. Exactly why this bear attacked, while others having similar backgrounds have not, is impossible to say beyond stating that the specific situation somehow interacted with the bear's experience and personality.

Grizzly bears usually enter camping areas at a walk and at night. Before an attack, a person seldom sees any signs of aggression. Such attacks typically occur when there is too little light for a person to see. No single course of action can be recommended. If you are suddenly bitten while your body is bulging out of the side of a tent, then perhaps the normal startled yell will be enough to let the bear know that you are a person and not a salami. Most campground marauding grizzlies still have enough "fear" of humans that they will flee when discovered.

But if you are camping in a remote area with a small party, the bear may press the attack. Under such circumstances playing dead would be akin to offering yourself to the bear. If you suspect a grizzly is about to eat you, you must do everything possible to deter the bear momentarily so you can escape. Shout at the bear. Throw things at or near it to try to distract it. Use every possible weapon or repellent you might have. Try to get somewhere that an attacking grizzly can't go, such as high up a tree, on a fairly hard cliff to climb, or on a big boulder.

5

Other
Attacks

A psychology professor I knew used to tell his classes, "Studying nuclear physics is child's play compared to studying child's play." He was saying the behavior of children, and all animal behavior, is complex and very difficult to predict. Anyone who studies behavior soon learns this truth. It applies to bears as well as people.

Because of this it was hard for me to write the previous four chapters on injuries inflicted by grizzly bears. Always I was torn between the more reassuring but possibly misleading statement, "these were the circumstances associated with injury," and the insubstantial "bears are unpredictable." I chose to group incidents that I believed had common, important antecedent factors. But the circumstances that I identified can't really be said to cause injury.

In Chapter 6 I document that circumstances associated with injuries also occurred many times without injury. In a given situation, a bear's personality, total life experience, and the specific conditions all interact. No one can say "that grizzly is going to injure someone." All I can do is point out situations in the past that were sometimes associated with injuries and identify what lessened the extent of injuries in some similar incidents.[1]

I have struggled for years trying to generalize about the behavior of grizzly bears during encounters with people. The preceding four chapters summarized the most important of my generalizations. But I can't reduce the circumstances of injurious encounters to a simple

74

formula. I just try to tip the odds in your favor. Regard me as a scientific handicapper. I study a bear's history—actually a lot of bears—and suggest where you should place your bets. I think I'm a good handicapper because I've been able to look at the track record of many grizzly bears throughout North America. And I am painfully aware that if I give the wrong advice, someone may suffer injury or death.

So far I've written mainly about common things people do that increase chances of injury. In this chapter I discuss other factors that haven't been associated with many injuries and I relate some encounters in which the contributing circumstances were unclear.

Norm Woodie and his wife may have felt that they offered little provocation on July 21, 1975. They had been out on backcountry patrol in a remote portion of Jasper National Park. I know Norm, and he is a mature and careful warden who at the time had forty-two years of experience in the wilderness. As he and his wife approached Cairn Pass on horseback, they saw a female grizzly with three cubs of the year about 500 to 600 yards away. The bears were hard to see clearly with the naked eye, but with binoculars there was no doubt that they were a family of grizzlies. The bears, or at least the mother, were digging and eating roots. Norm, who is always cautious around grizzlies, dismounted and took his rifle out of the scabbard. Because the bear family was near enough to the trail, Norm decided to try to get them to leave so he could proceed on patrol. He felt that they had lots of room in which to maneuver without feeling threatened. He started walking up the trail to let the bears know he was there. He shouted at them. The mother bear heard him, even from this distance, and stood on her hind legs for a few seconds. She then dropped onto all fours and charged straight at Norm. He shot his rifle into the air but she kept coming. Norm tells what happened next in his log for the day:[2]

> By this time she was out of my sight and I knew when she came over the hill she would be only 40 feet from me. I let my horse go as I could not fight both, and waited. I'm sure it was only a matter of seconds when she came over the hill 40 feet in front of me, still at a complete charge. I fired another shot at about 30 feet, which threw dirt in her face and stopped her momentarily. Then she came down again on all fours at a charge directly at me. She was ten paces or about 20 feet when I shot her, luckily between the eyes, which killed her instantly. During all this time of the charge the three cubs were always by her side. This was the main deciding factor—her having three cubs. At that final

instant I knew nothing would stop her and that I had to kill her instantly. If not being killed myself, or very badly mauled. I feel very sad that I had to kill her, but consider myself very fortunate, as I tried with all my endurance to give her every chance to run away.

In my 42 years in the wilderness, I have perhaps run into approximately 150-200 grizzlies and I have always used this approach—as mentioned—to scare them away, but as the saying goes "once in a life time." I hope that this very bad experience was that one time for me.

Some people might say that Norm provoked the incident by shouting at the bears. Clearly if he hadn't shouted and advanced, but had turned back, the bears wouldn't have seen him. Because of the great distance between him and the bears, he felt that the bears would have plenty of opportunity to flee. Indeed, this was not a sudden encounter at close range. The bear's charge from a great distance was unusual. This type of incident is uncommon, but I have records of several other incidents that fit the general pattern. As Norm implied, most grizzlies would flee under such circumstances. This one didn't.

Despite Norm's overall record of success with shouting and getting grizzlies to leave (he was usually on horseback and had a rifle too) if you see a grizzly before it senses you and you can retreat without attracting the bear's attention, then you are acting as safely as possible. I have made scores of such undetected retreats and detours. Even if a shout doesn't trigger a charge, the bear may approach out of curiosity.

Bears spend a lot of time exploring their environment, searching for food. Curiosity or just normal travel while foraging can bring a grizzly close to people. I believe that approaches out of curiosity are most often made by adult grizzlies that have little experience with people or by grizzlies that have been weaned but aren't yet adult and reproducing. Adult grizzlies sometimes force young bears without their mothers into marginal habitat. Such young bears do a lot of exploring and testing for things to eat. They can usually be made to flee but they are potentially dangerous, especially if they grow accustomed to people by getting food or garbage at campgrounds.

Another circumstance which might be associated with grizzly bear inflicted injury would be if grizzlies stalked and killed people as prey. A predator attacks its prey as a response to opportunity. Grizzly bears hunting elk or moose calves locate them by smell, sight, or sound and then attack. When a calf is caught, a few hard bites end its life and begin the bear's meal. Do grizzlies ever treat people like prey? When walking down trails in grizzly country should you worry about a grizzly crashing out of the bush with intent to knock down, kill, and eat you? Fortunately this type of incident is rare. I have, however, discussed how food- and garbage-conditioned grizzlies may prey on campers during the night. This is the stuff that nightmares are made of. I believe that familiarity with people and their foods creates the possibility that a grizzly will kill and eat a person in camp. But this is different from a bear stalking and chasing you during the day while you are walking. Certainly some such rare incidents have occurred. The killing and partial devouring of Harvey Cardinal, a guide and a member of the Doig River Indian Band, near Fort St. John in northern British Columbia, seems to have been such a case.[3]

Almost all grizzlies have entered their winter dens by January, especially in the colder parts of Canada. Harvey Cardinal must have been surprised to hear that a large grizzly was still active during mid-January 1970. He knew, however, that a bear's pelt is in prime condition at this time and that almost every piece of a dead grizzly was valuable—pelt, head, and claws. He set out to hunt the bear in sub-zero weather. There were no witnesses to the attack and killing, but Cardinal was apparently following grizzly bear tracks in the snow. Mike Crammond, in an interview with Jack Mackill, the wildlife conservation officer who investigated the case, recorded these details.[4] Cardinal was walking through the woods and had just passed a head-high mossy hummock when the grizzly attacked. "The grizzly had been lying behind the mossy hummock and had heard him coming. When he was just six feet past it, the bear circled behind the hummock into his tracks and hit him from behind. It ambushed him without warning." The attack appeared to have been sudden and deadly. The safety was still on Cardinal's rifle and his gloves were on. When found, Harvey Cardinal was frozen stiff. "Most of his abdomen was gone, up into his chest."

Shortly after Harvey Cardinal was found, the full retaliatory power of humankind was directed at the bear. It was hunted from helicopter and was finally flushed from the woods into an open muskeg area where it was repeatedly shot with shotguns and a high-powered .375 H & H Magnum rifle.

Jack Mackill described the condition of the grizzly. "It was fat, but it had its eyeteeth broken off near the gums. The others were loose, and some were filled with puss. It had a bad cut over its nose, some old scar tissue around its head, and a torn paw. It was probably a fighter and suffered the injuries that way." The bear was obviously not starving because Mackill noted that it had at least three inches of fat on its back and rump.

Perhaps the bear wasn't hibernating because of its injuries. However, the injuries as described are pretty normal for a mature, male grizzly bear, which is what I assume this animal was, based on its estimated weight of 575 pounds. Occasionally male grizzlies will be out this late, but it is unusual because there is little for them to eat. Berries and edible green vegetation are gone. Roots are frozen into the ground. When Cardinal walked close to the bear, the grizzly probably sensed that its only possibility for a meal was nearby. For a moment the bear may have disregarded its inborn fear of man.

The death of Harvey Cardinal is one of several that suggest that rarely some infirm or old grizzlies (and probably some "normal" ones too) may attack people without surprise, provocation, food conditioning, or habituation. The limited data on such attacks suggest that a grizzly that is having difficulty in normal feeding, either because of old age or some other reason, may try to prey on people. More often old or infirm bears will first seek out people's foods or garbage. The deaths of Michele Koons in 1967, and Harry Walker in 1972 were both inflicted by grizzly bears that were described as "old." The bear that killed Walker was twenty years old. I will discuss two other relevant incidents.

A bizarre noninjurious encounter with an old and apparently unhealthy grizzly happened on August 3, 1973, to an acquaintance of mine who was the chief park warden in Kluane National Park.[5] Despite its park status Kluane has almost no problem with bears being habituated or accustomed to feeding on human foods. The grizzly involved in this encounter could have had predation in mind.

Chief Warden Larry Tremblay was on backcountry patrol when he first saw two grizzlies about 450 feet away. One of them charged, followed by the other. The first bear pressed the attack, which Tremblay dodged and fended off with his rain slicker, poncho, and hat. Ten to twenty such charges were endured in this highly unusual incident, each charge beginning from a distance of five to thirty feet. During several of the charges the attacking bear leaped completely off the ground and launched itself into the air toward the warden. During the incident Larry used his slicker, poncho, and then his hat to slap the bear in the face after it charged him. Finally, after the attacking bear had grabbed both slicker and poncho, and Larry dropped his hat, the bears almost miraculously left.

Hours later Larry returned with a companion. The bears began to track them after they got the men's scent and discovered their camp. While the bears were in the camp, a shot in the air and a thrown rock triggered a charge. The bears were shot and later autopsied. The autopsies revealed a "very old female and a three- to five-year-old sub-adult grizzly." The female was "thin" (175 pounds) and in "poor shape." She had broken nasal bones and long claws indicating that she had not been digging very much. It was the female that led and pressed the charges at Larry and his companion. I consider it quite likely that the female's condition influenced her aggressive behavior.

Chief Warden Tremblay was fortunate to escape from his encounter without injury. Alan Precup, a twenty-five-year-old man from Illinois, was not so fortunate.[6] He died after being attacked by a young grizzly thought to be undernourished. Precup was last seen on September 9, 1976, when he left the tour vessel *Thunder Bay* at Wolf Point in Glacier Bay National Monument, Alaska. He intended to spend a few days by himself backpacking and camping in the monument. He set up camp on White Thunder Ridge.

When he failed to meet his arranged pickup on September 13, a search party set out the next day but found nothing. On September 16, four people from Seattle (Charles Jackson, Colin Milmer, Peter Talbot, and Leilani Vega) were camped along a lakeshore near White Thunder Ridge. Another couple was camped nearby and had gone hiking. The group of four was preparing soup and hot chocolate around noon when they noticed a grizzly (brown) bear approaching along the lakeshore. Banging pots and pans didn't deter the bear's approach, and so at 11:45 A.M. the group took their food and retreated to some cliffs.

The bear entered camp and tore it apart—ripping their tents and turning over camp items. It then approached the party, following their tracks, nose to the ground. They circled around the lake but couldn't shake the bear. By 1:15 P.M. they reached their camp again. They then left camp running toward a hill. The bear ran after them until it was only twenty feet away. They stopped and the bear approached to within ten feet. The bear walked back and forth, watching them. The party shouted and threw rocks at the bear. It retreated a short distance but continued to watch them.

At 2:45 P.M. the party of four saw the couple that had been off hiking. The two parties joined together at the bottom of White Thunder Ridge. From here they could see the bear investigating the hill where they were. All six people met the tour boat at 3:30 P.M. and reported the bear incident.

The Park Service helicoptered Ranger James Luthy to the area later that afternoon. He spotted a destroyed camp and was lowered to the ground. He noted it was Precup's camp, but since there was no sign of Precup he left.

A short while later a two-person search party arrived on foot at Precup's camp. They were confronted by a bear, which they threw rocks at, causing it to retreat. They left.

The next morning Luthy returned with two state troopers. Inspection showed that almost everything about camp had been disturbed and several items were bitten. Precup's journal was found with the last entry dated September 11. About 150 feet away, they found a bare skeleton, one intact hand, and both feet, still booted. There was no sign of a struggle at the death site. Inside Precup's camera there were two pictures of the suspected bear. It was a grizzly (brown), about three years old and its "appearance and behavior indicate the bear was undernourished."[7] This was thought to have been the only bear in the area, which was regarded as being very poor bear habitat with little for a bear to eat. It was almost certainly the same bear involved in the other incident.

It is quite likely that Precup took pictures of the bear that killed him. It is unknown whether the bear was in fact undernourished. When Precup saw the bear approaching he should not have waited and taken photographs. Since there were no trees big enough to climb near Precup's camp, this option was out, as was using a tree limb as a weapon. He either should have tried to avoid the bear, or if this was not possible, he should have improvised a weapon from rocks or from his camping gear. This might not have saved his life, but it could have helped his chances. Such actions have helped the other parties to avoid injury. Had Precup carried a bear-repellent device (see pp. 141–143), he might have used it to repel this young bear, whose attack seemingly began with curiosity and slowness sufficient to allow Precup to take pictures.

Rarely major attacks have occurred for no obvious reason and have been directed at people who have done everything reasonable to avoid attack. The following edited narrative was written by Joyce Thompson, a person involved in such an attack. The story was given to Larry Kaniut.[8]

Dying was the farthest thing from my mind in September 1972, when my husband Al Thompson and I planned our backpacking trip for trophy moose into the Kenai National Moose Range on Alaska's famed Kenai Peninsula, an area mostly closed to aircraft or tracked vehicles. We planned to catch the last ten days of moose season, which closed the end of September. Al was archery hunting; but if time ran out and he failed to get one, I would shoot one with my rifle.

The night before leaving, we gathered our gear together into one spot, double checking and eliminating any items we could get along without. Al was taking his 65-pound bow and glass arrows tipped with razor sharp, black diamond delta heads. He would carry his .44 Magnum revolver, and I would take my 30.06 rifle. We finished by stuffing our gear into two very full packs.

We adjusted our packs and started down the trail on a typically beautiful Alaskan fall day—the leaves were golden, it was warm and sunny, and the smell of Alaskan autumn filled the air.

Eight and a half bone-weary hours later we reached the area where we wanted to camp. Every muscle in my body ached and my feet were sore. As it was almost dark, we made a hurried camp, fixed something to eat and turned in for the night.

The next day we developed our camp into a very comfortable one. We built a lean-to out of logs and clear plastic, placing boughs on the ground for a mattress and covering them with a plastic floor. The front of the lean-to had a plastic flap to close out the cold night air. Al built a makeshift table from a piece of wood we found. We gathered an abundant supply of firewood and picked up paper and litter left behind by others.

On the third day, before crawling into his bag, Al located matches, a light, placed his .44 Magnum on a piece of yellow paper towel for easier spotting and laid my 30.06 by his side with the safety off and a shell in the chamber. Unlike me, he left his sleeping bag partially unzipped for quick access to a weapon. The combination of a warm sleeping bag, a tired body, and the crackling of the fire soon had me drifting off to sleep.

I was awakened about 4:00 A.M. by Al's whispering into my ear. He had sensed something and whispered to me not to move as something might be out there in camp. I listened, straining to hear a sound which might locate an animal. As I kept watching into the moonlight night, I saw the silhouette of a brown bear move alongside of me.

Al did not see the bear from his position. The animal was only inches from me, with just the plastic between us, and it didn't make a sound. It seemed to be moving away, when all of a sudden the bear was on top of me. He plunged through the top of our lean-to with a bellowing roar. This was Al's first sight of the bear.

Al grabbed the rifle; but with the impact of the bear, the rifle flew from his grip. For a fraction of a second the bear appeared confused as the logs broke and the plastic tore. He stood on his hind legs, towering over us. He was enormous, like a huge, gray driftwood log.

There was no time for Al to locate the .44 revolver. He knew the only way to save me was to immediately distract the bear from me to him. He also reasoned that if he turned his head in search of the revolver, the bear might instinctively go for his neck, thus killing both of us. As the bear dropped to all fours, Al grabbed its head with his left hand and slugged him with his right. The bear grabbed Al's left forearm in his jaws and by standing up, pulled Al out of his sleeping bag, tossing him through the air.

He landed at the foot of the lean-to. Like a flash the animal was over him. The claws ripped through Al's right side, almost penetrating the lung, and pinned Al to his chest. His teeth raked along Al's skull and managed to grip the scalp. The bear picked Al up with its mouth and one foreleg and ran on three legs.

With Al dangling by his scalp, the bear stood straight up shaking his head violently as a cat with a mouse. Al's feet never touched the ground. The bear ran a distance of approximately 25 yards, and a large portion of scalp tore loose from Al's head causing the bear to momentarily loose his grip.

While all this was taking place, I rose, realizing the heavy weight of the animal and horrible noise was gone. Al's sleeping bag was lying beside mine, empty. I had not seen Al's struggle with the beast because my head was covered, and I was baffled as to where he and the bear had gone.

I stood up in my sleeping bag, pulled it down and stepped out of it. Searching for a weapon, I saw the .44 revolver lying on the yellow piece of paper towel. The rifle was not in sight. Where was Al? Where was the bear? Even though it was not total darkness, I could not see any movement or forms nor hear any sound. I had a strong feeling of danger and of the bear charging me at any moment.

My first impulse was to run, to get away from the area. My common sense told me my best chance was to stay in this clearing and in camp as the bear would overtake me, and heading to an area of denser cover would only tend to give him a more secure feeling. My next thought was to stick the revolver in my waistband and try to climb a tree. Unlike black bears, brown bears do not climb trees unless they pull themselves up by using the limbs.
I was dressed completely in white, including socks, which must have made me very visible as I moved in the moonlight. The trees were large with no limbs low enough for me to reach. Dismissing any chance of escape, I cried "God, please help us," and braced myself holding the revolver in both hands. I may not kill a charging bear before he got me, but I would not give up my life without a fight.

As Al was being carried by the bear, he thought, "What a hell of a way to die." Then he thought of me, faced with the shock of my having a dead husband, miles from anywhere or anyone, and having to hike out of there alone. He became angry, and a strong will to fight for survival overcame him.

A brown bear is capable of dragging off a full-grown moose.

His strong legs and claws can move boulders and huge hunks of earth. A blow from his paws can break the neck of a moose or another bear. No man could come close to matching his strength. Al realized his only chance was to convince the bear he was dead.

When the scalp tore off and the bear momentarily lost his grip, Al fell onto a hump of moss. He grasped the hump with his right arm, holding his face and stomach down to keep from being ripped open, took a deep breath and held perfectly still. The bear cuffed at him, leaving horrible claw marks all along his side and shoulders. He bit into Al's back twice, while standing over him looking for a sign of life. There was none. Al's playing dead displayed remarkable self-discipline, as the pain was excruciating.

Then I heard the bear. He was moving away from me, heading toward cover in the direction of the little lake in the area. As I stood listening, trying to locate him, I heard Al call to me. He was running toward me. Moving closer to him, I could see his knit shirt was torn and he was covered with blood. "I'm hurt bad, but I'm going to live," he said. In the next breath he ordered, "Find the rifle, quick!"

"Where do you think it is?" I asked.

"Look at the end of the lean-to; it may have landed there," he replied. As he wiped the blood from his eyes, he held the revolver while I searched for the rifle. I had to feel around for it in the darkness. I found it and also a shirt for him to hold on his head, as blood was pouring down over his eyes.

Our minds were working fast, lining out immediate things to do. A fire! Got to get a fire going! Thanks to the dry wood, kindling and paper we had collected on our cleanup this was quickly accomplished. In a few seconds the flames were high.

Al slumped on the sleeping bag. He was cold and started to shake. The temperature was about 25 degrees. He must have lost a great deal of blood and was possibly starting to go into shock. Got to get him warm and look at his wounds. I pulled our sleeping bags close to the fire for him.

We started to check his wounds. He had been badly mauled. I looked for spurting blood, which would indicate bleeding from an artery. His legs were uninjured. He had a large hole in his side under his right arm from the bear's paw. This required a large compress, which we had included in our first-aid kit.

I had sewn large game bags from unbleached muslin for this hunt. The material was new and clean. I tore the bags into long strips to use for bandages.

Al's head was very bloody—half of the skin on his forehead was missing, from the bottom half of his left eyebrow extending back into his hair. Due to all the blood and poor light, I did not notice part of the scalp was gone. I thought it had been torn back and was still attached.

I wrapped his head around and around several times with bandages which were quickly soaked with blood. His left arm was badly chewed, and the pain was very severe. He instructed me to take my knife and cut off the shredded piece of flesh that was hanging from the largest wound. There appeared to be a great deal of muscle and nerve damage. . . .

Despite his extensive injuries, Al Thompson and his wife walked over ten miles for help. For a while Thompson was near death, but his will to live was tremendous and he survived.

Possible contributing circumstances in this incident were the "litter left behind by others" and possible prior wounding of the bear. The litter was there; the wounding possibility is pure speculation on my part. This illustrates why it is often difficult to understand the causes of bear attacks. Sometimes if we knew the history of the attacking bear, the cause of the attack might be clearer.

⌇ 6 ⌇

Aggression Without
Injury

MOST interactions with grizzly bears do not lead to injury. Most don't even involve aggression. Instead, either the bear is curious, or flees, or seems to ignore people. In this chapter I discuss interactions in which the person judged the bear to have acted aggressively but no injury resulted.

I caution against generalizations because my data on noninjurious encounters have been collected only when and where accurate records were available. I don't have a random sample or a complete catalog of noninjurious encounters. All but twelve of the incidents come from national park records and most of them are from Glacier National Park, Yellowstone National Park, Denali National Park, and the Rocky Mountain national parks of Canada.

I studied 135 noninjurious encounters. Most people involved in these episodes were hiking (46 percent, 62 out of 135 cases) or were in a frontcountry or backcountry camp (16 percent, 22 out of 135 cases).[1] Noninjurious encounters preceded by these different types of situations need to be discussed separately.

When such encounters were preceded by hiking I judged that the most common associated motives were either the bear responding to a perceived threat (62 percent, 28 out of 45 cases in which the associated circumstances could be judged) or the bear seeking the hiker's food (33 percent, 15 out of 45 cases). Females and cubs most often responded to the perceived threat (64 percent, 18 out of 28 cases in which the sex and social status of the bear was known). Bears responding to perceived threats probably did so because they suddenly discovered people nearby. In 95 percent of all cases (19 out of 20 cases in which the distance could be judged), people were unaware of such bears until they were less than fifty-five yards away. This statistic further supports the principle that a distant bear is normally nonaggressive and safe.

A charge was the most common aggressive action directed at people who were hiking and became involved with a grizzly responding to a perceived threat. Often such charges seemed as if they would lead to an attack because they came so close. In fourteen out of twenty of this type of incident in which the distance of the closest charge was known, bears came to within sixteen feet of a person; in the remaining such incidents bears came within twenty to sixty-six feet of a person. It is clear that close charges can occur without injury. Sometimes a person was charged again and again. In such incidents twelve parties were charged once, but three parties were charged three to six times, and Larry Tremblay (discussed earlier) was charged ten to twenty times—in every case without injury.

It is impossible to be precise about what a hiker should do if confronted by a rapidly approaching and apparently aggressive grizzly. Dropping a camera or other object may gain time. Especially if a bear is seeking food, it may stop to investigate the object. Drop a pack only if other objects aren't available. Remember, if you are attacked a pack may help to protect your body. In sixteen cases hikers confronted by an aggressive grizzly dropped some object. In eleven of these cases (69 percent) the bear stopped and investigated the object.

If trees are nearby and the bear is more than two hundred yards away, you may have time to climb a tree. You can climb a tree to escape an aggressive grizzly bear that is closer, but remember a grizzly can charge at a speed of at least thirty miles per hour, or forty-four feet per second. An Olympic sprinter doing the 100-meter dash in ten seconds flat is only traveling at thirty-three feet per second. If a suitable tree is nearby, you should get to it quickly and climb quickly. People climbed trees in seventeen cases out of the sixty-two noninjurious encounters with grizzlies. Try to climb the tree before, not after, the grizzly bear charges. My data through 1980 on encounters leading to injury yielded records of nine people being injured while starting to climb or after climbing a tree. The distance you can climb and the amount of time it takes to get up high enough are important variables. In only one case did a grizzly bear climb higher than sixteen feet and injure a person. Therefore, I would climb as high as possible given time and opportunity. Alternatively you may climb a lesser distance up a tree with limbs small enough to support you but too small to support a thrashing grizzly bear. Sometimes a person may be near a cabin or other secure shelter when confronted by an aggressive grizzly. In seeking any shelter the same considerations regarding distance and speed must be kept in mind.

But let's say that these options don't exist. You and a friend are out hiking in a lovely, small subalpine meadow. You've been quietly looking at the flowers and not thinking about bears. You top a small rise leading into another meadow and there, only forty yards away, is a mother grizzly with two young cubs. She sees you, momentarily stands on her hind legs, and almost in the same motion she drops onto her four legs and charges at you. What should you do?

Some of your options are:

1. Stand your ground or move slowly away while trying to intimidate the bear by shouting, yelling, banging objects, setting off a repellent device (if you're quick enough), or in the extreme hitting the bear;
2. Stand your ground or move slowly away but remain relatively quiet and attempt to be nonthreatening;
3. Immediately drop to the ground and play dead, or;
4. Run away.

Neither the data on noninjurious encounters nor my understanding of bear behavior permits me to strongly recommend any one course of action. Until experimental work is done, real incidents remain too complex to allow for conclusions.

Table 3 (p. 88) lists some of the actions of hikers during noninjurious encounters. From this list I conclude that there is no specific act that will provoke an attack in all such circumstances. I don't, however, recommend playing dead (unless attack is imminent) or running away. Both actions keep you from watching the bear and responding to its actions. Running may only make the bear chase you. One intepretation of the data is that the bear decides whether to attack a person before it charges. If this is the case it wouldn't matter what you did.

What I would do if confronted at close range by a charging grizzly bear would be to stand my ground or slowly back away and talk to the bear, trying to let it know what I am, not to threaten it. Avoid staring directly at the bear, which threatens it, but watch it closely. Many people have stood their ground and tried to intimidate the bear. Acting aggressively *toward* the grizzly may be appropriate if you face

TABLE 3
Actions by people during grizzly bear encounters
that *didn't* result in injury

	ACTION	NUMBER OF TIMES MENTIONED IN INCIDENT ACCOUNT
NOISE	Scream	4
	Shout	42
	Growl	1
	Fire gun (not shoot bear)	5
PASSIVITY	Faint, play dead, be passive	10
	Stand still	23
OTHER	Run away	39
	Drop a pack	15
	Climb a tree	28
ACTION TOWARD BEAR	Threw object at bear	9
	Hit bear	3

a young, single grizzly who is more curious about you than aggressive, if the grizzly appears sick or wounded, or if it has been stalking you. In these cases your aggression may repel the bear.

The data show that standing your ground and either making noise or being quiet were done in many noninjurious encounters between bears and hikers and didn't lead to injury. Two sudden encounters in which I know the people involved serve to illustrate this.

On July 18, 1972, Chris Dunkley was hiking in the backcountry of Banff National Park in the company of his wife and another couple. They were about three miles from Lower Waterfowl Lake on the trail to Cirque Lake, hiking in fairly open coniferous forest. At about 10:00 A.M. they met a female grizzly with one cub. Chris's written account follows:

> At first sighting the sow ran across our front, approximately 40 yards in front. She traveled from our right to our left and was hidden from view because she was lower, in a little creek bed. A few seconds after she was followed by her cub. Then she reversed and charged to approximately four feet of me (in the lead) before swerving off to my right. The first charge broke a fishing rod held in my hand. About 30 yards to my right she whirled and charged again because at this moment the cub was close to me but running to catch up with the sow. The third charge was just a swoop bluff which took her to my right again where she met

her cub and left peacefully. The second charge forced me to jump behind a tree. The 3 other persons, bunched, held ground and yelled loudly. We all stood firm and did not run. I in the lead threatened and yelled and had to jump behind trees, but generally held ground.[2]

Chris is a level-headed person with considerable experience as a backpacker and hiker. He had seen grizzlies before, but had never experienced anything like what occurred. Injury may have been avoided because the entire party responded well. Note that the party generally stayed together, held their ground, and shouted or yelled at the mother bear.

The closeness of the first charge, actually breaking Chris's fishing rod, clearly illustrates how close charging grizzlies may come without injuring people.

As described, my data show that many hikers have faced multiple charges and were not injured. Jenny Clark faced such a situation and escaped without injury. At the time of her encounter Jenny was a seasonal park naturalist in Jasper National Park. At ten on the morning of June 17, 1972, she was quietly hiking alone on the Maligne Canyon Nature Trail only five minutes from the parking lot when she suddenly saw a female grizzly with two cubs of the year feeding not more than thirty-three feet away. Jenny continues the story in excerpts taken from one of my incident report forms that she sent to me:

Because she had not heard me come up behind her while she was feeding, her first reaction was a very loud growl, as she spun on her hind feet and revealed for an instant two cubs of the year on her far side. She ran with them into the trees at the edge of the clearing and both cubs immediately climbed trees—it was definitely a grizzly despite this behavior. The sow then came out of the bush and charged down the trail. I had not moved and stood facing her but averting my eyes so as not to look her in the face. I made no noise or movement. She stopped her charge about 20 feet in front of me, turned sideways in an apparently ritualized, stiff-legged, hackles-up posture and went back to her cubs who were whimpering from the tops of their trees. She stood up at the base of the trees, talking back to them, then faced out at me and charged again. This happened 3 times. Then the cubs came halfway down the tree and I felt I could try backing out. Wrong move! Though she seemed to be turned away from me my first step initiated another 3 charges that froze me in my

The mother grizzly bear that charged Chris Dunkley's party near
Cirque Lake, Banff National Park, Alberta, came so close that she
broke Chris's fishing rod.

tracks. The cubs stayed at halfmast though and after the 6th
charge she simply gathered her cubs and cleared out, leaving me
alone in the clearing.[3]

Jenny might have avoided this incident by being more alert or by
making noise while hiking; but, given where the incident occurred,
few people would have anticipated meeting a grizzly bear. Jenny thinks
that possibly the bear was traveling to a nearby dump. Jenny's behavior
of quietly standing her ground and trying not to threaten the bear
seems to have led to the good results.

Unfortunately I haven't been able to determine "cause and effect" from such case histories. Don't confuse my lack of clear recommendations about what to do before a possible attack with my more certain suggestions about actual attacks.

So far I have talked mainly about noninjurious encounters between grizzly bears and hikers. I also examined twenty-two records of people who were camping before being involved in a noninjurious encounter. In fourteen of these twenty-two cases, the bear appeared to be seeking food. Grizzlies aggressively seeking food sometimes charged at people, but they also used other forms of aggression, such as slowly but deliberately approaching people. If you think that a bear is after food, you can often buy time by throwing an object away from yourself and toward the bear. You may then be able to leave the area or climb a tree or seek other shelter. Grizzlies aggressively seeking food may hang around for a long while. Three of fourteen such noninjurious incidents lasted from thirty minutes up to three hours. If in a tree, you should remain there until the bear has been gone for at least ten or fifteen minutes, and then quickly abandon the site and report the incident to proper authorities.

If you are armed and have repellent devices, you can try to chase away a food-seeking or curious grizzly. Use noisemakers such as "scaring" shells (see p. 143), freon boat horns (see p. 127), shout, rev engines, or bang pots. Keep making loud noises until the bear leaves or becomes aggressive. If it continues to approach or charges, keep up the noise but be ready with an appropriate firearm (see pp. 241–246). Without a proper firearm for back-up, repellents or human aggression should be used mainly from long distances and then only if you have a nearby tree to climb.

7

The Tolerant Black Bear

MOST people don't fear black bears as they do grizzlies. There are few if any accounts by pioneers and explorers depicting ferocious black bears that have withstood extensive wounds and attacked the hunter. Even though black bears lived in most areas where the pioneers settled, this bear rightfully never became the topic of fearsome legend.

When western Europeans came to North America, the black bear was distributed from the Atlantic to the Pacific and from northern Mexico to the limit of treeline in the northern Arctic, wherever there was adequate cover where the bear could escape potential harm.

The black bear has adjusted to the development of North America much better than has the grizzly bear. Today black bears live in forty of the contiguous United States and in Alaska, in a few places in northern Mexico, and in all of the Canadian provinces and territories except Prince Edward Island (see p. 95). For the most part they are found where habitat is suitable and are excluded only where extensive forest clearing has occurred, such as in parts of the eastern and central United States. In many areas, however, settlement without clear-cutting or dense population has provided black bears with new food sources—such as abandoned fruit orchards—that may have increased the bears' numbers.

The black bear has expanded its range to some degree in areas that were once populated by grizzly bears. The Ungava Peninsula of northern Quebec and the upper-subalpine-forest zone of Yosemite National Park are such areas.[1] Black bears have been successfully transplanted into Arkansas and Louisiana, where they have recovered from historical population lows to the higher levels they enjoy today.[2]

Once classified as a nuisance or pest species because of agricultural depredations, the black bear is now a big-game species in every one of the United States where it is found except Maine and in every province and territory of Canada except Prince Edward Island.

Bear populations are very hard to count, and most census figures are little more than extrapolations from knowledge of populations in small segments of similar habitats. A figure of 500,000 ± 200,000 black bears is a reasonable guesstimate for all of North America. This figure is in the same ballpark as Ernest Thompson Seton's estimate of 500,000 for the continent before the arrival of western Europeans, although Seton's figure was probably quite low.[3]

Between 1960 and 1980, black bears injured over five hundred people. This may make them sound more ferocious than grizzlies, which they are definitely not. The large number of injuries is partly because there are about ten times as many black bears in North America as there are grizzlies. Also, over 90 percent of the recorded black bear-inflicted injuries were minor. I found only thirty-five cases out of more than five hundred in which injury was major. These included twenty-three deaths through 1980, many of which are discussed in the next chapter. (Remember that records of deaths go back to 1900.) The small incidence of major injuries contrasts sharply with the grizzly bear situation, where more than half of the injuries were major.

Most black bear-inflicted injuries occurred in national parks, typically happening in campgrounds where black bears were seeking food or along roadsides where "panhandler" black bears begged for food. At least 90 percent of the injuries inflicted by black bears during the period between 1960 and 1980 I attribute to bears habituated to people and conditioned to eat human foods. Such bears will forage in campgrounds seeking out any edible garbage or inadequately stored food, even to the point of breaking into cars, where they can rip and twist the steel as if it were aluminum. Along roadsides they readily learn that begging leads to handouts unless feeding is strictly prohibited. Along some backcountry trails they have learned rob-and-run tactics that literally scare backpackers out of their packs.[4] In rural and remote areas they quickly discover anything belonging to humans that is edible.

The black bear's intense motivation to feed on human foods or garbage has probably set up hundreds of thousands of situations that could have led to human injury, yet only a few did. During the sixties and early seventies, I watched people hand-feed black bears along national park roadsides and at dumps. Black bears were sometimes made to stand on their hind legs and "dance" for small edible bits. I've seen people pet, poke, and even "shake hands" with a black bear. The restraint that the powerful black bear normally displayed in these circumstances always amazed me.

One incident, which I did not witness, comes from the files of Yellowstone Park and harkens back to the era of the bear feeding shows.[5] A "proper and matronly woman" repeatedly enticed a black bear to stand and "dance" on its hind legs for small food scraps. When the scraps were gone and the bear was dropping back to all fours, the bear's front claws gently raked along the front of the woman, giving her only minor scratches but baring her bosom. The woman, embarrassed and incensed by the incident, demanded to the superintendent that the bear be destroyed. The superintendent chose to protect the bear.

Black bear being hand fed by tourist, Great Smoky Mountains National Park.
Jane Eager

Present black bear range (approximate).

Mike Pelton and Jane Tate Eager, two researchers from the University of Tennessee at Knoxville, studied the hundreds of black bears and millions of tourists that are found in Great Smoky Mountains National Park each year.[6] Over a three-year period they observed what happened in 392 instances in which roadside bears were either fed or approached people for food. I discuss this interesting research in detail at the end of Chapter 15, but to summarize it here, they saw 624 aggressive acts directed by the bears toward people. Most acts of aggression were recorded from bears that were roadside regulars and had seemingly learned that aggression could bring food. Only thirty-seven aggressive acts out of 624 (6 percent) resulted in contact with a person. There were no major injuries observed. Crowding or petting preceded twenty-nine (78 percent) of the situations leading to contact.

Further research conducted in Great Smoky Mountains National Park, a focal point for black bear problems, showed that from 1964 to 1976 there were 1,028 reported black bear incidents for the whole park.[7] During this period 107 people were reported to have been injured. Most of these injuries involved bear-people concentrations,

Yellowstone National Park bear-feeding show of the 1930s.

Yellowstone National Park Archives

Yellowstone bear-feeding platform.   *Yellowstone National Park Archives*

such as occur along roadsides—thirty-two of the injuries involved people feeding bears, and three involved people petting the bears that injured them. There were only seven backcountry injuries during this period, and all occurred at heavily used sites, also suggesting the influence of human food or garbage.

In some national parks, black bears cause extensive property damage. They become clever and powerful nuisances whose ability to raid camps tests the wits and patience of even the most seasoned outdoorsman. In a two-year period during the mid-seventies, park research biologist Dale Harms estimated that 3,840 black bear camp raids occurred in Yosemite National Park.[8] Over three years, 1,493 reports were taken of automobiles being damaged by black bears seeking food. Some bears in Yosemite regularly smashed vehicle windows and pulled out window and door frames in pursuit of food. Harms found that vehicles with food stored in the passenger section, rather than in the trunk, were particularly vulnerable. Vehicles with

Black bears and attendant at Jasper Park Dump, 1968.   *Stephen Herrero*

food stored in the trunk had only 18 percent of the damages.

Irate campers escaping crime in the cities were not consoled to discover Yosemite break-and-enter artists cloaked in fur and standing on four feet. Action came fast, primarily through visitor education and information programs.[9] In 1975 Yosemite reported 879 incidents in areas near roads (frontcountry), with damages exceeding $100,000. By 1979 the number of frontcountry incidents decreased to 161, with damages estimated at $13,000.

In Yosemite backcountry, probably frequented by many break-and-enter bears that had left the frontcountry, the reported incidents increased from 100 in 1975 to 225 in 1979, with a high of 371 in 1977.[10] An estimated 60 to 80 percent of the bear population perfected their campground-raiding skills to the point where conventional food-storage techniques would not work. These bears have spoiled many a vacation and have inflicted minor injuries to people. Although the park is implementing a major campaign to return the bears to feeding almost exclusively on natural foods, once a bear has learned how to raid camps or force food from hikers it is hard to make it stop. Habituated, food- or garbage-conditioned black bears usually have to be killed.

Sudden encounters with black bears, even mothers with cubs, almost never lead to injury—further evidence of the bears' tolerance

Camper torn open by black bear, Yosemite National Park. *Dale Harms*

for human beings. In a sudden encounter the black bear's behavior is different from the grizzly's. When a wild black bear suddenly encounters a person, it frequently will charge toward the person, swatting the ground with a front paw or making loud, blowing noises. Although such actions may make your palms sweat and your legs shake, they are rarely followed by attack.

My records through 1980 show only four sudden encounters in which people were injured by female black bears with cubs. There were six injuries and no deaths. In these incidents the black bear mothers seemed to be defending their cubs.

One of these incidents, resulting in two injuries, occurred in a national park. It took place half a mile south of the Mountain Ash Creek campsite in Yellowstone National Park on August 10, 1973.[11] At about noon, Michael Whitten and his companion, Mark Seeley,

Black bear family begs by roadside, Yellowstone National Park, 1968.

Stephen Herrero

both nineteen years old, were out for a short hike. As they were crossing an open willow area, they observed what they thought to be a brown-colored black bear female. She had three cubs of the year with her. The cubs ran and climbed a tree as the female bear charged. The young men also ran to trees, and each climbed a different tree to a height of about ten feet. The bear climbed the tree that Michael Whitten was in and "pulled him down by his right foot and proceeded to maul and bite him in the chest, stomach, right upper thigh, left wrist and left ankle (seventy-one stitches total)."

Mark Seeley saw his friend being mauled and, while still in his tree, yelled to divert the bear's attention. In response, the bear left Whitten and dragged Seeley from his tree by the right foot. Seeley received injuries to his foot and to the right side of his buttocks (eight stitches). Both young men played dead, and the mother bear retrieved her three cubs and left. The area was closed for eight days, but the female bear was not killed. No further incidents occurred in the area.

The actions of the bear in this case were very much like those of a grizzly. The victims seemed convinced that the bear was a black bear, but I can't rule out the possibility that it was a grizzly.

In his book *Bears*, Ben East, a writer and field editor for *Outdoor Life* for more than thirty years, relates three other incidents that I consider to be the result of sudden encounters.[12] Each incident involved a female with young.

One of the incidents involved Maurice Day and Lloyd Hilborne who were running a survey line in the Warroad district of northern Minnesota. Ahead of them in the bush they saw a black bear cub, which at first they mistook for a black wolf. East describes what happened:

> The cub disappeared and before they had gone thirty feet farther, an adult bear that they later estimated to weigh five hundred pounds [almost certainly far too high—SH] stood up from a bed two hundred feet away and made a determined rush for them.
>
> They were in a stand of small trees, only three or four inches in diameter. They scrambled up the nearest two, but Hilborne did not make it high enough. The bear stood on her hind legs, grabbed him by a heel and yanked him down.
>
> She bit him around the legs, arms and shoulders. Both men yelled, and she dropped Lloyd and climbed after Maurice. The tree bent with her weight and he jumped and ran. But she overtook him and closed her jaws on his neck. Only a miracle of chance saved him. Her teeth went into the back of the neck and out under the side of the jaw.
>
> Then Hilborne started to get back on his feet, and she let go of Day and went back to her first victim. For the ten or fifteen minutes the attack lasted she mauled first one man, then the other, turning time after time on the one that was trying to get up.
>
> Hilborne finally fought back with his jackknife, stabbing her around the neck and shoulders, and Day fought her off with a four-foot club broken from a dead tree. At the end she broke off the attack, stood and looked at the two men, then ran into the bush.
>
> Day's throat was torn and he was bitten about the head, shoulders, back and hips. Hilborne had more than two hundred tooth and claw wounds.

Other versions of this incident exist, but all suggest the involvement of a female with cubs. Both men recovered from the attack, although it was severe enough that they could have died. Again, I have no records of people being killed as a result of black bear attacks preceded by a sudden encounter.

Researchers studying black bears confirm that black bear females are seldom aggressive, even when harassed. Al Erickson, who made the pioneer study of black bears in North America employing live trapping, captured 96 bears 109 times.[13] He stated that, contrary to the popular belief at that time,

> Most female bears did not display strong maternal protective instinct, and quickly abandoned cubs when danger was imminent. In only 3 of 10 cases was the female detected in the vicinity of where cubs of the year had been captured. Two of these mothers attempted to drive off the handling crew by rushing forward, snorting and rapidly chomping their teeth. At no time did they approach closer than ten feet. A particularly aggressive charge could be terminated by making a great deal of noise, particularly loud shouting, which seemed to unnerve the animal.

Ed Harger, a Michigan wildlife biologist who studied black bears after Erickson, reported that in trapping and handling more than three hundred bears, only four times did females run them off while the biologists were removing cubs from a live trap.[14] Lynn Rogers's experiences with handling black bear cubs offer conclusive evidence regarding the reluctance of black bear mothers to attack people:[15]

> In 18 cases during our black bear studies we treed or otherwise captured cubs with their mothers present. None of the mothers made contact with us even when we held their cubs and the cubs bawled. The mothers typically stayed in brush cover and huffed. None approached closer than seven meters; one repeatedly bluff-charged to that distance, retreating after each charge. One mother may have left the scene with her remaining cubs after I chased one cub up a tree and captured it; at least I did not detect her again.
>
> In nine cases in addition to the above 18, I released cubs that various trappers had trapped. In these nine cases the mothers did not appear to be present. However, in two of these cases, both the mothers and the cubs were radio-collared study animals,

and in each case the cubs rejoined their mothers in less than an hour.

In developed areas, however, where black bears have become habituated to people and accustomed to feeding on human food or garbage, there is evidence of increased danger from females with cubs. Research biologists in Great Smoky Mountains National Park examined the age and sex of black bears involved in 107 human injuries between 1964 and 1976.[16] They found that productive females were involved in eighteen (17 percent) cases involving personal injury but only thirty-seven (6 percent) of nuisance problems. This suggests that females with young are less likely to become involved in nuisance problems but that if they do and find themselves in close proximity to people, injury is more likely to result than with other age/sex classes of bears. Nuisance problems in Great Smoky Mountains National Park most often involved feeding bears or bears doing damage while trying to get at human foods. In these cases females with cubs may be drawn very close to people and injury may follow.

Even provoking black bears by approaching, chasing, or wounding them seldom leads to injury. During August 1968, I watched three thrill-seeking teenagers chase the two cubs of a blond-colored black bear up a tree. They did this by pelting the cubs with rocks. At no time did the female even act aggressively toward them. Such behavior would almost certainly lead to injury by a mother grizzly bear. Eventually the mother bear climbed the tree and wrapped her body around one of the cubs to shelter it. At this point the dispassionate scientist in me gave way to the animal protector. I ran over to the boys and told them to stop throwing rocks at the bears. They quickly redirected their aggression from the bears to me, threatening me with chains and a tire iron, but I stood my ground—as if I were confronted by a bear—and in the end they left.

Historical records exist of black bears having injured people who wounded, trapped, cornered, or otherwise harassed them[17], but I found only a few incidents since 1900 in which harassment appeared to have been an important circumstance associated with major injury. One of these involved a hunter who was injured by a black bear he had shot. This is the only example I found of a black bear injuring a hunter. This incident was investigated and related by Ben East.[18] A sixty-five-year old Athabascan Indian named Alexie Pitka who had, in his life, killed ten or twelve black bears was hunting along a slough of the Yukon River in the interior of Alaska in 1950. He stalked a black bear until he got close enough to drop it with one shot. Pitka then waited for a little while to make sure that it was dead. He then approached. As East tells the story:

> For reasons he himself did not understand, he leaned his rifle against a bush and went the last few steps with no weapon but a belt knife. He was three yards away when the bear rolled to its feet and leaped on him.
>
> It knocked him unconscious with one blow, which proved a merciful happening. When he came to he was lying on the ground, the bear was standing over him, he could feel its fur against his arms and smell its foul breath. The bear's face was only a foot from his, but the luckless Indian no longer had a face.
>
> As he floated up out of unconsciousness he remembered his knife. He freed it and drove the four-inch blade into the bear's belly as hard as he could. The bear gave no sign that it felt the knife thrust. It was probably dying on its feet from the bullet wound.
>
> Pitka stabbed the animal repeatedly. He could feel blood spurting down on him. Finally, as he put it, he went to sleep again, and when he awoke the bear was no longer standing over him. He could hear it thrashing and bawling in the brush a few yards away. When the noise died out the Indian knew the bear was dead.
>
> He had taken incredible punishment. The entire right side of his face from the eye across to the nose and down to the chin had been torn away. The right eye was ripped out of the socket, and he could barely distinguish light with the left. His nose was torn off, with cartilage sticking out of raw flesh. The right cheek and part of the left were gone, and his mouth was so mangled he could not manage a drink of water. Three teeth were left in the jaw; the rest were dangling loose. All the torn flesh and skin of his face were hanging down beneath his chin like a grisly, bloody bib, and the pain in his head was beyond description.

Somehow Pitka survived. More than fifty hours after the attack, his wife found him near death. He spent a total of ten months in the hospital and was left crippled and mutilated. As the Indian said later, "What remained was not a very good face, but it was better than none."[19]

As I wrote this book I questioned whether I should include details of such a gruesome incident. I decided to do so because of the casual manner with which many people treat black bears. The mauling of Pitka is a stark reminder of the power that black bears can unleash.

⤳ 8 ⤳

The Predaceous
Black Bear

ALTHOUGH black bears are normally tolerant, they are dangerous under certain circumstances. They can bite through live trees thicker than a man's arm. They can kill a full-grown steer with a bite to the neck. Rarely, however, do black bears use their power to injure or kill people. I have records of twenty people who were killed by black bears from 1900 through 1980. Sergeant Robert Brown of the Alaska Department of Public Safety, Anchorage, and Larry Kaniut have cursory records of an additional three deaths in Alaska. This brings the total to a minimum of twenty three. Which is about half the number of recorded grizzly bear-inflicted deaths during the same period.

Most black bear-inflicted deaths and serious injuries fit into a pattern that is different from the pattern of major injuries inflicted by grizzly bears. Only one of twenty black bear-inflicted deaths that I studied occurred within a national park, where food conditioning and habituation are most common. In contrast, food-conditioned and habituated grizzly bears killed at least ten people in national parks. Clearly most black bears can become accustomed to people and their foods without endangering human lives.

Another feature of major injuries inflicted by black bears was that predation appeared to be the motive for eighteen of the twenty (90 percent) black bear-inflicted deaths. In these incidents the bears treated the people as prey. In the fifteen black bear-inflicted deaths for which data were available on the time of day of the attack, I discovered that fourteen (93 percent) of the fatal attacks took place during the day. This too contrasts with incidents of grizzly bear predation which typically occurred at night.

In one of the predatory instances, protection of young by a female may have also been a contributing factor. Another death was due to a person falling out of a tree while being attacked by a black bear. In another case I could not ascertain the circumstances.

Of the twenty people killed by black bears, ten (50 percent) of the victims were age eighteen or under. Five were younger than ten years old, suggesting that young people may be more subject to fatal black bear attacks. Of the other victims killed by black bears, nine were adult males, and so it is clear that on occasion they will attack a full-grown man.

Three of the fatal attacks involved young children who were playing out-of-doors. Typical of these rare incidents was the death of three-year-old Carol Ann Pomranky, near Sault Sainte Marie, Michigan, on July 7, 1948. Carol Ann lived with her parents and her brother, Allan, in a cabin at Mission Hill. The cabin was in the woods and was owned by the Forest Service for which Carol Ann's father worked. July 7 was hot and Carol Ann was playing outside in the yard. The account of Carol Ann's mother, Mrs. Arthur Pomranky, as given to a forest ranger and published by S. C. Whitlock,[1] tells what happened:

> On July 7, 1948, at approximately 2:30 P.M., I was in the kitchen of our cabin at Mission Hill in company with Mrs. Merlin Summers, a friend. I was sitting about four feet from the back door with my back to the south wall of the kitchen, and Mrs. Summers was in the middle of the kitchen ironing clothes. Mrs. Summers was facing south or to the rear of the room, and in line with the back windows, although from her position, could not see the rear yard. My son, Allan, was playing in the basement which is directly under the kitchen, but which has an outside entrance. My daughter, Carol Ann, was playing in the back yard, and had been for most of the time she was outside, in the close vicinity of the back porch. My first indication that anything was wrong was when I heard Carol Ann utter a cry of alarm. I ran to the back door, which was open with the screen door closed.
>
> Carol Ann, when I reached the door, was on her hands and knees on the porch with one hand touching the screen in the door, and a bear was about mid point of the three steps of the back porch. The bear growled showing his teeth and grabbed

Carol Ann with his mouth and pulled her off the porch onto the ground where he picked her up by the arm with his mouth. At this point, Mrs. Summers pulled me from the door and shut the inside door.

I ran for my husband's pistol, a 32-20 Colt revolver, but in my excitement could not load the pistol. I ran to the door, but the bear and child had disappeared into the bushes. I did not see in which direction the bear went. I ran to the telephone, and called the Ranger Station at Raco, and told Mr. Elliott what had happened. They went into the woods to look for the bear as soon as they arrived.

Further details of the case are gruesome but offer strong evidence that the bear treated Carol Ann as prey. Soon after Carol Ann was dragged away by the bear, Mrs. Pomranky called her husband and he quickly organized a search party. The party was headed by Alex Van Luven, a former state trapper, widely recognized as a competent woodsman. A selection from Van Luven's account describes the search and the condition of the victim when she was found:

I drove to my home in Brimley, a distance of nine miles, to get my dog, Tower. No one except three men had as yet gone into the woods as the searchers who had assembled in my absence were instructed by Alex Goldade and Deputy Sheriff Randolph Wilson to wait until I had returned with the dog. I took four men from the group, instructing the men to stay behind me and the dog and instructed the balance of the men to stay out of the woods until I sent word to them as to what to do. I traveled in a westerly direction from the cabin, as no one at the cabin could definitely say as to which direction the bear had gone. At a point approximately 100 yards west of the cabin the dog apparently scented the bear, and almost simultaneously one of the three men who had preceded me into the woods shouted from a distance of about sixty yards, and in a southerly direction. I went to where the men were and discovered blood spots, one of the child's shoes, and noticed that the leaves had been disarranged at that spot. The dog at this point pulled strongly in a northwesterly direction and I followed the dog about one hundred fifty feet and discovered the child's body. The body lay face upward, with the head reclining against the foot of an 8-inch scrub oak. Part of the clothing remained, a shirt still worn, but rolled down on the arms from the top, and rolled up from the bottom to form a ring around the child's chest. The child still wore pants, but they were pulled down about the ankles. Neither article of clothing was badly torn. The abdomen was completely removed as well as the stomach and intestines, and the front part of both legs eaten away to the knees, also the left calf. No blood was in evidence and leg bones were clean and visible. One length of intestine about eight feet long was caught on a piece of brush near the body, but was disconnected from the body. Numerous deep gashes appeared about the head and neck; however, little damage had been inflicted on the face. One tooth mark appeared about an inch behind and in line with the left eye and had an appearance of depth sufficient to reach the brain.

A short while later a 125-pound black bear was shot nearby. Autopsy revealed fragments of human flesh and bone in the bear's stomach. Microscopic sections of the bear's brain and spinal cord revealed no abnormalities. The bear was, however, "very thin," and no fat was found in any of the normal places. Considering the time of year this was not unusual, but it does suggest a hungry bear. The blueberry season, when bears in that area begin to fatten, was said to be still a few weeks away.

The woods came within forty feet of the house. The bear may have used this cover to get close to the Pomrankys' house. Once there, the evidence suggests that the bear sensed Carol Ann and attacked and killed her as if she were prey, such as deer. The disembowelment of the girl is something typically done by bears to prey. After making a kill bears often will begin feeding on the contents of the digestive system.

I don't know if it would have been possible, but had Carol Ann's mother immediately attacked the bear, she might have caused the bear to drop her daughter. One need not be a prizefighter to deter a black bear.

On September 1, 1976, a ten-year-old girl was attacked and injured by a black bear about forty miles northeast of Williams Lake, British Columbia. A British Columbia Fish and Wildlife memorandum regarding the attack tells what happened:[2]

The attack occurred when the girl was carrying a water bucket back to a lonely hut from a nearby creek. When the bear approached her she dropped the bucket and grabbing an axe laying nearby on the ground, hit the bear twice, then ran for the house. The bear followed and swatted the child knocking her down. She managed to reach the door of the cabin. The bear attempted to follow her inside. With a good presence of mind and in spite of her injuries she managed to reach and throw a pot of boiling water into the face of the bear. The bear fled.

This young girl did everything right once she was attacked by the bear, which was probably attempting to prey on her. She fought the bear with the nearest available weapon, an axe. She then headed for nearby shelter, where despite her injuries (she suffered broken ribs) she continued to fight the bear by throwing water into its face. She caused the bear to flee and probably saved her own life.

While black bears have had countless opportunities to kill people in national parks, only one death has been recorded since 1872.[3] Again a child was the victim. On August 12, 1958, seven-year-old Barbara Coates was playing with her sister outside their cabin at Sunwapta Bungalows in Jasper National Park, Alberta. A black bear walked into the area where the girls were playing. Barbara, startled by the bear, grabbed a small tablecloth and some cookies and ran to the cabin steps. The bear chased and caught her on the steps. Two teenaged girls who worked at the bungalows heard yelling and ran to the site. They hit the bear with branches until it dropped Barbara. The girl died of her injuries shortly thereafter.

The bear was a young female believed to have been a "highway bum," accustomed to receiving handouts. It had no history of aggressive action.

If a black bear stalks and attacks during the day, a person should try to fight it off using any available weapon. Even young children have fought enough to have deterred potentially fatal black bear attacks.

When the girl ran, a predatory response may have been triggered in this bear. The cookies, or past experience, may have attracted the bear onto the site. This was one of two incidents in which human foods and habituation were known to have been associated with a black bear-inflicted death.

The other incident was the only such case involving a camper who was asleep prior to attack. During the night of July 25, 1971, John Richardson and Linda Moore were sleeping in a mountain tent near the Holzworth Ranch steak-fry area of Colorado (now part of Rocky Mountain National Park).[4] At about 1:55 A.M. a bear attacked them. Linda Moore was bitten on her right buttock, and John Richardson was dragged 150 feet. Gus Wedell, who was sleeping nearby in a motor home with his family, was awakened by Linda Moore. Gus grabbed a frying pan, ran to Richardson, and beat the bear with the pan, causing it to flee. Richardson was dead.

The bear responsible for the attack was hunted and killed. Autopsy showed an apparently healthy, large, male black bear, weighing 306 pounds. The contents of the bear's stomach was entirely garbage. The bear's teeth were worn, indicating an old animal.

This type of incident, in which a bear apparently accustomed to feeding on human foods or garbage attacks and kills a person in the middle of the night, occurred often enough with grizzly bears to confirm the danger of this situation. Since this is the only incident of its type that I have found regarding black bears, the odds of a person being killed by a black bear under these circumstances are slight. The fact that the bear ran off after Gus Wedell hit it with a frying pan further demonstrates the value of human aggression with whatever weapons are at hand.

A terrible encounter seemingly involving attempted predation happened in Alaska on August 13, 1977. During the summer of 1977, Cynthia Dusel-Bacon was participating in her third summer of geologic field mapping in the Yukon-Tanana Upland of Alaska. All five geologists in her group, after being helicoptered to an area, usually worked alone. Cynthia was concerned about the added risk of working alone, but she enjoyed the work and the solitude in wilderness areas.

She had encountered bears during her previous field work. In 1975 she had seen five black bears and managed to avoid them all. She doesn't think that any saw her. In 1976 she saw a black bear forty feet away on the trail. The bear ran off. Earlier in 1977 she had seen two grizzlies. During her work she tried to remain aware of bears. She looked ahead for them while traveling and regularly clapped and yelled to warn or scare off bears. She relied on these techniques instead of carrying a firearm.

In having reviewed two accounts written by her of her attack, I concluded that there is no doubt that Cynthia Dusel-Bacon is a very level-headed, intelligent professional. As events showed, she is also very brave. I quote extensively from her account (as given to Larry Kaniut)[5] because it clearly depicts the nature of what I consider to be an act of attempted predation by a black bear.

During the morning of August 13 she was let off by helicopter pilot Ed Spencer near the top of a rocky, brush-covered ridge about sixty miles southeast of Fairbanks.

I descended the ridge slowly for several hundred yards, moving from one outcrop of rock to another, breaking off samples and putting them in my pack. I stopped at one large outcrop to break off an interesting piece and examine it. A sudden loud crash in the undergrowth below startled me and I looked around just in time to see a black bear rise up out of the brush about 10 feet away.

My first thought was, "Oh, no! A bear. I'd better do the right thing." My next thought was one of relief: "It's only a black bear, and a rather small one at that." Nevertheless, I decided to get the upper hand immediately and scare it away.

I shouted at it, face to face, in my most commanding tone of voice. "Shoo! Get out of here, bear! Go on! Get away!" The bear remained motionless and glared back at me. I clapped my hands and yelled even louder. But even that had no effect. Instead of turning and running away into the brush, the bear began slowly walking, climbing toward my level, watching me steadily. I waved my arms, clapped and yelled even more wildly. I began banging the outcrop with my hammer, making all the noise I could to intimidate the bear.

I took a step back, managing to elevate myself another foot or so in an attempt to reach a more dominant position. By this time the bear had reached the trail I was on and was slightly uphill from me. It slowly looked up the hill in the direction from which I had come and then stared back at me again. I knew that in this moment the bear was trying to decide whether it should retreat from me or attack. Suddenly the bear darted around behind the outcrop and behind me. My next sensation was that of being struck a staggering blow from behind. I felt myself being thrown forward, and I landed face down on the ground, with my arms outstretched.

I froze, not instinctively but deliberately, remembering that playing dead was supposed to cause an attacking bear to lose interest and go away. Instead of hearing the bear crashing off through the brush, though, I felt the sudden piercing pain of the bear's teeth biting deep into my right shoulder. I felt myself being shaken with tremendous, irresistible power by teeth deep in my shoulder. After playing dead for several minutes, I came to the horrible realization that the bear had no intention of abandoning its prey.

"I've got to get my radio in the pack. I've got to get a call out," I thought.

My left arm was free, so I tried to reach behind myself to the left outside pocket of my rucksack to get at the walkie-talkie. My heart sank as I discovered that the buckled flap on the pocket prevented me from getting out my radio. My movement caused the bear to start a new flurry of biting and tearing at the flesh of my upper right arm again. I was completely conscious of feeling my flesh torn, teeth against bone, but the sensation was more of numb horror at what was happening to me than of specific reaction to each bite. I remember thinking, "Now I'm never going to be able to call for help. I'm dead unless this bear decides to leave me alone."

The bear had no intention of leaving me alone. After chewing on my right shoulder, arm, and side repeatedly, the bear began to bite my head and tear at my scalp. As I heard the horrible crunching sound of the bear's teeth biting into my skull, I realized it was all too hopeless. I remember thinking, "This has got to be the worst way to go." I knew it would be a slow death because my vital signs were all still strong. My fate was to bleed to death. I thought, "Maybe I should just shake my head and get the bear to do me in quickly."

All of a sudden, the bear clamped its jaws into me and began dragging me by the right arm down the slope through the brush. I was dragged about 20 feet or so before the bear stopped to rest, panting in my ear. It began licking at the blood that was now running out of a large wound under my right arm. Again the bear pulled me along the ground, over rocks and through brush. Now it walked about four feet away and sat down to rest, still watching me intently.

Here, I thought, might be a chance to save myself yet—if only I could get at that radio. Slowly I moved my left arm, which was on the side away from the bear, and which was still undamaged, behind me to get at that pack buckle. But this time the pocket, instead of being latched tight, was wide open—the buckle probably was torn off by the bear's clawing or from being dragged over the rocks. I managed to reach down into the pocket and pull out the radio. Since my right arm was now completely numb and useless, I used my left hand to stealthily snap on the radio switch, pull up two of the three segments of the antenna, and push in the button activating the transmitter. Holding the radio close to my mouth, I said as loudly as I dared, "Ed, this is Cynthia. Come quick, I'm being eaten by a bear." I said "eaten" because

I was convinced that the bear wasn't just mauling me or playing with me, but was planning to consume me. I was its prey, and it had no intention of letting me escape.

I repeated my message and then started to call out some more information. "Ed, I'm just down the hill from where you left me off this morning . . ." but I got no further. By this time the bear had risen to its feet; it bounded quickly over to me and savagely attacked my left arm, knocking the radio out of my hand. I screamed in pain as I felt my good arm being torn and mangled by claws and teeth. [When found she had no flesh on her left arm for about five inches between her shoulder and elbow.]

It was then I realized I had done all I could do to save my life. I had no way of knowing whether anyone had even heard my calls. I really doubted it, since no static or answering sound from anyone trying to call had come back over the receiver. I knew I hadn't taken time to extend the antenna completely. I knew I was down in a ravine, with many ridges between me and a receiving set. I knew there was really no chance for me. I was doomed. So I screamed as the bear tore at my arm, figuring that it was going to eat me anyway and there was no longer any reason to try to control my natural reactions. I remember that the bear then began sniffing around my body, down my calves, up my thighs. I could read the bear's mind as it tried to decide whether it should open up new wounds or continue on the old ones.

I didn't dare look around at what was happening—my eyes were fixed upon the dirt and leaves on the ground only inches below my face. Then I felt a tearing at the pack on my back, and heard the bear begin crunching cans in its teeth—cans I had brought for my lunch. This seemed to occupy its attention for a while; at least it let my arms alone and gave me a few moments to focus my mind on my predicament. "Is this how I'm going to go?" I remember marveling at how clear my mind was, how keen my senses were. All I could think of as I lay there on my stomach, with my face down in the dry grass and dirt and that merciless, bloodthirsty animal holding me down, was how much I wanted to live and how much I wanted to come back to Charlie, my husband of five months, and how tragic it would be to end it all three days before I turned thirty-one.

It was about ten minutes, I think, before I heard the faint sound of a helicopter in the distance. It came closer and then seemed to circle, as if making a pass, but not directly over me. Then I heard the helicopter going away, leaving me. What had gone wrong? Was it just a routine pass to transfer one of the other geologists to a different ridge, or to go to a gas cache to refuel and not an answer to my call for help? Had no one heard my call?

The bear had not been frightened by the sound of the helicopter. Having finished with the contents of my pack, it began to tear again at the flesh under my right arm. Then I heard the helicopter coming back, circling, getting closer. Being flat on my face, with both arms now completely without feeling, I kicked my legs to show whoever was up above me that I was still alive. This time, however, I was certain that I was to be rescued because the pilot hovered directly over me. But again I heard the helicopter suddenly start away over the ridge. In a few seconds all was silent; it was an agonizing silence. I couldn't believe it. For some reason they'd left me for the second time.

Suddenly I felt, or sensed, that the bear was not beside me. The sound of the chopper had frightened it away. Again—for about ten minutes—I waited in silence. Then I heard the helicopter coming over the ridge again, fast and directly toward me. In a few seconds the deafening, beautiful sound was right over me. I kicked my legs again and heard the helicopter move up toward the crest of the ridge for what I was now sure was a landing. Finally I heard the engine shut down, then voices, and people calling out. I yelled back to direct them to where I was lying. But the birch brush was thick, and with my khaki work pants and gray pack I was probably difficult to see lying on the ground among the rocks.

Ed was the first to spot me, and he called the two women geologists down the slope to help him. Together they managed to carry me up the hill and lift me up into the back seat of the helicopter. I remember the feeling of relief and thankfulness that swept over me when I found myself in that helicopter, going up and away over the mountain. I knew that my mind was clear and my breathing was good and my insides were all intact. All I had to do was keep cool and let the doctors fix me up. Deep down, though, I knew the extent of my injuries and knew that I had been too badly hurt for my body to ever be the same again.

Cynthia survived this, and after several months of hospitalization and surgery she was able to state:

The bites on my head have healed, and my hair has grown back and covers the scars completely. My right side is covered with new skin; my left stump is strong and has good range of motion. I'm fitted with artificial arms, and I'm ready to resume my interrupted life as both wife and geologist. It will be difficult for me to operate a workable arm on my right side, where I have no stump, and to manage the use of the arm and hook on the other side, where I have no elbow. But with practice, I know that I will eventually be able to make my prosthetic devices and my feet and mouth do many of the things my hands did for me before. I plan to continue my job with the U.S. Geological Survey. Both Charlie and I have loved our work there, and our colleagues have been tremendously supportive of me throughout the ordeal. I'd like to stay with the Alaskan Geology Branch, perhaps specializing in petrography—the examination of sections of three-hundredths of a millimeter thick wafers of rock under the microscope to determine their mineral composition and texture. With only minor adaptations to the microscope, I should be able to do this work as effectively as I was able to do it before my accident.

I am determined to lead as normal a life as possible. I know that there are certain limitations I can't get around, having to rely on artificial arms. But I'm certainly going to do the best I can with all that I have left. And that's a lot.

Cynthia Dusel-Bacon's courage, level-headedness, and determination are an inspiration. Her actions during the encounter always seemed to have been guided by what she thought was the right course of action. At first she tried to intimidate the black bear and get it to flee. In 99 percent of such encounters she probably would have been successful. Where she erred, in my judgment, was in playing dead after the attack occurred and the bear began chewing on her. I don't know if by this time she still had the strength to fight back, but if she could have grabbed a stout stick or rock, she might have had some chance of deterring the bear if she could have struck it. Overall, her calm, collected presence—which helped her to reach her radio and call for help—no doubt saved her life.

There is some doubt concerning whether the bear that mauled her was shot. Fish and Game officials shot and killed a 175-pound female black bear near the scene of the incident. The bear had blueberries in its stomach and appeared to have been in good health. "Unidentified substance" was also in the stomach. This could have been parts of Cynthia or her clothing, although this was not proved. Fish and Game officials also saw a one-year-old cub in the area. Although a cub of this age should have been weaned by its mother, it possibly was still with the female that supposedly attacked Cynthia. Because of the age of the cub and the nature of the attack on Cynthia, I consider it almost certain that Cynthia was not attacked by a mother bear defending her cub. Rather, Cynthia was probably the victim of the rare situation in which a black bear decides to prey on a human being.

Not quite two years later, On July 4, 1979, another woman, Karen Austrom, was hiking in Mt. Robson Provincial Park of British Columbia and was attacked and badly mauled in a similar incident.[6] Karen too was hiking alone during the day and was confronted at close range by a 125-pound young, male black bear. The bear showed considerable vacillation before attacking. It even climbed a tree, as if to escape. Once it attacked, Austrom played dead and repeatedly offered the bear one of her arms to protect her vital areas. When a large party arrived forty-five minutes later, the bear had mauled and eaten much of her arm but her other injuries were minor. The bear retreated into the bush. To me this is another clear case in which the victim should have used every possible means to fight and intimidate the bear.

Very rarely will a black bear kill two or even three people. During the summer of 1980, Leeson Morris, age forty-two, and Carol Marshall, age twenty-four, were working and were based at Cantex "Rig 10" near Zama in northern Alberta. Morris, the geologist for the camp, had apparently left around five in the afternoon and had not shown up for supper by seven. About this time Carol Marshall and a companion, Martin Ellis, went for a walk to look for Morris. Ellis's statement describes what happened next:[7]

> We stopped for a smoke and had just sat down and Carol noticed a black bear about 10 feet in front of us in the bushes. We started to run a few yards and Carol stumbled. I told her to climb a tree and she sort of panicked and couldn't get up it. I climbed up a tree right beside it and got up about 6 feet and then I reached down and grabbed Carol by the arm. I still couldn't get her up so I reached down under her bum and she slipped so I had a hold of her around her waist. The bear was at the base of the trees and took a lunge and clawed Carol's bum. She then fell to the ground and the bear immediately grabbed her by the neck and shook her several times. He used his mouth and I could hear her neck break. He then immediately dragged her by the neck into the bushes. I stayed up the tree for about 10 minutes and then the bear came back. He climbed up the tree again and I kicked him in the head. He was up the tree about 13 feet. The bear then went back down the tree. He came up 2 more times but I got rid of him once by grabbing a smaller nearby tree and pushing it against him, and the other time by kicking him in the head. He then just chewed on branches like a crazy bear . . . He went down the tree again and left for about 10 minutes. He circled around the back and came up the tree for about 5 or 6 minutes and then Reagan Whiting came walking by. I saw him and told him that the bear got Carol so he ran back to camp for help. The bear went to take a look in the direction of where Reagan was, saw nothing, then came back up the tree. He went

really crazy chewing on the branches. Then Bud Whiting came and the bear headed in his direction. Bud shot him once; the bear let out a scream and headed off in the bushes. . . .

Later the body of Carol Marshall was found nearby as was the partly eaten body of Leeson Morris. Morris was apparently walking along a streambed, stopping occasionally to chip off rock with his geologist's hammer. He was attacked from behind and his chest was crushed. There were also bite marks on his neck, apparently from where he was dragged. The next day a mature male black bear, in apparent good health, was found and killed near the site of the attack. Evidence clearly linked this bear to the killings. Further investigation of the attack site revealed that every branch was removed from the two trees (one nine inches, the other five inches in diameter).

These incidents illustrate several important things. In my opinion the deaths of Leeson Morris and Carol Marshall were both clear cases of predation. The bear's behavior suggests that it would have tried to kill more people if it could have. In this regard the behavior suggests what zoologists call "surplus killing" or a killing frenzy—the killing of prey beyond the immediate needs for food.[8] The bear's behavior in biting the tree limbs also indicates that it was very excited. Perhaps this was the result of having overcome its inborn tendency to avoid people.

The success of Martin Ellis in fighting off the bear further supports my contention that under such circumstances a person should use every inner resource and available weapon (even if it is only your foot or fist) to try to fight off a black bear. I have come across several other incidents in which people have successfully kicked black bears in the head and have knocked them out of trees, but sometimes black bears have grabbed people by the foot and pulled them out of trees. Black bears are much better tree climbers than are grizzlies. If a person climbs a tree to avoid an aggressive black bear they may have to fight the bear in the tree.

The deaths of Carol Marshall and Leeson Morris occurred about two hundred yards from the rig camp. The possibility exists that the bear had gotten some food from the camp or was otherwise familiar with people; although camp personnel felt that it had not been seen before. I consider it likely that it was a wild black bear with only a modest amount of experience with people.

This is a clear example of the general type of incident in which a black bear sees a person and decides to try to kill and eat its victim. The worst of this type of incident occurred in Algonquin Park, Ontario, on May 13, 1978.[9] Four teenaged boys, who were off on a fishing trip, never went more than four hundred feet from their car. The oldest of the party was Richard Rhindress, age eighteen. He survived to tell the story of the deaths of the other three: his brother Billy Rhindress, age sixteen, and their friends, George and Mark Half-kenny, ages fifteen and twelve.

The youths arrived at the park entrance around four in the morning after driving from the nearby Canadian Forces Base at Petawawa where they lived. They tried fishing in several creeks. By late afternoon George Halfkenny had caught four speckled trout, which he carried in his pocket. About 5:30 P.M., at Stone Creek, George decided to fish some more. The others remained in the car while he walked a short distance along the bank of the stream. A little while later George's brother, Mark, and Billy Rhindress, decided either to also try fishing or to look for George. Richard Rhindress, the oldest boy in the group, decided to stay behind and catch up on sleep.

At about 6:30 P.M., Richard woke up and wondered where his companions were. He shouted and honked the horn, but there was no response. A bit later he drove around looking for them, thinking that perhaps they had come out elsewhere along the road. Later on he returned to where he had last seen them and explored along the creek bank. Mike Crammond, a journalist who later investigated the incident, thinks that Richard Rhindress could have been within one hundred feet of the bear and his dead companions.[10] Finding no one, he returned to the car, drove home, and reported what had happened. A search party was soon organized.

The subsequent discovery of the boys' bodies and the killing of a 276-pound male black bear, which was positively linked to the deaths of the boys, allow the following interpretation of events: George Half-kenny, who had gone fishing alone and had four fish in his pocket, was probably the first to be killed. He seemed to have been attacked from behind, probably while intent on fishing. Generally the woods were thick enough that a bear could have stalked close to George without the boy being aware of it. George may have put up a fight, because branches were found broken at the scene of the attack. The bear dragged its victim away from the creek in a semicircle and stored the body about fifty-five yards upstream. A short while later, Mark Halfkenny and Billy Rhindress had apparently proceeded about 110 yards up the stream when they either surprised the bear, who by now had dragged George across the creek, or were ambushed by the bear while they were hiking. There were signs of a small struggle, but the boys' broken necks suggested instantaneous death. All three bodies were then dragged into the bush, 100 to 150 feet from the creek and up a low ridge. When searchers found the bodies they were partially covered with brush, and the bear appeared to be "standing guard over them."

Persons investigating the incident felt that the first boy who was killed, George Halfkenny, may have been attacked because he resembled another bear.[11] George wore dark clothing and was black. Others suggested that the bear attacked George to get the fish he had in his pocket, although the fish were still in his pocket when found. I don't consider either of these explanations to be valid, although fish odors may have served to attract the bear in the first instance. There was also a high density of bears in the area at the time of the attack. One observer reported having seen twenty-nine bears during three hours of searching from a helicopter. This may have led to increased agitation in the bear that killed the boys.

Strong evidence suggests that this is another surplus-killing incident in which the bear treated the three boys as prey. The boys were killed, rather than injured. All were dragged to a common place, and two of the bodies had been partially eaten. There seems to have been little they could have done to avoid this tragic incident.

Since 1980, when my systematic data collection ended, I have received information concerning three additional black bear-inflicted deaths.[12] Two of these, the deaths of Melvin Rudd and Clifford Starblanket, took place in central Saskatchewan in late May 1983. This year there was a late green-up and black bears were probably having trouble finding food.

Melvin Rudd, age fifty-five, who was fishing, was apparently stalked and killed by a black bear. The bear that killed him subsequently attacked Keith Ecklund and Larry Reimer while they too were fishing near to where Rudd's partly consumed body lay. When the bear attacked, Ecklund fought it off by kicking it in the head. A short time later it attacked Reimer when he came to help his friend. Reimer fought the bear, eventually killing it with his filleting knife. Autopsy of the bear revealed parts of Rudd's body in the bear's stomach.

The circumstances of the Starblanket attack were less clear because he was not found until about five days after his death. Starblanket, a trapper camping in the forest reserve, had a lot of garbage and hides strewn about. He was also rumoured to have been feeding a bear prior to his death. When Starblanket's body was found he had multiple and severe injuries to the head and neck, most likely caused during a black bear attack. The bear was never found.

The circumstances of the third death are also vague. On July 5, 1983, David Anderson, age twelve, was part of a group camped on the shore of Lake Canimina in La Verendrye Wildlife Reserve, Quebec. The party had suspended their food between two trees about

165 feet from the site but sometime during the night a bear climbed one of the trees and broke a two-inch diameter limb, causing the food to fall to the ground. It subsequently ate some of the food. A bear, probably the same one, visited the camp three times during the night of July 5–6. On the last visit, at 3:30 A.M. the bear ripped open a tent and pulled young Anderson out. Anderson's dead body was found about one hundred feet from the tent.

My conclusions about known cases of predation and attempted predation by black bears on people are that habituation or garbage and food conditioning have only infrequently been primary contributing circumstances. In fact, the habituated black bear, found so commonly in some of the national parks, seems almost always to be involved only in incidents of minor injuries. Nor have black bears suddenly confronted by people been responsible for deaths, although this may have been a contributing factor in one case. Rather I conclude it is mainly wild black bears found in rural or remote areas—where they have had relatively little association with people—that occasionally try to kill and eat a human being. This behavior must be exceedingly rare, since I have found so few records of it, given that the population of black bears in North America has probably never been less than my estimate of 500,000 ± 200,000.

Warning signals of aggressive intent by black bears have seldom been reported to precede cases of apparent predation. Instead a typical predation scenario might involve the bear slowly approaching a person during the day, perhaps partly circling and then rushing toward the person, trying to knock the intended prey down and inflicting injuries with jaws or paws and claws. Multiple charges are not seen in these instances as, for example, frequently occur when a black bear suddenly encounters a person on a trail. Instead, the predaceous black bear typically charges a person only once and at the end of this charge it has caught its prey. Such attacks may be of prolonged duration because the bear usually does not leave unless it is scared away, overpowered, or injured by the person.

One final circumstance that may cause some black bears to attack and injure people is failure of natural food crops for the bears. Incidents of property damage by black bears increase during years of low production of wild berries on which the bears normally feed.[13] This is understandable enough, since black bears are strongly motivated to secure adequate foods in order to fatten before hibernation. It would also not be surprising if, during years of food-crop failure when black bears are aggressively seeking human foods and garbage, they also were more likely to injure people. Scientific evidence of this actually happening is, however, weak.

David Hatler describes what happened in the interior of Alaska during 1963, a year when blueberries were "generally scarce."[14] Failure of the berry crop caused black bears to concentrate in the few areas where blueberries were available. The bears also sought food from people's camps. Four people were injured and one person was killed by black bears. All injuries took place during the time when the bears would normally have been fattening on berries. The possibility of berry-crop failures being associated with increases in human injury merits research. If true, it might be possible to monitor berry production in a given area and to anticipate which years black bears will be a problem.

I have found almost no evidence that injury or infirmity are important factors predisposing black bears toward attacking people. I consider this a possible factor leading to attack. Rabies and trichinosis are two bear diseases that *might* influence attacks on humans. Many black and grizzly bears involved in attacks on people have been tested for rabies, and a few have been tested for trichinae levels. No association has been proven between either of these diseases and attacks on human beings.[15]

Since I have discussed in detail several of the very rare fatal attacks by black bears, it is important to reestablish perspective on the chances of injury. John O'Pezio, a black bear specialist with New York State's Wildlife Resources Center, provided me with some of the best data to do this.[16] He estimates that there is a relatively stable population of 4,100 black bears in New York State. During the period from 1960 through 1980, he was able to tally a minimum estimate of 77 million recreation days spent by people in areas occupied by black bears. During this twenty-year period only three bear-related injuries occurred. In all three cases a bite or a swipe was made through a tent while the injured party was asleep or resting. All injuries were minor. One was only a scratched toe.

What should a person do if attacked by a black bear? When discussing grizzly bear attacks, I tried to show that the response to an attack depends on the reason why the attack occurred. The same thing holds true for black bear attacks. While this may sound as if everyone visiting bear country should be a registered bear psychologist, it is not this complicated.

If a black bear attacks in a campground or alongside a road, or in any place where many bears appear to be habituated to people, then the first assumption should be that the bear is attacking because you have gotten too close to it and it wants more space, or it is trying to get at food that you have. In the first instance simply backing away and watching the bear should end the attack. In the second case, in which a black bear is trying to get at your food and injures you, it is best to give up the food. A person who is very familiar with black bear behavior might choose to act aggressively and get the bear to back down, especially before it attacks (see pp. 141–142). However, a black bear that has become so habituated to people that it will actually injure someone to get at food can be very difficult to deter.

The most dangerous black bear appears to be one that attacks a person who has been hiking, walking, berry picking, fishing, or playing during the day in a rural or remote area. The bear's motivation in this unlikely event most often appears to be predation. The exceptions to this are the very rare instances of females with cubs in backcountry areas attacking to defend their offspring. In this case one should play dead or passively resist, as if a grizzly bear mother were attacking.

If predation is the motive for an attack, the attack typically continues until the bear is forced to back down, or the person gets away, or the bear gets its prey. People who run away, unless they have somewhere to go, or people who act passively or play dead, are simply inviting the bear to continue the attack. If a bear does not take just a minor bite or swipe at a person and leave but instead appears to be pressing an attack, then the unarmed person should either try to escape, for example, to a nearby hard-sided shelter, or fight back. Climbing trees is a possibility but the agile black bear climbs well. Heavy objects such as axes, stout pieces of wood, or rocks are possible weapons. They can be used to hit a bear on the head, with the hope of stunning it and causing it to leave. Other aggressive actions by a person might include kicking, hitting with a fist, yelling or shouting at the bear, or banging objects, such as pots, together in front of a bear's face. This is an action plan of last resort—in close combat, a bear has the advantage over an unarmed person. But in the rare situation in which a person might face such a black bear, fighting off the bear could save that person's life.

I know of three incidents in which black bears were likely trying to prey on people and were killed by the people they attacked. None of these people had a firearm handy. In two cases the people knifed the bear to death, and in the third case a small boulder was used to crush the bear's skull.[17]

The situation might arise when one is attacked during the day while out hiking and the species of bear involved can't be determined. If it is a grizzly, then probably it is a response to a sudden confrontation of a female with cubs and therefore the person should play dead. If, on the other hand, it is a black bear looking for a meal, then fighting back is indicated. I suggest studying this or other books that explain how to tell a black bear from a grizzly.

⎾9⏌

Avoiding
Encounters

Your best weapon to minimize the risk of a bear attack is your brain. Use it as soon as you contemplate a trip to bear country, and continue to use it throughout your stay. In national parks and other areas where bears are protected from hunting, you will not have firearms, and so your brain will be your most effective bear deterrent.

Gather information and lay careful plans before your trip. What species of bear live in the area you will be visiting: black bear, grizzly bear, or both? I have already documented that black bear females with cubs are much less dangerous in sudden encounters compared to grizzly bear females with cubs. Because black bears climb trees with greater ease than grizzlies, your thoughts about tree climbing should be influenced by the species of bear you might encounter. In areas where both species are found, it is sometimes difficult even for the experts to identify whether a given individual is a black bear or a grizzly. When in doubt, assume the most dangerous case—that it is a grizzly.

Learn something about the behavior, ecology, and management of bears. Read the pamphlets put out by various resource-management agencies on bears. Go to a naturalist talk on bears. Try to see the film *Bears and Man*, produced by Parks Canada and the National Film Board of Canada.[1] I helped with the script writing and scientific content of the film. The information is accurate, and the images are powerful. If you are unaware of what a bear can do to people or property, this film will inform you. By learning about bears you will be able to develop a feel for where you might encounter them. People traveling on foot through bear habitat can increase both their safety and enjoyment by learning to interpret the various traces that bears leave when using an area. (I develop this topic in Chapter 13.)

Now that you have some general familiarity with bears, find out more about the bears in the area you intend to visit. Because bears addicted to garbage and human food are particularly dangerous, I suggest asking local land or resource managers if there are any garbage or human-food problems related to bears in the area where you will be. If you are car camping and you see culvert or other kinds of traps set for bears, realize that your chances of having a tent torn open (or worse) are increased. If grizzlies are involved, I recommend leaving. In some areas, such as Yosemite National Park during the period between 1975 and 1980, black bears became expert in the art of packsack and food cache thievery.[2] Advance knowledge may allow you to anticipate and outwit these clever rob-and-run bears and can save you later grief. In most areas where natural bear populations exist, the kind of extreme precautions required in Yosemite are unnecessary.

In some park areas certain individual bears may be known. The behavior of a given bear is as characteristic as is its color and markings. Each grizzly bear mother has a distinct personality. Although all grizzly bear mothers are protective of their cubs, some do so by scrupulously avoiding human signs, sights, and smells, whereas others will forage close to human activity. In our eight years of studying grizzly bear families we have come to know certain mother grizzlies who seem very aggressive whenever threatened. Other mother grizzlies we watched came within sixteen feet of people and didn't act aggressively.

Both grizzly bear and black bear adult females have predictable home ranges, general areas where they can be found year after year. The boundaries are subject to modification with changes in the environment or the bear population, but there is still a good chance of being able to identify at least the neighborhood where a known female and her family might be. Information concerning individual bears, or specific areas, is often available from wardens, rangers, or researchers.

Land managers will also be able to advise you about areas where bears are unlikely to be found. Even in parks famed for their bears, such as Yellowstone, there are some areas where at certain times of the year you would be about as likely to meet a bear as you would a hippopotamus.

Assuming that you know something about bears in general and the area you intend to visit, my next recommendation has to do with mental preparation related to injury. It holds whether you are car camping or wilderness backpacking in bear country. Wherever bears are found there is some chance of human injury. You should think about how to avoid it and what to do if you or someone else is injured. Panic by the person who discovered Monte Adams was one factor contributing to his death. Monte, a southern Alberta hunter, was mauled by a female grizzly bear with cubs in fall of 1979.[3] (See pp. 245–246.) In contrast, I mentioned how quick action by a companion saved Barrie Gilbert's life. First aid training and a good first-aid kit are important, as is thinking out in advance what you might do in such situations. Spare food and drink can be vital after an attack.

Communication is also important. In remote areas radio communication can mean the difference between life and death, as it did in Cynthia Dusel-Bacon's case. Where VHF communication networks are in place, persons working in bear country should carry receiver-transmitters. If one can afford them and get permission, I also recommend that certain recreational travelers carry these for emergency use.

Flares can be useful in attracting search aircraft. Signal mirrors and bright orange ground markers such as ponchos may also be invaluable. Without such tools to attract the attention of aerial searches, you may not be seen.

The most reliable means of obtaining outside help is a companion. Larger parties have enough people so that some can attend to injuries while others go for help. In bear country large parties have the additional bonus of either making enough noise or appearing formidable enough to help to keep bears from attacking.

TRAVEL IN BEAR COUNTRY

The discussion that follows focuses on grizzly bears because they are the species most often involved in sudden-encounter incidents.

Careful travel in grizzly country requires alertness, attention, intelligence, and knowledge. Alertness and attention to your immediate environment are important. Where are you? Are you traveling along a tunnel-like trail through dense vegetation? Is there a rushing stream nearby? While traveling look for traces that bears have been active. Knowledge concerning traces of bear activity and of their preferred travel routes (see pp. 180–182) will help you to anticipate where bears might be.

What else can you do to avoid sudden encounters with bears, especially grizzly females with cubs, or any bear protecting a carcass? Try to detect bears when they are distant. If the country is open enough so that you can scan ahead for several hundred yards, you should use binoculars. Without binoculars I have sometimes confused bears, porcupines, and wolverines at distances of several hundred yards. While scanning look carefully at suspicious "animal-like" objects. If any are seen watch them for a few minutes to see if they move.

If you see a grizzly (or any bear), your response depends on how far away the bear is and whether you think it has sensed you. If the bear is unaware of you, try to detour quietly yet quickly downwind and away from the bear. Use cover if it is available. If you do this, chances are the bear won't sense you. Watch for the bear anyway, and remember that tree climbing is also a possibility.

If the grizzly is aware of you but is still several hundred yards away, then my recommendation isn't so clear. You may act as I suggest above, or you may detour upwind, at a slow or fast walk—not running but putting distance between yourself and the bear. By getting upwind the bear will be able to smell you when you are still distant. This may make it feel less threatened. Waving your arms may help it locate and identify you.

If the bear is aware of you and nearby but hasn't acted aggressively, slowly back away, talking in as even a tone as possible to the bear, while waving your arms. Don't stare at the bear. Your actions should help the grizzly determine what you are, but they shouldn't threaten it. Look for possible trees to climb. If the bear acts aggressively, then you should follow the suggestions I gave in Chapter 6.

As soon as visibility becomes restricted, such as in dense brush, and there is a chance of suddenly confronting a grizzly, I often start making noise. Some people shout or chant their favorite protective mantra; others sing, wear bells, blow whistles, or bang pots or sticks together. I prefer to yodel. The more you know about bears, and where you might confront one, the more selective you can be in your use of warning noise. Remember that the bear is supposed to hear your sound when it is still far enough away from you that it does not feel threatened. Keep in mind that most sudden encounters leading to injury have occurred when the person was not aware of the grizzly until it was less than fifty-five yards away. Supposedly the bear was not aware of the person any sooner, and when it became aware, the person was already too close.

I recommend making loud noise, as opposed to a few small bells hung from your pack and left tinkling.[4] Near rushing water, in a strong wind, or even in dense forest, the noise of such bells and even the human voice does not carry very far. Low frequencies are supposed to travel better around trees. I sometimes use a combination of deep guttural sounds combined with a yodel and a short, explosive, high-pitched sound at the end. Your friends may think you are crazy or paranoid, but let them have their opinions. In Alaska, fisheries biologists surveying salmon streams sometimes walk while discharging a firearm into the air every hundred yards or so.[5] Also in Alaska, John Vania, ex-Regional Supervisor for Alaska Fish and Game, south-Central District, told Larry Kaniut:[6]

> During the summers of 1961 and 1962, I supervised a salmon tagging program in the northern end of southeast Alaska. As part of the program I had two- and three-men crews walking salmon streams in July and August looking for salmon we had tagged earlier in salt water. During the two summers more than 100 salmon streams were walked on Admiralty, Baranof and Chichagof Islands as well as a few streams on the mainland between Juneau and Petersburg. Records were kept of all bear sightings. Nearly 200 bears were recorded sighted during the two-year study. Most of them were brown bear.
>
> The crews were made up of college students who were majoring in fisheries or wildlife. All had little or no experience with bears. When we first started the project, I was concerned about the possibility of crew members getting mauled by bear. Most people I'd talked to said that the "danger was in surprising a bear; to avoid that, make lots of noise." As a result I equipped each crew with a small horn purchased in a boat shop and powered with a small cannister of gas (believe it was freon). The gas cans were replaceable. The horn and gas can measured about six inches and weighed less than a pound.
>
> Crews would walk up a stream and toot the horns occasionally, especially when the brush around the stream was dense. When the crews did this, they never encountered a bear, even though there was a great deal of bear sign along the streams. After walking a number of streams and not seeing any bear at all, some of the crew decided they would like to at least see a bear. So they stopped tooting their horns. They immediately began to run into bears along the stream.
>
> For people who really are afraid of bear, who are in brushy country and want to avoid running into them, I highly recommend a gas powered boat horn or some similar device. When walking along streams that are noisy (lots of rapids, etc.), you need something that makes a loud noise. . . .

I tried police-type whistles on bear, blowing both the police whistle and the silent dog whistle. These whistles had no effect, but the boat horn really got the bears' attention! The police whistle is better than the human voice or a can or rocks but not as good as the air horn.

There may be danger in making noise. While you are trying to avoid sudden surprise, especially of females with cubs, you may attract some grizzlies. Young adult grizzly bears are particularly curious, and their curiosity is often not yet tempered with a knowledge that humans can mean trouble. This type of bear *may* be attracted to human sounds. Bears may also be attracted by high-pitched squeaking sounds, which may sound like distressed animals to the bear.

Chuck Blyth, the illustrator of this book and one of the botanists working on our Banff grizzly bear project, relates the following story. Toward evening he was shouting and whistling while walking down a road that cuts through a good area for grizzlies. Somehow he felt uneasy and, looking behind him, saw a grizzly about thirty feet away. The bear stood up on its hind legs, waved its head back and forth, and pawed its nose. The bear then dropped onto all four. Chuck stood his ground and then slowly took four steps backward. The bear ran at Chuck who dropped his notebook and ran for a tree ten paces away. The grizzly and Chuck reached the tree at about the same time but the bear didn't attack while Chuck climbed the tree to safety. Did Chuck's shouting and whistling attract the bear? I think it possible. What would the bear have done if Chuck hadn't climbed? I don't know. I still make noise when my vision is restricted and I think that I might encounter a grizzly bear at close range. As mentioned, the response of grizzly bears to noise could, and should, be investigated scientifically.

A non-obtrusive noisemaker would be one that a person couldn't hear but a bear could. Bears probably hear in the ultrasonic range of 16–20 megahertz, perhaps higher. Some people can hear these frequencies but most can't. The affect of ultrasonic emitters on bears deserves study.

Since climbing a tree offers reasonable protection from grizzly bears, I keep a sort of inventory of available trees while I am hiking. While a bear's reach may exceed ten feet, a tree that allows you to get your feet thirty-three feet or more above the ground will provide protection from grizzlies that may climb a short distance. How far away is the nearest tree of acceptable height? If there are none, then I find myself doing a lot of visual scanning of the landscape looking for bears. If trees are available, you should keep in mind the speed

This book's illustrator, Chuck Blyth, takes refuge in
a tree from grizzly bear.

of grizzlies. Do you have enough distance to beat the bear to the tree
if necessary and then to get your feet up beyond a bear's reach?

Adult grizzlies seldom climb trees, but some of them can and do.
For example, Terry Skonsberg, a trail maintenance worker, was injured on September 16, 1976, in Banff Park when a female grizzly,
who had yearling cubs on the ground, climbed fifteen feet into a tree
and pulled him down.[7] He made the mistake of shouting at her when
less than one hundred yards away to try to get her to leave a trail that
they were both using.

A cautious traveler in bear country is usually aware of which way
the wind is blowing. Because bears have such acute senses of smell,
they commonly detect a person by scent. But they cannot smell you
unless the wind carries your odor to them or they encounter odor
traces that you have left behind. If you are traveling with the wind
blowing into or across your face, then bears ahead cannot smell you.
If you think that a bear ahead of you might not be able to smell you,
then make noise. Some people claim that they know bears are nearby
because they smell the bears. I have never been able to do this. Some

horses and dogs do have good enough noses to tell if a bear is nearby.

Sometimes your first indication that a bear is near will be sound. A crashing in the bushes may indicate that you have come too close to a bear or a deer or a moose. Or you may suddenly hear some of the aggressive sounds made by bears. These include snorting, loud blowing or huffing, and, less frequently, deep gurgling growls. They all indicate cautious retreat for you.

Dr. Milo Fritz of Anchor Point, Alaska, has treated several mauling victims. He told Larry Kaniut that many of the victims were men between the ages of forty and sixty who suffered from high-frequency hearing loss.[8] These men might not have heard a nearby bear and may have continued to approach. If you are over forty and you spend a lot of time in bear country, it is probably worth having your hearing tested.

Most likely the best suggestion related to safe backcountry travel in bear habitat is to use horses. If safety is a primary concern and you like traveling by horseback, then this is for you. In the entire history of the North American national parks I have discovered no record of a person on horseback being thrown and then mauled by a grizzly. I do, however, have two records, both from the Rocky Mountain parks in Canada, where people have been injured by being thrown from horses that were startled by grizzlies. Inexperienced horse riders and horses increase the chances of being thrown, because most horses react to a nearby bear. A horse usually senses a bear's presence before a person does.

The best indication of the risk reduction that horses confer to travelers in grizzly country also comes from Canada's Rocky Mountain parks. Here park wardens have used horses for hundreds of thousands of hours, in regular backcountry duty over about seventy-five years. I have heard of wardens occasionally riding up on their horses and closely approaching a bear family to get a good look for individual identification or just to "play cowboy." There is no recorded bear-inflicted injury related to wardens on horseback.

Finally, here is Adolf Murie's tongue-in-cheek suggestion regarding safe foot travel in bear country: Ade suggested that you travel with a companion whom you can outrun.[9]

CAMPING IN BEAR COUNTRY

It is late at night, and you and your family have spent a long and tiring day on the trail. You come into the officially designated campsite and it is a beauty. Lake view, running water nearby, and not a bug to be seen, heard, or felt. But what is this? The campfire remains have been disturbed. About thirty feet away you find a fresh bear scat with a telltale plastic bag and kernels of corn in it. If you know that there are only black bears in the area, you may choose to camp and risk the loss of your food and packsack or two and perhaps accept a small chance of injury. If it is grizzly country, you should just pack up and leave no matter how tired everyone is.

A garbage-addicted grizzly bear can become a terror that strikes in the night, when its senses are working well and yours are hampered not only by dark but also by fear. Such a bear is a product of human activities. At some point it was shy and wary of the smell, sound, and sight of people. Then a camping party may have left some unburned garbage in a campfire. After a week the human odor was gone and only the odor of food remained. The bear was attracted by the odor. It ate the food. The situation was repeated several times. The bear came sooner after people left and began to get accustomed to their odor. Nothing bad happened to it and the food was a reward.

You do not know how far the situation has gone when you look at the area as a possible campsite. Perhaps natural foods are scarce this year, and a few days ago the bear smelled the odor of people's food in someone else's pack and tore it apart. Or maybe the bear came into camp at night and smelled a child's candy bar through a tent wall and tore into the tent to get the food.

But you are sure that park or forestry officials would have closed the campsite if this had happened. Maybe they *did* close the campsite where it happened. Different parts of a male grizzly's home range may be up to one hundred miles apart.[10] Perhaps this is just one of several campsites on the bear's travel route. To look after your family's safety as well as your own, you have no choice but to leave, camp elsewhere, and to report the incident as soon as possible.

The irony of this type of situation is that the people to blame are seldom injured. Is the bear to blame? It is doing nothing more than following a foraging strategy, which, before the introduction of human recreational use of its habitat, was successful for many generations of ancestors. Despite this the bear will ultimately have to be killed if it persists in its new role of campsite scavenger.

For these reasons I recommend total cleanliness when camping in bear country. When backpacking, cook downwind and well away from where you will sleep. Plan your meal quantities so that what is cooked is eaten. If you must store leftovers, place them in your food cache. Wash your dishes and pots thoroughly, and if significant amounts of food particles remain in the dishwater, hike several hundred yards before emptying the dishwater. Burning is all right for small bits of

Do's and Don't's for backcountry campsite location in bear country:

DON'T
1. Camp near a bear trail or seasonal feeding ground.
2. Cook near your tent.
3. Camp in places where food or garbage has been left.
4. Camp where bear sign (droppings, tracks, etc.) exists.

combustible leftovers and garbage, but make sure that combustion is complete. With the emphasis today on low-impact camping, one dimension of which is doing without a fire, you may have to forgo burning garbage. Without a fire, all leftovers should go into sealed plastic bags and join your food cache. Garbage should not be buried in the backcountry. A thin layer of soil only partly masks its odor, and bears and other scavengers will dig it up. "Pack it in, pack it out" is the right policy. Odor and previous experience get bears foraging for human food and garbage. You can do little, if anything, about the bear's previous experience, but you can control the odor of your foods. For the backpacker, there are many dried foods available that offer a reasonably balanced diet and low odor.

After cooking is the time not only for dishwashing but also for washing yourself to remove any lingering food odors or even the odor of insect repellents or cosmetics. I know of no incidents where it is clear that bears have been attracted by such chemicals, but some of

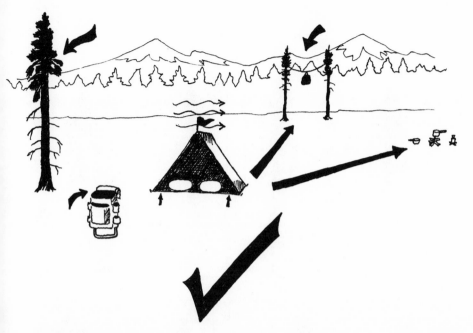

DO

1. Locate cook area at least 100 yards downwind of tent.
2. Camp where trees allow for proper food storage, at least 100 yards downwind of camp—or, if there are no trees, store food well away from camp in ABS cylinders or in airtight plastic bags.
3. Camp near a possible escape tree in grizzly country—or camp in open, well away from any cover for bears.
4. Leave pack outside with flaps open.

them are highly odorous and this could possibly elicit a bear's curiosity. After cooking you should also change your clothes if you think they are odor-impregnated.

Even in stormy weather try to avoid cooking in your tent. If you do a lot of winter camping and cook inside your tent, consider having both a summer tent and a winter tent. I do, because of food-odor impregnation into my winter tent—and I eat big, sometimes highly odorous meals while snow camping.

Where to store your food in the backcountry can be a problem to test your, and a bear's, ingenuity. The first rule is to store your food well away from where you will sleep. Proper food storage should not be a challenge for you if the park has provided storage facilities such as a cable or platform between two trees or a "bear pole." Most often these luxuries are not available, and when they are provided they may indicate a history of troublesome bears in the area. The experience of the bears in the area where you are camping is critical

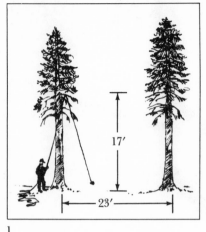

FOOD STORAGE IN BACKCOUNTRY AREAS WITH TREES

Suspending foodbag between two trees

Materials needed:
- About 100 feet of ⅛″ or larger nylon rope
- Weight at end of rope to help throw it over tree limbs
- Ability to attach food sack to rope (a carabiner is handy)

1. Pick two trees about 23 feet apart. Throw weighted end of line (or climb up and place weighted end of line) over a limb about 17 feet up.
2. Tie off line on first tree. Throw weighted end of line over limb of second tree.
3. Attach food bag near what will be the middle of the line between the two trees.
4. Secure other end of line to second tree and check to see food is about twelve feet above the ground.

This system works in most areas, but if the bears are experienced food robbers they may have learned to rip off the line from the tree trunk.

1

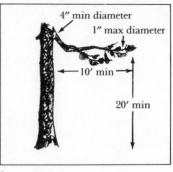

4″ min diameter

1″ max diameter

10′ min

20′ min

2

4

5

5′

12′

6

7

Suspending Foodbags from One Limb
The Yosemite National Park System—developed to foil robber bears

1. Find a tree with an appropriate branch.
2. Select a live, downsloping branch only and be sure there is no object below the branch that could support a bear's weight.
3. Balance the foodsacks with equal weight (10 pounds maximum per sack).
4. Position rope as far out on branch as will support the weight of the food, but not a cub. Branch diameter should be a maximum of 1″ at point of suspension. (Note: This and the following drawings not drawn to scale.)
5. With one sack hoisted to branch, tie second sack as high as possible. Tie a secure loop in rope near one sack for retrieval; put excess rope in sack.
6. Toss sacks into position.
7. To retrieve sacks, hook loop with stick and pull down.

Using a "bear pole" for food storage. A lifting pole is being used to raise a pack onto one of the four hooks at the top of a food-storage pole. Note aluminum collar to prevent bears from climbing the pole.   *Martha McCallum*

to how you store your food. If the bears are not used to feeding on people's food, then it is unlikely they will tear open a pack containing no food or odors. In many areas an easy way to keep food away from bears is to string a line between two trees and suspend your packsack from the line or to suspend your food from the end of a tree limb. See pp. 134–135.

Because grizzly bears do not climb as well as black bears, you can often successfully store food in grizzly country in a cache tied to a tree trunk. This system is easier to rig than is a line between two trees. Remember that young and (rarely) even older grizzlies will sometimes

Food cache, Kluane National Park, Yukon Territory.   *Stephen Herrero*

climb trees to get at odorous food. Whenever storing food off of the ground, place it in well-sealed plastic bags or you will increase odor transmission by wind.

When there are no trees around and there are still bears, chances are that you will encounter only grizzlies. Under such circumstances I follow the normal procedure of keeping my food cache several hundred yards away from camp. First, place your food inside several layers of plastic bags and close them carefully. This will help trap odors inside the bags. But where to put it? Big boulders and cliffs offer interesting challenges for people adept at climbing. Most people are better rock climbers than are bears. Deep crevices between rocks can also offer safe storage. If you have waterproof bags, food can be stored inside and submerged. Although doing this further helps to remove odors, it does not preclude a bear seeing your aquatic food cache. Barney Smith, bear biologist for the Yukon Government, suggests the possibility of burying plastic bags full of food in frozen soils, but these are hard to dig. Sometimes I just carry my plastic bags well away from camp and hide them on the ground if nothing better can be found. I've never lost food this way, but in Denali National Park grizzly bears have learned to raid this type of food câche. I never simply give up in frustration and sleep with my food to protect it. I would rather lose the food than risk injury. Yosemite, Sequoia, and Denali National Parks have tested lightweight, cylindrical ABS plastic pipe with a tight-fitting but removable end for food storage for back-

Black bears can easily climb trees to get at improperly stored food, Yosemite Valley, Yosemite National Park.   *David Graber*

packers.[11] The toughness and diameter of these containers make it difficult for black or grizzly bears to bite or break them. With food or garbage inside they should be stored on the ground well away from camp. In preliminary tests these containers were quite successful. They weigh a little more than three pounds, so backpackers going into treeless areas can carry them.

The car camper may feel that it is permissible to use odorous foods. I generally agree. However, in campgrounds where bears have become accustomed to feeding on human food or garbage, they can become aggressive in trying to get at something that smells edible to them. Put food in the trunk rather than in the passenger section of a car.[12]

There are other odors not directly related to human food that may lead to campers being injured by bears. Menstrual blood as a bear attractant has been the subject of much speculation. Vaginal secretions and odors are known to change with the onset of menstrual flow.[13] In my analysis of grizzly bear-inflicted injury, I did not find a correlation between attacks on women and any particular stage of their menstrual cycles. The data, however, are very incomplete and the chances of not discovering a real relationship are high. Experiments on bears' reactions to menstrual blood have been done, and knowledge of the results helps to further understand if a relationship might exist between menstrual odors and injury.

Recently the attractiveness of menstrual blood to polar bears was compared with their attraction to several other odors.[14] In a laboratory in Churchill, Manitoba, seal scent, which is the odor of the natural prey of polar bears, and menstrual blood odors both elicited maximal interest from all captive bears. In field tests, used tampons were detected by odor about two-thirds of the time. Both in the lab and in field tests, other animal odors and nonmenstruating human female blood were presented to polar bears. These elicited minimal or no response.

One should not assume that attraction to and ingestion of menstrual blood-soaked tampons is the same as an attack on a menstruating woman. This question was not answered. Also, the responses of bear species other than polar bears were not studied. Polar bears are far more carnivorous than are black or grizzly bears. The experimental results regarding menstrual blood odor and polar bears do, however, suggest caution for menstruating women who choose to camp in bear country. A basic precaution should be to wear internal tampons, not external pads.

Absence of garbage with no signs of scavenging by bears is the first criterion for choosing a backcountry campsite. Other important characteristics have to do with the relationship of the site to seasonal bear habitat.[15] Knowledge of the travel routes, food habits, habitat preference, and signs of activities of bears should allow you to take a quick look around an area and to rate its natural attractiveness to bears. Both black and grizzly bears prefer to approach uncertain situations by using trees, bushes, or other landscape features for cover. You therefore may want to camp in open areas. If you camp in treed sites, an escape tree is a good idea in grizzly country (see pp. 132–133).

One of the worst possible campsites is in the middle of or just off a trail through dense bush. Bears travel lines of least resistance. Where understory vegetation is dense, they will often use trails built by people. If constructed trails aren't available, then bears develop their own tunnel-like systems or modify game trails made by other animals. When vegetation is dense, sparsely vegetated river or stream edges, beaches, or ridges also become travel routes. In open country, trails and roads may be used or avoided, apparently depending on the experience of a bear with people, or perhaps even depending on a bear's mood.

I have mentioned that another technique for minimizing risk while backcountry camping around bears is to sleep in a tent rather than without shelter. Sleeping under the stars is one of my favorite things to do while camping, but I choose areas in which to do this carefully. My data strongly suggest that people sleeping without tents were more likely to be injured, even killed, than were people who slept in tents.

Some tents are safer than others. When camping in bear country, I like to have a foot or two between me and the tent wall. Curious or garbage-addicted bears will sometimes bite or claw the sides of a tent as if testing to see if something edible is inside.

A flashlight is important when camping around bears. Noise in the night can cautiously be investigated by using a flashlight. A marauding black bear can usually be chased away by making noise, such as by shouting or by banging pots. A marauding grizzly should not be provoked in this or any other manner. If you have to leave the tent at night to go to the bathroom, or for any other reason, a flashlight allows you to check the general area for bears.

Some people would like to have a bear-detection system so that they know, especially during the night, if an animal such as a bear has entered the area where people are sleeping. Electronic detection systems have been developed for polar bears, which sometimes enter remote camps in the north.[16] Gordon Stenhouse, a bear biologist for the Northwest Territories, Canada, has developed a good, inexpensive and lightweight system that could be rigged around a tent.[17]

Both horses and dogs will normally sense a bear before a person will and thus increase your chances of early detection of a marauding bear. Horses will usually become restless if a bear is nearby. Horses can be good for warning you of bears if the horses are tied near a tent. The right dog can give you a valuable extension of your senses in bear country. Some dogs, like bears, have an acute sense of smell and can serve as an early warning system that a bear is around. Sometimes, however, even trained dogs will sleep while a bear enters a camp.[18] A further possible help from a well-trained dog is that it can be taught to chase a bear, or at least hold it at bay, while the dog's owner has time to retreat, climb a tree, or seek a weapon. But it is only a well-trained dog, experienced around bears, that is an advantage to its owner. An untrained dog can trigger an attack (see pp. 49–50).

In national parks dogs are either banned on trails or must be kept on leashes or otherwise controlled because of their potential for disturbing not only wildlife but also other people. Some lands under other jurisdictions also have similar dog-control rules.

BEAR REPELLENTS AND ATTRACTANTS

Campers or hikers may be faced with a bear that is either curious or is just testing to see what a person will do. In such a circumstance it might be possible to get the bear to leave by using a repellent. Sometimes just waving your arms and talking is enough to cause such a bear to leave. As previously mentioned, extremely loud and sharp sounds such as are emitted by freon-powered boat horns were one of the most promising long-range repellents tested under a limited range of lab and field conditions.[19] A less readily available repellent, which was almost 100 percent effective in repelling hundreds of polar bears after they had been feeding on seal bait, was a 38-mm, multipurpose riot gun that shot rubber bullets.[20] Most bears returned to the bait site more than once but after being repeatedly hit with rubber bullets they eventually stopped returning. The rubber bullets were apparently painful but did not seriously injure the bears. However, this riot gun has killed people and requires training to use.

Research carried out in Yosemite National Park on black bears that were used to both people and campground raiding showed that human aggression toward black bears was effective in getting unwanted bears out of camp.[21] Running toward and throwing objects at an approaching bear were two of the most effective techniques. Other effective methods were yelling, clapping hands, and banging pots together. Combinations of these mildly aggressive acts seemed to be particularly effective. The further a bear got into camp, and especially if it was already eating people's food, the harder it was to chase away.

There is no question that black bears can often be repelled by using these means. It should be obvious that if human aggression toward black bears is carried too far, even the tolerance of black bears can be exceeded and an attack could be triggered.

People should not normally act aggressively to try to repel or displace a grizzly bear. I discuss some of the exceptions to this rule (see pp. 87–88).

Electric fencing can be an effective means of keeping grizzly or black bears away from beehives, garbage dumps, or campgrounds (see p. 234). However, high standards for equipment quality, installation, and maintenance are required. Bears experienced in feeding at such areas may not be kept out.

Of the many chemical compounds such as mothballs, ammonia, and mace, that have been tested as bear repellents, those containing capsaicin, an active ingredient of cayenne peppers, have shown the most promise.[22] Capsaicin spray has been shown to stop fighting dogs when sprayed into their eyes.[23] It is widely used by mail carriers. Lynn Rogers, summarizing various tests conducted by researchers on capsaicin products, reported that all twelve black and all five grizzly bears who had capsaicin sprayed into their eyes were repelled without aggression.[24] The effectiveness of capsaicin has been tested on caged and free-ranging black bears, on caged grizzly bears, but not on free-ranging grizzlies. Whether capsaicin would repel a bear, such as a mother grizzly, that was highly motivated to attack has not been tested. Toxicity tests of capsaicin have shown no persistent damage to the skin or eyes of people, dogs, or albino rabbits.[25]

Among the commercially available forms of chemical sprays containing capsaicin, "Phaser" is the most consistent repellent. It also has the most reliable and effective spray system.[26] "Halt" and "Dog Shield" are proven repellents but they have less range.[27]

Another commercially available chemical repellent which has shown promise with limited testing on black bears is called "Skunker."[28] It uses the active ingredient which skunks spray to defend themselves.

The major current limitations of all chemical repellents are the preliminary nature of testing, their short range, the difficulty of accurate delivery if a person is excited, and their potential for abuse. Their seven-to-thirty-foot range means last-minute delivery to a bear and this would have to be done under very difficult conditions if a bear were charging full out. Wind could aid or severely deflect the spray. Chemical repellents are no substitute for avoiding bear confrontations, but they may be useful in repelling curious bears, especially black bears, that might become aggressive if not repelled.

Another potentially useful repellent is the "Schermuly" bird-scaring cartridge.[29] These shells will go for about four hundred feet, leaving a white trajectory. They then explode, illuminating about a one-hundred-foot radius. They can be shot from either a twelve-gauge shotgun or a special pistol. In tests on polar bears conducted during 1983, they repelled sixteen, about two-thirds, of the bears tested from approaching a seal bait.[30] Nine bears continued their approach. These shells have not been tested with black or grizzly bears, but they would probably have some repellent ability and would be particularly valuable at night because they illuminate a large area.

One means of stopping an aggressive bear from attacking might be to attract it to something else. Several species of lizardlike animals lose their tails when attacked by a predator. The tail flops wildly, supposedly to attract the predator's attention, and the tailless animal moves slowly for cover. A self-inflating and "jumpy" air-filled plastic animal might help to attract an aggressive bear away from a person— at least for a few seconds. No tests of this idea have been conducted.

Because of the limited amount of information available, I recommend no repellents except caution and understanding of bears, acting aggressively toward black bears, electrical fencing for specific uses, chemical sprays in some circumstances, and proper firearms in the hands of experts.

BERRY PICKING AND FISHING

These recreational pastimes deserve special mention in the context of avoiding injuries from bears. Productive berry patches are the most likely places to find bears in the summer or fall. Some species of berries, such as huckleberries (*Vaccinium* spp.) and salmonberries (*Rubus spectabilis*), are preferred by bears and are also favorites of people. Be alert while picking these berries. Watch for bears and fresh bear signs in berry patches. Make noise. If you are picking with young children, keep them close to you. Documented cases exist of black bears killing young children who were berry picking.[31]

Fish are natural food for bears as well as for people. They are odorous once out of the water. It is easy to get the odor from fish onto your body and clothing. Fish guts left after cleaning are a special challenge in bear country. If fishing in a large-volume stream with little human use and almost no pollutants entering into it, I suggest dumping fish guts directly into the stream or river. This may be contrary to local regulations, so check in advance. A large flowing body of water has the capacity to assimilate and decompose a limited quantity of organic matter such as fish guts. Larger quantities would pollute the water. The fish's air bladder should be pierced before throwing the remains into a water body. If this isn't done the remains may float to shore.

If this option is not available, then fish guts may be thoroughly burned in a very hot fire. In some places, if you are far from camp and other people, they may simply be left on the land to decompose or be eaten. Thought is required in choosing an appropriate place to dispose of fish guts.

In some protected areas, such as Katmai National Park, recreational fishing is popular and Alaskan brown bears, the large cousin of the grizzly, are numerous. To avoid attracting bears, the park managers have installed a special fish-cleaning house and disposal facilities.

10

Characteristics of Bears

IN this chapter and in the next five, I discuss basic information that people interested in safety might want to know about bears. I try to present enough information so that you can start to sense the environment as a bear does. You will not be able to think and feel like a bear, but you should have a better idea of the ways in which a bear responds to some elements of its environment, including people.

Philosopher Ludwig Wittgenstein said, "If a lion could talk, we could not understand him." A lion's language and actions, like a bear's, evolved from the way in which they adapted to and survived in their daily environment. Since we people face different challenges in life than do bears, it is difficult for us to understand the world of a bear. What we can do is understand the bear's world in human terms. We describe what they look like to us, test the acuity of their senses, measure the extent of the area used by certain age/sex groups of bears, and observe the visual signals, sounds, and smells with which they communicate with one another.

Black bears, as their accepted common name designates them, are not always black. An individual bear's coat color may range from blond, cinnamon, or light brown to dark chocolate brown or to jet black. Many intermediate color combinations exist. Along a portion of coastal Alaska and British Columbia, bluish-tinged black bears are found.[1] White- to cream-colored black bears have been described, especially from coastal islands and the adjacent mainland of southwestern British Columbia.[2] In addition to this, albino individuals are known.[3]

In moist areas black is the predominant coat color. Only black-colored bears have been reported from New England, New York, Tennessee, and Michigan.[4] In Minnesota 94 percent of the black bears are black in color and 6 percent are brown.[5] In coastal Washington State, over 99 percent of the coat colors were black, but 21 percent of inland Washington bears were brown.[6] In more arid interior areas, brown and blond shades become more prevalent.[7] Brown and blond are the most common coat colors in southwestern United States.[8] In arid Yosemite National Park, only 9 percent of a large sample of bears had a black coat color;[9] 91 percent were some shade of brown to blond.

It has always bothered me to look at a handsome blond-colored bear and to have to refer to it as a black bear. No wonder people are suspicious of zoologists. In fairness, zoologists are equally suspicious of common names, because they can vary from region to region. The alternative—calling members of this species *Ursus americanus*—works out well in technical literature but will never make it into our spoken language. So be prepared to see black bears in a variety of colors, depending on where you may be.

Ursus arctos bears are only sightly less confusing. *Ursus arctos* bears from the coast of Alaska, and sometimes from the coast of British Columbia, are usually called brown bears, or big brown bears. In this book I have used the term grizzly bears to apply to all *Ursus arctos* bears found in North America. This is contrary to common usage, but it is a practical necessity so that you always know what species I am talking about. When I talk about *Ursus arctos* bears from coastal Alaska, I have referred to them as grizzly (brown) bears to keep from alienating Alaskans (and so they will also know what bears I am talking about).

Zoologists recognize two subspecies of *Ursus arctos* bears in North America.[10] Those found in Alaska's three Kodiak Islands—Kodiak, Afognak, and Shuyak—are reproductively isolated and have distinctive cranial characteristics. These bears have been designated as *Ursus arctos middendorffi*. All the rest of the *Ursus arctos* bears vary from one another mainly according to gradients that reflect the energy available for growth. Therefore the vast majority of these bears in North America have been given the subspecific name of *Ursus arctos horribilis*,[11] the scientific name most often associated with the grizzly bear. This is another reason why I chose to use this common name. If having two recognized subspecies and several common names is confusing, just be thankful that the views of C. Hart Merriam weren't accepted. Merriam recognized eighty-six species and subspecies of *Ursus arctos* bears in North America.[12] If his views prevailed, I might never have finished this chapter!

The common name *grizzly* is derived from the term *grizzled*, which refers to hair that is either flecked with gray at the ends or is a mixture of gray and darker colors. Many, but not all, grizzly bears show this grizzling as a flecking of white on the ends of dark hairs on their coats. A black bear almost never has it. Because of the possibility of grizzling being superimposed on basic coat color, the color patterns of grizzly bears are many. Grizzlies may be pale—almost luminous blond, or reddish blond or light brown, or medium to dark brown, or even black. Color combinations are common. Fortunately black is probably the least common coat color, but it occurs frequently enough in areas where both black and grizzly bears exist that one should not assume that a black-colored bear is, in fact, a black bear! Also, black-colored grizzly bears are seldom heavily grizzled. Albino individuals have been seen.

To confuse the novice further, there are also variations in color patterning on the coats of each species. Pure brown or blond bears seldom exist for either black or grizzly bears. As many as ten genes may control coat color in black and grizzly bears,[13] and this yields many possible shades and patterns. Distinct white chest patches or blazes are sometimes present in black bears but are never found on grizzly bears. Grizzlies may, however, have an indefinite white chest patch that extends as a collar from the chest to the shoulders. Grizzly bears are typically grizzled, mainly on the back and about the shoulders, though the grizzling may extend well down onto the flanks. From a distance the grizzly usually seems to have darker legs and lighter upper parts.

Coat color is a relatively unreliable characteristic for identifying

Young grizzly (brown) bear with salmon. The bear has molted almost all the sun-bleached blond hair from last year and the new, darker coat is obvious.

Derek Stonorov

individual bears over a period of several months or more. The reason is that both species of bears molt during the summer. The new outer (guard) hair is the darkest that the individual will have. On most bears, especially of the brown-to-blond color types, an obvious lightening of color or bleaching of the coat occurs between molts. So beware of people's description of a mean brown-colored bear—by the time you meet it it may be a bleached blond.

None of our human confusion regarding species identification based on coat color has rubbed off on the bears. There are no known cases of mating between grizzly and black bears in nature, even though both species sometimes live in the same geographic area. When held in captivity, however, the two species have interbred and have produced cubs.

Other external characteristics are useful for field identification of bear species. Grizzly bears show a fairly distinctive hump between their shoulders as compared to black bears (see p. 150). The hump is a muscle mass covered with relatively long guard hairs and is tangible evidence of the grizzly's greater ability to dig into earth. While this is a reliable species characteristic, often useful because it can be discerned with field glasses at several hundred yards, it too can be confusing. Black bears frequently have this appearance when they drop their heads below the level of the rest of their bodies.

The facial profile of each species is different (see p. 150). Grizzly bears typically have a somewhat concave profile from between their eyes to the end of their nose whereas black bears normally have a "Roman" profile, more convex than the grizzly's. Most black bears have a light-colored area just behind their noses and extending around the snout. Grizzly bears often have this, too, but it is not as distinct.

Bear tracks can be useful in telling black bears apart from grizzlies (see pp. 186–191).

When you see a bear, you want to know not only the species but also whether it is a female with young. Fortunately cubs are normally less than one hundred yards from the female and usually at least one of them is visible when a female is seen. But females will sometimes leave their cubs and go at least several hundred yards away.[14] A grizzly bear mother temporarily separated from her young in this way still has her protective instincts. Also, bears less than a year old may be resting, and being motionless, be almost impossible to see—or they may be resting out of sight in a nook or hollow. If a grizzly is seen at a distance it may take as much as an hour or more to reveal whether the bear has cubs.

Adult male bears of both species are heavier and longer than

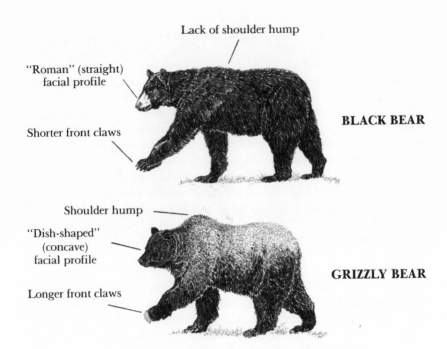

Lack of shoulder hump

"Roman" (straight) facial profile

Shorter front claws

BLACK BEAR

Shoulder hump

"Dish-shaped" (concave) facial profile

Longer front claws

GRIZZLY BEAR

Identifying characteristics of black and grizzly bears.

females. A male grows during each year of its life. A female reaches her near-maximum size in early adulthood,[15] which means that adult males may range from slightly heavier to up to twice as heavy as females.[16] Art Pearson studied a population of grizzly bears in the interior Yukon.[17] He found that the average weight of forty mature males was 306 pounds whereas that of twenty-one females was 209 pounds. The maximum size of each sex showed greater differences. The largest male weighed 529 pounds, nearly twice the weight of the largest female, 276 pounds. These interior grizzlies are one of the lighter-weight populations that have been studied. The largest living grizzly (brown) bears in the world may come from the Alaska peninsula or the Kodiak Island group.[18] Al Erickson reported that exceptional adult males from these areas may weigh up to 1,300 pounds.[19] Lee Glenn studied the size and growth of 344 different grizzly (brown) bears on the central Alaska Peninsula.[20] He determined that the mean weights of five adult males and twenty-five females over nine years of age were 858 pounds and 456 pounds. The heaviest male weighed 974 pounds but was only ten years old, and so if he lived he would get heavier. The heaviest female weighed 611 pounds at fifteen years. (Black bear weights are discussed later, pp. 172–174.)

We have watched mating pairs of grizzly bears that at first we

A black bear grazing, showing the grizzly-like hump that black bears sometimes appear to have. *Stephen Herrero*

mistakenly thought were a female and her cub. Because of the size differences between males and females, the female looked like a cub to us! The same female when with her cubs the next year would "grow" vastly in apparent size, especially if encountered on foot.

It takes a very competent observer, and special circumstances such as observed mating, to be able to identify the sex of a bear from limited observation of a single bear. With black bears it is sometimes possible to get close enough to observe the genitalia.

Bears share an ancient but relevant common ancestry with dogs. Some taxonomists stress the similarities between the dog and bear families. George Simpson has referred to bears as being like large dogs with short tails.[21] The phylogenetic relatedness of dogs and bears yields clues about the senses of bears. The dog's senses have been studied much more intensively than have the bear's.

Dogs and bears alike have acute senses of smell. People, with their limited powers of olfaction, can marvel at, but not imitate, the olfactory prowess of bears. An Indian saying goes: "A pine needle fell. The eagle saw it. The deer heard it. The bear smelled it."

The evidence for black and grizzly bears having an acute sense of smell is anecdotal but extensive. We have observed grizzly bears repeatedly testing the air for the scent of recently born elk calves. The calves are thought to be relatively odorless. While hunting for elk calves, bears will often walk back and forth across a calving area, periodically thrusting their noses into the air and sniffing. It has appeared to us that once they smell a calf it will soon be located and killed. Both species of bears can also apparently distinguish between human beings and nonhuman animals by the scent traces left by people's footfalls. Bears can smell carcasses from several miles away.[22]

Males can also locate some females who are coming into heat by finding and then following their scent trails.[23] If a bear sees or hears something, it will often move downwind to get more information.

The extensive evidence that bears have an acute sense of smell makes it clear how futile it is to try to hide a candy bar by putting it under a camp pillow. You may escape the eye of mother but not the nose of bear.

Smell is the fundamental and most important sense a bear has. Bears find much of their food and many of their mates by smelling. When a bear encounters a person, final knowledge for the bear concerning the strange biped standing before it often seems to require the bear to get the person's odor. A bear suddenly confronted with a person may stand on its hind legs, not as a spoof of the biped it faces, but to better smell, see, or hear a person. A bear may also charge, sometimes repeatedly, or may partially circle a person to gain a position where it can smell the two-footed animal. Usually a bear that acts like this will flee once it has caught scent of a person.

A bear's nose is its window into the world just as our eyes are. But what of a bear's eyes? Most people and many scientists believe that bears have poor eyesight. Some people interpret a bear standing and then circling a person to better smell the person as clear evidence for poor vision. There is, however, some scientific evidence to suggests that bears have reasonable visual acuity. Perhaps they just do not trust their eyes as much as they trust their noses!

Experiments have shown that black bears learn visual-discrimination tasks based on hue (color) more rapidly than do chimpanzees and as rapidly as dogs, when tested under similar conditions.[24] While foraging during the day, black bears appear to use their eyesight much more than has been assumed.[25] Their acute color vision probably is an aid in locating small bits of food and differentiating these from inedible objects. Black bears have also been shown to have the ability to rapidly learn to discriminate forms such as small squares, circles, and triangles.[26] Their retention of this learning was excellent up to the maximum time tested—eight months. This visual-form retention, coupled no doubt with other sensory retention of learned information, probably helps to explain why bears are able to remember a given food source for so long.

Are bears nearsighted and only able to recognize form at relatively close distances? I do not know. The apparent confusion of bears seen by humans at distances of say between one hundred and six hundred feet might be interpreted in this way. An alternate explanation would be that they try to get evidence from other senses such as smell,

Black and grizzly bears locate almost odor-free ungulate newborn by smell.

hearing, and even touching before reaching a conclusion. Experiments conducted on European brown bears, a close relative of the grizzly, showed that they could recognize their keeper moving toward them at a distance of 361 feet.[27] More experimentation is needed.

Hearing in bears is probably good although most of the evidence is anecdotal. A brief bleating by an elk calf was sufficient for two grizzly bears about 1,600 feet away to hear the sound and then to locate and kill the calf.[28] European brown bears have been shown to be able to hear an auditory signal at 490–510 feet, whereas a person can only hear it at 263 feet.[29] As mentioned earlier, limited evidence suggests that bears, like dogs, can hear sounds in the ultrasonic range—too high for a person to hear.[30]

To avoid sudden confrontations with bears at close range, a prudent person can use the known information about a bear's senses and try to convey advance information to bears. Traveling with attention to which direction the wind is blowing and making noise in bear habitat when vision is restricted are examples of this. Controlled movements such as slowly waving a hand may also help a bear that has seen you to sense what you are. How a bear responds to its perception of you as a person depends on many factors and cannot be predicted simply from a knowledge of the senses of bears.

Bears normally walk on all four legs. When trying to sense something, however, they will often stand on their hind legs. Sometimes they will walk a few steps while still standing. No doubt the ability of bears to stand on two feet has influenced some people's perception of them as being humanlike or even "cute." It has also led to many bears being conscripted as circus performers.

The most persistent rumor I have heard regarding the running ability of bears is that they cannot run downhill without stumbling. Many people have either told me this or asked me if this were true. Apparently some naturalist talks contain this information. The rumor is untrue. I have watched grizzly bears chase one another, and I have watched grizzly bears chase elk and bighorn sheep—downhill, uphill, sidehill—wherever the pursuit leads. I have never seen a grizzly bear stumble, although they may do so occasionally. I suspect that the same is true for black bears.

Bears are strong. Although confirmation of this is mostly by inference and anecdote, formal testing is hardly required. Adult bears have a predator's strength and ability to subdue and kill large ungulates. The jaws of adult bears are very powerful and are sometimes used to crack open ungulate leg bones to get at the marrow. I've listened to bears doing this. From a distance the sound reminded a friend of mine of a child eating hard candy. Even young bears are surprisingly strong. A six-month-old cub is a pretty good match for most people.

John Romansky, a student of John Craighead, told me that in Yellowstone Park he saw two adult male grizzlies, each probably weighing more than 400 pounds, engaged in a dominance contest that included one bear grabbing the other with its jaws, planting its feet, and lifting the opponent completely off the ground and throwing it into the air. Derek Stonorov saw one large male Alaskan brown bear "pick the other bear up in its teeth" and throw it down a riverbank.[31]

Trying to physically subdue an enraged adult black or grizzly bear is like wrestling with a tank. Occasionally you may find a vulnerable spot and stop the bear but, generally, you are better off trying to avoid or outwit it.

Curiosity is as much a part of a bear as is its fur. I've mentioned how young bears, and some older bears, inexperienced with humans, may approach people or their belongings out of curiosity. Usually avoidance prevails and the curious bear flees when a person is sensed, but sometimes bears seem to bite tents, packs, coolers, cans and even people just to see if such things are edible. An overly curious bear, especially if it is also aggressive, usually doesn't survive for long around people.

Bears, especially when young, play a lot. Although this trait has little relation to human safety, no description of black or grizzly bears would be complete without mentioning play. One of the most humorous play sessions I've observed occurred during June 1968 when two black bear cubs of the year came upon a young sapling pine tree. One bear climbed to near the top. Then the other bear followed, and their combined weight bent the tree to near the ground where one cub hopped off and the other was catapulted up as the tree straightened. Soon both cubs were up the tree again to repeat the sequence.

Grizzly bear cubs are just as playful. When they encounter a snow-covered hillside, play usually follows. I've spent many happy hours watching them roll, wrestle, jump, and repeatedly slide on snow. Even adult bears sometimes launch themselves onto snow for a good slide. In Waterton National Park during the spring of 1982, we watched a male grizzly following a female with large cubs. Their route went up a snow-filled gully that was several hundred yards long. Near the top he seemed to tire of following her, and he turned around and launched himself onto the snow, rolling and tumbling downward. She turned and watched his antics, and within a few seconds she too was rolling down the snow toward him. The cubs stared downward, but their caution toward the male probably kept them from joining in.

Play among bears is part of their social and physical development. It doesn't really make them at all like people, even though some people see it this way. Behind the bear's sometimes playful behavior there always beats the heart of a carnivore.

Play is part of the essence of bear cubs.

11

The Evolution
of Bears

To further understand the nature of a bear, we can look at how bears came to be—their evolution. The facts that scientists gather about bears today take on broader meaning when we know how these animals changed over time in response to their environments.

Most mammals are either vegetable eaters (herbivores) or meat eaters (carnivores). Black and grizzly bears are the end products of meat eaters that were redesigned over millions of years to eat mainly vegetation. Functionally they are omnivores, which means that they will eat a wide range of foods including both animals and plants, but they clearly belong to the mammalian order Carnivora, which also includes specialized predators such as wolves, weasels, and tigers. Black and grizzly bears show their Carnivore* ancestry in their opportunistic predation on animals ranging in size from ground squirrels to moose. Compared to specialized predators, bears are inefficient, relatively unsuccessful predators of large mammals. The bears' ancestors had smaller and more lithe bodies and were no doubt more effective in killing small animals. Modern bears, with the exception of polar bears, have become somewhat chunky and unspecialized for killing.

---

*When *Carnivore* is capitalized, it implies that an animal is classified in the order Carnivora. When *carnivore* is not capitalized, the term is used to describe the meat-eating food habits of a species.

The major trend in the evolution of bears was the development of interrelated adaptations that allowed a Carnivore to feed relatively efficiently on vegetation.[1] In both black and grizzly bears, the molar teeth are today characterized by elongated, relatively flat grinding surfaces that are given additional detail by a wrinkling of the enamel. Numerous low, rounded cusps are found on the molars. This is typical of Carnivores, such as European badgers and black and grizzly bears, that eat a lot of vegetable food. Bears are the extreme of this trend, and their molar surfaces have come to resemble those of omnivorous pigs.[2] Understanding the significance of this evolutionary trend is a cornerstone to understanding black and grizzly bear ecology and behavior.

Since in bears most chewing takes place on the molars, relatively far back in the mouth, massive muscles have evolved to facilitate grinding by the molars. Jaws fall open by gravity when muscles are relaxed, but strong muscles are required to close them and then to grind a root or blades of grass into small fragments. This is why bears can bite hard.

The grizzly is adapted for heavier chewing than is the black bear. A primary difference in diet between the two species is that grizzlies include far more roots, bulbs, corms, and tubers in their diets than do black bears. Eating these items requires jaws and teeth to crush and grind more than does eating green vegetation and berries.

Both species will eat mast, the nut crops of various trees, and so there is also some adaptation for heavy grinding in black bears. This specialization is carried further in grizzly bears. The longer claws and greater shoulder musculature—the hump—are additional interrelated adaptations that assist the grizzly in digging foods out of the ground.

Why did this strong trend toward eating vegetation develop in bears? By knowing something about the lives of predaceous Carnivores, I can suggest a possible answer. Predaceous Carnivores live from feast to famine. When a kill is made, an amount of prey weighing up to one-fifth of the Carnivore's body weight can be eaten during a single feeding. But prey are often hard to catch, and in some areas or at certain times of year prey become scarce.

Many Carnivores will ingest some vegetation, especially easily digested fruits, in their diet. Bears have taken this occasional herbivory practiced by most Carnivores and turned it into their essence. I imagine that ancestral bears that were best able to ingest and process vegetation were most successful in surviving periods when game were scarce or were hard to catch. Once this trend was started, it continued.

Bears began as small-bodied carnivores but eventually became large-bodied omnivores. The cave bear *Ursus spelaeus*, which has been called *le moins carnivore des Carnivores et le plus ours des Ours*—"the least carnivorous of Carnivores, and the most bearish of bears," exemplified this trend.[3]

In nature a successful organism is one that survives and contributes more of its genes to succeeding generations than do other individuals. For black and grizzly bears, genetic fitness is directly related to getting enough of the right foods to eat. Even though bears are the most efficient vegetation eaters among the Carnivores, they are relatively inefficient at processing coarse vegetation when compared to ruminants such as sheep or moose. Ruminants have multiple-chambered stomachs and helpful bacteria that assist them by breaking down cellulose. Aided by these bacteria and the ability to rechew partially digested plant matter (ruminate), they can survive by eating relatively large quantities of what is in winter low-quality vegetation. In northern temperate zones, mountain sheep can survive on a diet of dried forbs and grasses. Moose survive winter by eating small-diameter twigs or even ingesting the needles of conifers such as subalpine fir if deep snow confines their movements.

The simple gut of a bear, even though it is elongated compared to other Carnivores,[4] still lacks the ability to digest nutritionally poor vegetation.[5] For this reason, black and grizzly bears typically forage on vegetation when it is near its peak of nutrient availability and when it is easy to digest.[6] When food is nutritious and abundant the bear's simple digestive system has advantages over the ruminant system. After a ruminant eats, it must spend several hours not eating but digesting its food. When there is lots of food, bears often eat large quantities without much of a break for digestion. The bear's simple gut very rapidly processes foods such as berries, extracting calories and nutrients, putting out fecal matter, and making way for more food. In this way bears are able to make the most out of abundant and nutritious food that is only available for a relatively short time.

People's food and garbage are so attractive to bears not because bears will "eat anything" but rather because people's food and garbage are so easily converted into calories by bears. Human beings too are quite inefficient at digesting unprocessed, complex carbohydrates. To aid digestion of carbohydrates such as starch, we cook our rice, potatoes, and pasta. Bears have never learned to cook, but they readily learn where cooks throw away easily digested leftovers.

A successful bear is a well-fed bear. For example, reproductive success for female black bears is strongly related to nutrition. In 1976

Lynn Rogers published results that elegantly demonstrated that female black bears had to reach a certain body weight before they could successfully reproduce.[7] He reported that in Minnesota none of the sixteen adult females that weighed less than 147 pounds on October 1 produced cubs, whereas twenty-eight out of thirty adult females that weighed more than 176 pounds and were without cubs from the previous season produced cubs. I suspect that nutrition affects reproduction in grizzly bears in a similar manner.

Adequate quantity and quality of food not only makes the difference between whether or not adult female black and probably grizzly bears are able to produce cubs in a given year, but good nutrition also hastens the age of first reproduction. In food-rich areas bears reproduce by as much as one to three years earlier than do their counterparts in less productive areas.

The size of a litter that a female bear has is another measure of reproductive success. Litter size ranges from one to four for both black and grizzly bears. Some black bears have been seen with litters of five,[8] but since adoption is known to occur occasionally, this possibility has to be ruled out before natural birth litters of five can be accepted. The most common number of offspring in a given litter (the mode) for females of both species is two. The mean number of cubs varies from a low of 1.65 to a high of 2.29 for black bears in different areas and from a low of 1.70 to a high of 2.36 for grizzlies.[9] Low mean litter sizes for both species occur in areas where food is scarce, especially in those interior areas that lack major mast crops. Black and grizzly bear litter size is fairly constant, but the small size variation that does occur is clearly related to nutritional factors.

Many more pieces of evidence could be presented to substantiate the close relationship between reproductive success in female black and grizzly bears and their diets. Female black bears that have fed on dumps were found to be significantly heavier than counterparts that existed exclusively on natural food. They also reproduced at earlier ages (5 females who had access to dumps first reproduced at a mean age of 4.4; 9 females subsisting without garbage first reproduced at a mean age of 5.6) and had litter sizes that averaged 3.10 versus 1.99 for other females that existed on a more natural diet.[10]

We can now clearly see the basis for the attraction of female bears to garbage-food sources. Provided that they are not shot or run over by motor vehicles as a result of feeding at dumps, they are able to increase their body weights and hence produce more offspring.

What does food mean for males? They neither give birth to cubs nor play a role in raising the offspring. In interpreting the importance of food for male bears, I have to use more inference than I did for females. Still, a clear suggestion emerges.

Bears are promiscuous given the opportunity. Each adult male can potentially inseminate several females during a breeding season, which lasts for about two months. Adult "females" can be seen as being a scarce "resource" for the males because each male "wants" to mate with more females than are available. For both species in most years, a significant proportion of adult females will be unavailable for breeding because they are accompanied by cubs. Females available for breeding thus become a scarce resource if there are equal numbers of adult males and females present in the population. Older, bigger, and more aggressive males tend to mate the most.[11] To gain this privilege, they first must dominate other male bears. So male bears, like female bears, have a strong drive to grow. In both sexes adequate quality and quantity of food are the cornerstones of reproductive fitness. Because of this, food availability is a primary determinant of where bears are found except while breeding or denning.

12

Bear Foods
And Location

WHERE are bears most likely to be found? Near their food. By learning to recognize feeding areas, people traveling in bear country can improve their ability to avoid sudden encounters with bears. I have stressed that both black and grizzly bears select foods that are relatively high in nutrients and are easy to digest. Bears normally move until they find these foods.

Seeking and eating food is the main factor that influences the movement and location of both black and grizzly bears. However, there are other important influences. Some of these other factors are: cover,* which is used for escape and protection; bedding areas and thermal microenvironments, which are places where bears rest or go to cool or warm themselves; den site areas, which are where bears spend the winter; and mating areas, which, in some places, seem to be an integral component of the grizzly bear's reproductive behavior. Discussion of these nonfood factors follows a discussion of bear foods. Because I am writing this chapter to cover the general factors influencing the movements and location of black and grizzly bears throughout North America, I cannot adequately describe the specific areas used by bears in different geographic regions. These areas, however,

---

*Cover refers to trees, shrubs, or other landscape features that allow an animal to partly or fully conceal itself.

have similar, general biological characteristics. For example, they are areas of early green-up in spring or areas where there may be many berries in fall.

SPRING AND SUMMER FOODS

Both black and grizzly bears in northern temperate zones emerge from their winter dens from March through May having lost from between 15 to more than 40 percent of their body weight over the winter.[1] Female bears with newborn cubs will have nursed their offspring since the time of birth in mid-January or February. During this entire period the mother bear typically has nothing to eat or drink. By human standards they should emerge ravenously hungry, but there is no evidence to indicate that this is so. If adequate fall foods were available, bears leaving their dens in spring still have a significant layer of back and rump fat.

After emerging from their dens, bears may remain in a hibernationlike state for a few weeks,[2] but they soon move to areas where there is something for them to eat. Natural spring foods for both black and grizzly bears seldom allow them to gain weight. Studies have shown that in many areas bears continue the weight loss begun during denning until berries begin to ripen in summer or fall.[3]

Spring and summer foods for bears may include grasses and other green vegetation, flowers, the sapwood (cambium) of trees, the underground storage organs of plants, insects, mammals, fish, berries that ripened the previous fall and are still on bushes, and a variety of people-related foods such as garbage. Which food is eaten depends upon many factors, such as nutritional content, taste, and whether cover is present. One thing hikers can watch for is the size of a food patch—the more food there is, the greater the chance of a bear being there.

Grasses and Other Green Vegetation, Flowers, and Sapwood

Bears normally eat the above-ground portions of green, herbaceous plants when the plants are in early growth stages. Growth typically occurs after the dormant winter period. During early stages of growth, the shoots, leaves, and stems of most herbaceous plants and a few shrubs and trees are succulent, easily digested, and are high in nutrients compared to later growth stages when flowering, fruiting, or dormancy have occurred. Bears often move to, and forage in, areas where preferred plants are in early growth stages.[4]

The plants eaten by bears vary from area to area, but the principle of foraging on early growth stages is a general rule. It has exceptions such as feeding on flowers. Bears probably eat plants that are just beginning to grow because bears lack a caecum* and the accompanying bacteria to digest cellulose.[5] For this reason bears cannot easily digest most mature plants.

During early growth stages, plants are highest in protein, an essential nutrient in bear growth and tissue rebuilding. At high elevations, plants grow very rapidly, and this creates a greater percentage of protein in plant tissue compared to lower-elevation sites.[6] Hence, during summer, bears prefer to feed at high elevations. Where black and grizzly bears coexist, the grizzly dominates the high country in summer and may completely keep out black bears.[7] In the absence of grizzlies, black bears feed at higher elevations in summer.[8]

Feeding on herbaceous green vegetation generally begins in early spring and may persist until fruits begin to ripen. Vegetation development occurs with different timing and character, depending upon local climate, soils, and other factors. In mountainous areas the timing of green-up varies with elevation, orientation to the sun, depth of snowpack, and other factors.

Some specific examples of early green-up sites particularly attractive to grizzly bears in the mountains of western Canada are south-facing avalanche slopes in areas where heavy snowfall exists, and windswept south- and west-facing mountain meadows all along the eastern slopes of the Canadian Rockies. In sites having either of these characteristics, the snow melts earlier than at other areas at similar or even lower elevations. Because of their southern exposure and slope angle, such sites receive more of the sun's energy and plant growth begins early.

On the forest floor earliest green-up occurs on small meadow hills facing south and along the edges of watercourses and roads. These sites often attract black bears. Many national parks have road right-of-ways that green-up early and attract black bears. Once the bear is there, it is easy—but illegal—for tourists to feed the bears and to make panhandlers out of them.

In moist coastal areas, early season green-vegetation foods for both black and grizzly bears include the shoots of perennial shrubs

---

*The caecum in many herviborous mammals is a large digestive organ that contains many bacteria and Protozoa capable of digesting cellulose.

such as salmonberry (*Rubus spectabilis*) and devil's club (*Oplopanax horridum*). Salmonberry shoots may grow a yard or more in the spring. They are a very important spring food.

By moving from place to place, bears can usually find sites where plants are just starting to grow. For example, moving from the south side of a valley to the north side and up a thousand feet may take a bear from vegetation that is approaching dormancy, because it has completed its growing cycle, to vegetation just emerging from a cloak of snow. In the interior mountains of most of North America, green-up may begin as early as February and extend into July, depending on local climate. Although feeding on green vegetation is interspersed with feeding on other foods, from early spring until berries are prevalent, green plants are always important to both black and grizzly bears.

Because moisture encourages a prolonged growing season and maintains succulence and nutrient levels in plants, moist meadows tend to produce green vegetation attractive to bears.[9] This is true especially later in the season when sites having an early green-up have become dry. Bears' preference for moist meadows can lead to conflict with people, especially in grizzly bear habitat. In the mountains during the late spring and summer, but before berries are readily available, grizzly bears feed in moist meadows and other moist sites. These same areas that are emerald green when other areas are browner and drier are also attractive to hikers and campers.

The conflict may be particularly sharp if findings by Dick Russell and his co-workers reflect a general principle.[10] They believe that female grizzly bears and their cubs in Jasper National Park were most often found during the summer in moist subalpine meadow environments and that the less dangerous adult males more often frequented major valley bottoms. Whether or not this finding is substantiated, there is no doubt that moist meadows in early stages of green-up are very attractive to grizzly and black bears alike. In coastal Alaska grizzly (brown) bears were observed to spend six weeks in a moist-meadow environment where they fed on emerging sedges as the snowpack gradually receded up a mountain slope.[11]

Other sites that also maintain moisture and are important for green-vegetation feeding are forest-meadow edges and avalanche slopes, especially slopes that accumulate a deep snow cover and have a prolonged melt with different portions of them becoming snow free over a period of weeks or more. Although most hikers avoid such areas because they are hard to travel through, constructed trails sometimes go through them. Because visibility is often restricted, precautions are strongly recommended. Trail relocation, or widening to increase

A biologist works in a moist avalanche slope habitat favored by
grizzly bears.   *David Hamer*

line-of-site distances, may be appropriate. Sometimes, while studying
an avalanche slope with binoculars or a telescope before visiting it, I
have detected the presence of bears, at first only by seeing shrubs
moving and—as much as an hour later—by actually seeing a bear.

In moist areas plants are sometimes eaten in mature as well as
early stages of growth; among them the cow parsnip (*Heracleum lanatum*) is an important food for both black and grizzly bears. While
cow parsnip feeding is most prevalent during early growth stages,
feeding is also common on more mature plants. The part of the plant
most often eaten is the main stem, although the stems of the leaves
(petioles) are also eaten, and later in the year even flowers are occasionally eaten. A similar feeding pattern exists for angelica (*Angelica
arguta*), a close relative of the cow parsnip.

In addition to cow parsnip flowers, which are sometimes eaten by
both black and grizzly bears, black bears (but not grizzlies) commonly
eat dandelion flowers. I love to watch a black bear walking through
an expanse of yellow dandelion flowers, the bear's head bobbing up
and down as it nips off the flower heads. Flowers of a few other plant
species are also minor foods for bears. Grizzly bears faced with a
restricted springtime diet will in some areas eat the flowers of willows
(catkins).[12]

Also in springtime black bears, and to a lesser extent grizzly bears,

Plants important as grizzly bear foods.

Horsetail (*Equisetum* spp.)   Hedysarum (*Hedysarum* spp.)   Buffaloberry (Soapberry)
                                                                 (Shepherdia canadensis)

will sometimes strip the outer bark off trees to feed on sapwood.[13] This occurs when few high-energy foods are available. The sapwood has a concentration of the tree's nutrients.

Underground Storage Organs of Plants

Some plants store nutrients and next season's growth potential in underground storage organs such as roots, bulbs, tubers, and corms.* Black bears seldom if ever feed on these underground foods, but for grizzly bears, where these foods are abundant they are usually important, especially when above-ground portions of the plant are small or dried up.

In the early spring, feeding on these subterranean foods either occurs before or simultaneously with feeding on the first green shoots. In many, but not all, interior mountain ranges of western North America, grizzlies locate and feed on the roots of what is, to them, an important plant. This is hedysarum (also called bear root or eskimo potato) (*Hedysarum spp.*).[14] Hedysarum roots, like other such subterranean foods, are dug and eaten primarily when the plant is dormant, during spring or fall, or during early growth. At these times hedysarum has the most energy stored in the roots. As green-up progresses, grizzly bears move to find areas, such as north- and east-facing slopes, where hedysarum, or other plants having underground food storage, is still immature.[15]

Insects and Other Invertebrates

Ants, bees, beetles, and other insects also may be important food for both black and grizzly bears. In Banff National Park, grizzly bears often fed on ants and larvae in deadfall from previous fires, especially in summer. During these months you would do well to keep a sharp eye while traveling through windfall, especially since human travel through windfall is slow and awkward. Old-timers call windfalls "grizzly sidewalks," because grizzlies supposedly walk on top of the downed logs. I have not observed this myself, but Barney Smith has seen grizzlies walking on large timbers left as part of logging waste.[16]

Bees and their larvae and honey may become highly sought after, especially where people keep bees. Without adequate protection by electric fencing or other means, these hives become like lively ice-cream parlors for bears and disaster areas for people.

---

*A *corm* is a short, fleshy underground stem resembling a bulb and covered with several scalelike leaves.

Rotten log torn apart by grizzly bears which fed on the ants within, Banff National Park.   *Stephen Herrero*

Black bear turning over rocks in search of insects, which can form an important part of a bear's diet.

Both species of bears also frequently turn over rocks in search of insects. In 1972 Jay Sumner observed one grizzly female with three cubs which for a month fed heavily on Noctuidae moths that were obtained by turning over rocks. As many as two hundred of the moths were found under an area covering approximately two square feet.[17]

Lynn Rogers was studying black bears in Minnesota during 1975, a year when the summer berry crops were poor. One radio-collared female spent nearly three-fourths of her foraging time eating ants and their larvae. Lynn points out that insects are important sources of fat and protein for bears.[18]

Adolf Murie, one of America's great naturalists, observed that during the summer of 1935 crickets and grasshoppers were more abundant than usual in the Jackson Hole–Yellowstone region. Apparently for a while the bears in the region were living largely on these insects, especially the crickets. Murie further stated, "It was thought by some that the bears had deserted park garbage piles for the purpose of gorging themselves on these entomological sweets."[19]

In coastal areas both species of bears readily forage in the biologically rich intertidal zone where they eat crabs and other marine invertebrates. This feeding is not restricted to spring.

Mammals

Live or dead mammals will be eaten by bears any time they can be secured. If ungulates that have died during winter are available, bears of both species feed on them. Sometimes bears will dig animals like mountain sheep, goats, or elk out of snow avalanches that have killed them.

Later, during spring or early summer, ungulates have their young. Ungulate birthing grounds are places to be avoided or approached with care if grizzly bears also live in the area. Both black and grizzly bears can be significant predators on newborn ungulates. In some areas, black bears have killed and eaten up to 50 percent of newborn elk[20] and 42 percent of moose calves.[21] In the Rose Lake study area of the Yukon, grizzly bears killed at least 61 percent (25 out of 41) of radio-collared, newborn moose which died between birth and June 21, 1983.[22]

Two injuries in Mt. McKinley Park were possibly caused by grizzlies which were "keyed up" from hunting moose calves near the time of birthing.[23]

Once the newborn are a few days old, these quick-to-develop young appear to be able to evade predation by bears provided they are healthy. The period of easy hunting for bears is then over. For the rest of the year, bears only kill ungulates when the prey are sick or wounded or when otherwise catchable individuals are found. Some bears, however, especially in the absence of competition from wolves, may become successful predators of adult ungulates.[24] More often bears will scavenge dead ungulates. I earlier stressed the danger of suddenly coming upon a carcass that a grizzly has claimed.

In some areas ground squirrels, marmots, or other rodents become bear food. These ground-dwelling rodents are mainly the prey of grizzly bears because of this bear's superior digging ability. Ground squirrels and marmots are eaten primarily during summer and fall.

Fish

Fish make good food for both black and grizzly bears but, like mammals, they are usually hard for bears to catch. The exception to this is during spawning, or when fish bunch up on their way to spawn. Fish spawning may occur in spring, summer, or fall, depending upon the species.

Some salmon streams are famous for the bears that fish in them. One such spot, the McNeil River Falls Game Sanctuary, Alaska, has become a significant tourist attraction because it is a major fishing hole for grizzly (brown) bears.

Berries That Ripened the Previous Fall

On the eastern side of Canada's Rocky Mountains, a berry-producing member of the heath family, *Arctostaphylos uva-ursi*, has the appropriate common name of bearberry. (*Arctostaphylos uva-ursi* translates from its Greek and Latin roots into English as bearberry berrybear.) Despite the name, the fruits are only moderately important for bears. In the fall when the fruits mature they are mealy and only have a trace of sweetness. Bears occasionally eat them then but, in contrast to most other berries, many of these red-colored fruits stay on the plants over the winter. By spring their sugar content may have increased two- to threefold.[25] Both black and grizzly bears in the Rockies feed on them in spring. As far as I know, they are the only major berry available then. A similar species, *Arctostaphylos rubra*, also has berries that persist over winter. Black bears in Nahanni National Park, Northwest Territories, have been observed eating these berries in spring.[26] In Denali National Park and in the Yukon, grizzly bears eat overwintered crowberries (*Empetrum nigrum*),[27] and along the Northwest Coast and in the Yukon, both black and grizzly bears may eat overwintered low-bush cranberries (*Vaccinium vitis-idaea*).[28]

People-Related Foods

Garbage may be the first substantial meal that a bear gets in spring. Garbage feeding may also continue until bears hibernate. During our study of grizzly bears in Banff National Park, we recorded journeys of over twenty-four miles from backcountry denning areas to the Banff Sanitary Landfill. Despite its name, the Sanitary Landfill always had something for a bear to eat during the entire five years of our research. I've already thoroughly documented the safety problems related to garbage-feeding bears.

The influence of garbage on bear movements and location has been extensively documented. For example, during the Craighead study in Yellowstone Park, they found that "almost all park grizzlies visit one or more of the six major refuse-disposal areas at some time within a year."[29] As previously mentioned, some nights up to seventy grizzlies were observed to feed at the Trout Creek dump in Yellowstone.

The tremendous attraction of garbage was also confirmed in Yellowstone in other ways besides the sheer number of bears that fed at dumps. Even females with cubs of the year fed at the heavily used Trout Creek dump. Their cubs were left on the edge of the dump while the females went in to eat. Since male grizzlies have on occasion preyed on young grizzlies,[30] the females' willingness to leave their offspring must have been driven by a very strong attraction for garbage.

One of the strongest statements about how important it is for bears to get concentrated nutrients is shown by their occasional feeding at sewage lagoons. (They can digest some things better than we can.)[31]

Many other things that people grow or like to eat will attract bears. Bees and honey, cattle, sheep, pigs, carrots, corn, strawberries, raspberries, apples, plums, and pears are only a few things from a long list. I even investigated one situation in which bears took both marijuana plants and the planters they were growing in. The bears apparently took them to eat the fish fertilizer used on the plants. The marijuana wasn't eaten.

FOODS TO FATTEN ON: MIDSUMMER THROUGH FALL

Where available, berries and mast are some of the primary foods that bears fatten on in preparation for denning. When berries or mast are abundant, bears spend most of their time feeding on them or resting nearby. Art Pearson, based on his work in the Yukon, was the first to report an estimate of the number of berries ingested in one day by an adult grizzly bear.[32] The important berry in the grizzly's diet in the Yukon is soapberry (*Shepherdia canadensis*, also called buffalo-berry). This berry only has one seed in it, and so by counting the number of seeds in a scat and estimating the number of times a grizzly defecated in a day, he was able to estimate the number of berries eaten daily. Pearson found that grizzlies during peak feeding periods ate an incredible number of berries, about 200,000 per day. Scats from grizzlies eating these berries may occur as red splotches extending up to fifteen feet along a trail or as discrete red piles. Art Pearson documented that one immature female grizzly bear gained an average of 1.40 pounds per day over a sixteen-day period while feeding exclusively on soapberries.[33]

In productive buffaloberry areas in Banff National Park, we have observed up to nine grizzly bears within 1.2 square miles. In Glacier National Park, Montana, Cliff Martinka noted densities of up to 0.5 grizzly bears per square mile in rich huckleberry (*Vaccinium* spp.) areas.[34]

Some of people's favorite huckleberry patches are, of course, also favorites for bears. One such patch is found on a five-acre, thirty-year-old burn in British Columbia, where I and my family regularly pick berries. Fresh black bear droppings and other bear signs are always present when we pick. Although I have never seen or heard of grizzly foraging at the site, it is an area where one might show up. For this reason I usually leave our poorly trained dog at home and rely on my own and my family's alertness. I keep the children close by.

Almost all nonpoisonous berries, fruits, and nuts that occur in large enough quantities are attractive to both black and grizzly bears.

The list of berries that bears will eat is long. Other favorites, depending upon local availability, are mountain ash, salmonberries, devil's club berries, wild sarsaparilla, raspberries, wild cherries, wild strawberries, wild cranberries, and crowberries. Failure of a major crop of berries that bears feed upon in most years can motivate them either to undertake long-distance movements in search of food[35] or it may cause bears to den early.[36] I have already discussed how black bear-inflicted injuries increased during a berry failure year in the interior of Alaska (see pp. 120–121).

Mast refers to a crop of nuts, especially those such as beechnuts and acorns, that fall from trees after maturing and accumulate on the forest floor. Such nuts are a rich energy source for bears to fatten on. Compared to fruits, which have little fat, most nuts have about 50 percent fat. Fat has a caloric density about two times that of carbohydrates or protein. Black bears will sometimes ascend trees to feed

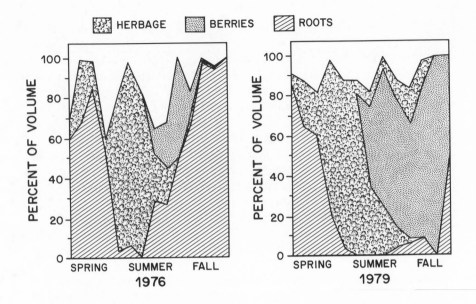

Seasonal composition of grizzly bear diet (major foods only) in Banff National Park, Canada, 1976 and 1979. In 1976 the buffaloberry crop failed and in the fall grizzly bears mainly ate hedysarum roots. In 1979 buffaloberries were abundant.[45]

on nuts,[37] but this has not been reported for the less arboreal grizzly.

When grizzlies still survived in California, they had acorn mast to feed on in much of the nonmountainous portions of their range. Indians also fed on acorn mast, and somewhat of a standoff took place regarding whether people or bears were dominant at a given feeding site.[38]

Today the grizzly's main source of mast comes from white-bark pine nuts in mountainous portions of Montana and small portions of nearby states. Red squirrels climb trees and do the harvesting. The grizzly comes along later and robs the squirrels' winter food caches.[39]

Black bears, however, still have good access to mast throughout portions of their range in central and eastern North America. In areas where mast is prevalent in the black bear's diet, bears have large numbers of young and adult body weights are high. Adult male black bears weighing 582 pounds and 600 pounds have been reported in mast feeding areas of New York.[40] In a similar area in Pennsylvania, a ten-year-old male (which would have continued to gain weight) weighed 650 pounds.[41]

During late summer and fall in Pennsylvania, Gary Alt reported weight gains of about 0.5 pound per day for cubs, 1.0 pound per day for sub-adults and adult females, and 1.5 to 2.0 pounds per day for

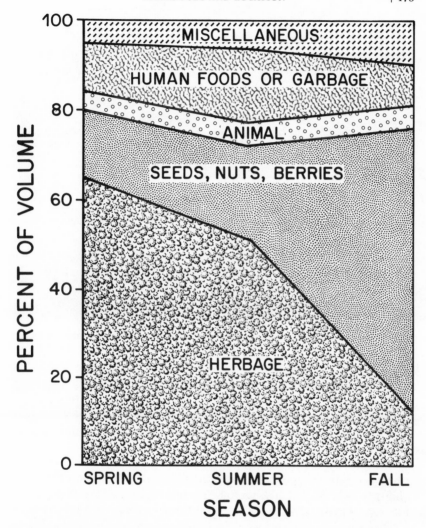

Average seasonal composition of black bear diet in Yosemite National Park, California.[45]

adult males.[42] One adult male studied by Alt gained 128 pounds in 60 days—from 348 pounds on July 19 to 476 pounds on September 19. Much Pennsylvania bear habitat produces both beechnut and acorn mast as well as blueberries.

A very heavy mast crop may alter the normal movement to den sites by black bears. Alt reported that during one such year in Pennsylvania, a black bear mother with five cubs of the year stayed out and fed all winter long.

Mother grizzly bear and one of her two cubs of the year digging for roots of yellow hedysarum in loose soil in Banff National Park.   *Frank Raimer*

The black bear's final fattening before denning is usually accomplished by eating fruits or mast. For grizzlies the final fattening may be similar to that of black bears if fruits or mast are available. Where they are not, the grizzly has the option of eating roots, bulbs, corms, or tubers.

By the fall, as plants approach dormancy, nutrients are once again transferred underground in certain plants. Depending on the availability of berries, which seem to be preferred, grizzlies return to feeding on plants that have subterranean energy-storage organs. Underground foods are available until the ground becomes too frozen to dig. In Banff National Park, the buffaloberries fall from the bushes and become unavailable as the frost deepens. Feeding on hedysarum roots continues until the ground is frozen and grizzlies enter their dens.[43]

Ungulates, either as prey or carcasses, can contribute substantially to the fall fattening of any bear. Huge male black bears (675 pounds and more) have been captured and weighed on the island of Newfoundland. Here black bears are major predators on adult woodland caribou.[44] I have speculated that one seven-hundred-pound bull elk could make the difference between whether or not a pregnant grizzly would have cubs the next season. No wonder such food sources are so aggressively defended by grizzlies. The availability of ungulates varies so much from area to area that local conditions have to be known in order to anticipate where ungulates may be fed on by bears.

The annual cycle of foods eaten by black and grizzly bears varies between biologically different areas and from season to season.[45] (See pp. 172–173). Major shifts in diet can occur from year to year. In 1976 in Banff National Park, when buffaloberries were scarce, grizzly bears fattened on hedysarum roots (p. 172). The berry crop also failed that year in Minnesota. As a result, ants became particularly important for black bears.[46] In each area the nature of the food eaten is always the same in that it is relatively easy to digest and high in nutrients. The specific foods eaten, however, include hundreds of different species depending upon what is locally available. The interested hiker or naturalist should learn to recognize the foods that are most important to bears in their region. These foods are often eaten mainly where they are particularly abundant or where some other habitat feature, such as cover, makes a given site attractive to a bear.

OTHER FACTORS INFLUENCING A BEAR'S MOVEMENTS AND LOCATION

Cover

Cover, such as dense trees or shrubs, hides a bear from other animals or from people. Black bears are seldom found more than several hundred yards from cover. By contrast, grizzly bears don't require as much cover as black bears. Normally if foods exist in open areas, such as extensive subalpine meadows, grizzlies will forage there. However, if grizzlies have been hunted or harassed by people, they will either use open areas less or will venture into them using the dark of night as cover. Both species of bears are able to shift their twenty-four-hour cycle and will forage during day or night, or both, depending on whether they are trying to avoid detection by people. Rarely do people venture into areas used as cover by bears because the dense vegetation makes travel difficult. For people, such as hunters, who travel through dense bush or forest, particular caution is needed in grizzly country. Grizzlies don't expect to encounter people in such areas, hence surprise could lead to attack.

Bedding Areas and Thermal Microenvironments

After feeding, both black and grizzly bears either lie down for a time or travel.[47] The areas chosen for bedding vary with the time of year and the specific location, but they serve some common functions and have some common characteristics. For grizzly bears, when it is hot, or if they are harassed, such beds are normally in cool, dense vegetation, especially forest, which offers bears cover.[48]

Bears use these beds during portions of the day or night. Grizzly bears sometimes lie on cool beds or are otherwise relatively inactive during the warmest part of hot days.[49] For both black and grizzly bears peaks of activity may occur either during cooler daylight hours or may be shifted into twilight or night depending on weather and human harassment. The recreational hiker who remains on well-used trails should not have to worry about surprising bears on their "beds" since the beds appear to serve as a retreat area for bears.

Denning Areas

In the temperate and subarctic zones, black and grizzly bears will spend from two to seven months either at den sites or in dens. The duration of denning is related to the duration of winter. In subtropical Florida some black bears do not den.[50] Black and grizzly bears kept in zoos often remain active, although somewhat lethargic, unless deep cold develops.

Denning appears to be largely a response to decreased food supply in winter rather than an inability to survive cold. Unlike ungulates, which survive winter by ingesting coarse, low-quality forage and by becoming relatively inactive, bears fatten in the summer and fall on energy-rich foods and then stay in one place living on stored energy. If they had to survive by foraging, their Carnivore's gut could not efficiently digest the stuff that ungulates eat, and as predators bears are not effective enough to survive on meat.

During hibernation both black and grizzly bear adults can decrease their heart rates from summer sleeping levels of about forty to fifty beats per minute to eight to ten beats per minute.[51] Their body temperatures fall very little, from 37 degrees Celsius to 32–35 degrees Celsius. Perhaps because of the near-normal temperature, both species of bears can be easily aroused and can defend themselves.[52]

While in their winter sleep, they metabolize primarily fats, decrease urea synthesis, and reabsorb urine from the bladder, thereby avoiding accumulation of nitrogenous waste products,[53] which could

Black bear den dug under a tree root.

be fatal, since during denning they don't urinate, defecate, or drink. Diets for human beings with dysfunctional kidneys, but lacking artificial kidneys, have been developed based on knowledge of the winter metabolism of bears. Astronauts on long flights may someday try to mimic aspects of the bears' winter metabolism.

Throughout North America dens for grizzly bears are found at different elevations and have varying compass orientations. Within a given area, or in ecologically similar areas, however, the compass orientation and the elevation of winter dens are similar. The slope angle at which dens are dug is usually between 25 and 45 degrees, with some being dug on slopes as steep as 60 degrees.[54] Usually grizzly bear dens are found in snow accumulation areas.[55]

Because of the nature of the location of grizzly bear dens, it is unlikely that recreational hikers or skiers would stumble on them. (Some of them are in "trigger zones" for avalanches.) I know of only two injuries—both fatalities—that occurred in one incident near a grizzly bear den. This was a provoked incident in which the victims were hunting the bear that killed them.

Denning sites for black bears are different. Whereas grizzlies typically den on mountain or other slopes, black bears normally den on the forest floor.[56] Black bear dens are sometimes excavated under the roots of trees.[57] The excavation is not as extensive as for a grizzly bear den. In the cold Michigan winter 14 out of 219 black bear dens were nothing more than unsheltered depressions on top of the ground.[58] These ground beds lacked the insulating qualities of a subterranean or other small-cavity den.

I observed a ground bed being constructed and used during the spring of 1968.[59] A black bear female and her newborn cub were

Black bear female and cub at den entrance, Banff National Park. *Stephen Herrero*

flooded out of a den site in a culvert. When she left the den she built a ground bed nearby. To build the bed she bit off and pulled out trees up to three inches in diameter, dragged them back to the site where she chose to build the bed, and laid them on top of each other. Except for the diameter of some of the spruce and fir boughs used in its construction, it could have been mistaken for a bald eagle's nest mistakenly built on the ground rather than in a tree or on a cliff.

Although this site was used for only three days, other black bears spend their entire winters in such structures. The energy costs of passing winter in this manner must be greater than passing winter in a typical grizzly bear den and should be greater than if the black bear denned in some kind of cavity. The reason that such dens are constructed remains a mystery. In some areas black bear dens have been found in old trees that are big and rotten enough to allow a black bear to excavate a cavity.[60]

I don't know of any black bear-inflicted injuries that have occurred near dens. Significant opportunity for injury has been presented by some research biologists; they locate dens by radiotelemetry and then crawl into the excavated dens in order to shoot a hypodermic syringe into the bear inside. The syringe contains a drug to sedate the animal so that the biologist can soon crawl all the way in and pull the animal out to measure and weigh it and to replace the old radio collar with one containing new batteries. The biologist, while maneuvering into position to shoot the syringe, will have anywhere from half to all of

Some black bears den in trees in Great Smoky Mountains National Park.

his body in the den and is normally anchored to a buddy who is ready to pull him out in an instant should trouble develop. While black bears in their dens are slowed down, they still occasionally act aggressively toward intruders. Some lightweight researchers have been popped out of dens like "jack-in-the-boxes." Despite these scientifically useful theatrics, no injuries have occurred. This further illustrates the lack of aggression shown by black bears even when harassed by people.

A few years ago, we wanted to change radio collars on female grizzly bears in their dens, and I called other researchers who had been doing research on grizzlies for a longer period than I had. None of them had ever carried out the crawl-into-the-den maneuver on a grizzly. We abandoned the project, preferring to let someone else do the experiment!

Mating Areas

In Banff National Park and the Yukon Territory, grizzly bears sometimes mate on isolated mountain ridges or mountain tops (see p. 180).[61] Mating usually occurs from May through June when there is still snow on the ground at or nearby the mating areas. Perhaps because of the remoteness and the snow nearby, there have been no recorded encounters with people at these mating areas. Distinctive mating areas apparently don't exist for grizzly bears in some other parts of North America and they have not been noted for black bears.

The sun-illuminated ridge in this photograph was used as a grizzly-bear mating area in June of 1978, Banff National Park.   *Stephen Herrero*

TRAVEL ROUTES OF BEARS

What routes do bears use to travel, and why and how often do they move from place to place? Such questions are hard to answer even when radiotelemetry is used. I shall interpret what I think is known, but I caution you regarding the overall ignorance on this topic.

Unharassed black and grizzly bears travel routes of least resistance, usually following trails constructed by human beings, game trails, open edges, stream bottoms, shorelines, ridges, open forest, and even roads. If harassed or pursued, both species may take to areas where they don't anticipate encountering people, such as dense shrub fields, closed forest, or swamps. Gary Alt describes the route taken by a radio-collared adult male black bear that he tracked on foot while Gary's father guided him from an airplane:[62]

> I came across his nest less than five minutes after entering the swamp. A fresh set of bear tracks led away. Close inspection left no doubt in my mind they had been made by an adult male; they were too large for anything else. I checked my watch. It was 10:30 A.M. and the chase was under way.
>
> After leaving the blueberry swamp I tracked the bear 2.8 miles, generally south, to a blueberry-spruce swamp where he was constructing another nest. At 1:15 P.M., the bear fled his second nest site, which he was building of spruce browse and

swamp grass. While in the second swamp, he made a loop, several hundred yards in diameter, but did not quite return to his earlier trail. He stopped only 50 feet shy and built a nest downwind, where he could watch for and smell anything following his old trail. As I came down the trail he spooked. I heard him, but wasn't sure what it was at that time and continued to follow his tracks around the loop, eventually coming to his new nest. By the time I found the nest, he was probably over a mile away.

The bear traveled northeast after leaving the second swamp, following a stream about three-fourths of a mile. He frequently jumped into the stream where the water was deepest, sometimes leaving it where he had entered, other times traveling as much as 50 yards in the stream. He apparently did this to cool himself, or perhaps to confuse the tracker. On several occasions when moving north along the stream, his tracks disappeared in the water. I assumed he would either cross the stream or continue north in the water. However, he did neither. He turned and walked south in the stream, then left the water heading in a different direction.

As the late afternoon progressed, I realized the bear was reaching into his bag of tricks. The bright afternoon sun was melting the snow from the rocks, and he began to use this to his advantage, jumping from rock to rock. He left little sign this way, making tracking much more difficult.

After a while he reached even deeper into his bag of tricks and came out with something new—back tracking. The first time it happened, I was moving along his trail at a good rate when, suddenly, his tracks simply vanished.

There were no rocks, no water, nothing to conceal his tracks. My first thought was that he had climbed a tree. After scanning the treetops until I was dizzy, I half expected Captain Kirk or Spock to appear and tell me that ol' 501 had been beamed aboard the Starship *Enterprise*.

I sat down and tried to think of a logical explanation. There had to be one, but I couldn't come up with it. I went back to the tracks. This time I noticed there were toe marks at both ends, even though there was no evidence in the snow to indicate the bear had turned around. I followed them back about 50 yards and found where the bear had jumped off the main trail, walking away in a direction perpendicular to his old tracks. He pulled this backtracking stunt on six separate occasions during the day, successfully slowing the tracker. Each time he placed his feet accurately in his old tracks and changed direction by about 90 degrees when leaving the original trail.

At 4 P.M. tracking was terminated for the day. Bear 501 had been trailed 5.5 miles through two swamps, across five streams, three jeep trails, and one paved highway. The bear crossed Route 390 within 50 yards of where my vehicle had been parked all day.

Using his plane, my father radio-located the bear before dark that evening. He was in a rhododendron swamp about one-half mile southwest of the point where tracking had been terminated. . . .

David Hamer and I often radio-located what was apparently a successful, wary, older female grizzly. For nearly a month she fed on natural foods within about a mile of a large horseback riding/camping operation. It appeared that she never even approached the camp. In the Swan Hills region of Alberta, which is one of the few remaining regions where grizzly bears survive in the boreal forest vegetation zone, Dick Russell and his colleagues used radiotelemetry to follow grizzly bear movements.[63] Most of the grizzlies they studied were young, because the bears were heavily hunted. The few old grizzlies avoided areas of human activity. It therefore appears that the greater the human pressure on either black or grizzly bears, the more the bears choose travel routes that avoid contact with people.

Knowledge of the travel routes of grizzly bears can obviously contribute to human safety. The tragic incident in which Jane Ammerman and Kim Eberlee were killed by a grizzly bear in Glacier National Park (see p. 64) was at least partly related to their being camped on what was apparently a bear travel route.

Male bears travel extensively during the spring–early summer breeding period.[64] These wide-ranging movements have not led to an increase in injuries, but could.

The frequency of movements from one feeding area to another, and the extent of these movements, is too complex to yield to simple generalization. A productive feeding site may cause bears to remain in one area for a week, or even a month, but at other times feeding sites which to me have appeared to offer forage enough for a week or two have been left by grizzlies after a few minutes or hours of feeding. I and others have speculated that these movements from apparent sources of plenty may be part of the grizzly's opportunistic foraging strategy.[65] Perhaps they try to find out about the location and quality of as many foraging sites as possible. By doing this, they may locate rich sources such as dead ungulates, or they may be able to find something to eat during food-crop failure years. However, why bears travel, and what routes they follow, remains largely unknown.

HABITAT DIFFERENCES BETWEEN BLACK
AND GRIZZLY BEARS

The black bear is primarily a forest-adapted animal. The grizzly, although able to utilize the forest, has the additional advantage of being adapted to eat foods found in open environments, sometimes far from the forest edge.[66] (The black bear has, however, moved onto the "barren grounds" of the Ungava Peninsula since the grizzly was extirpated there[67] and has also moved onto the relatively open chaparral-shrub and subalpine zones of Yosemite National Park since the extirpation of the grizzly.[68])

The black bear moves throughout the forest, often seeking small openings such as hillsides, meadows, or stream edges where the sun's energy breaks through the canopy and stimulates plant growth. Although there are many nutritious foods beyond the edge of the forest, the black bear needs cover as well as food. The more the black bear is hunted or harassed, the more important cover is to its survival. In the eastern United States most black bear populations are intensively hunted. For example, in Pennsylvania, since 1973, the hunting season has only lasted for one day. This is still enough time for up to 859 (during 1979) bears to be killed.[69] This kill is estimated to be an annual harvest of about 26 percent of the population.

Good quality forage is only one component of successful survival and reproduction for bears. They must also avoid predators. Just as the grizzly has a body adapted for digging, it also is adapted to protect itself from predators when in the open. The black bear, by contrast, usually climbs trees or goes into cover to escape from predation or harassment. In Chapter 15 I discuss how habitat differences between black and grizzly bears probably influenced the evolution of the differences in aggression levels that exist between the species.

Despite their adaptations for foraging in open areas, grizzlies also inhabit some heavily treed environments. Where meadow and forest areas are interspersed, the grizzly may spend most of its time foraging along the edge of forest and meadow. I believe that the more grizzlies are harassed, the more they retreat to the cover of the forest. In the contiguous United States, where fewer than a thousand grizzlies still survive, studies have shown that most grizzlies in Yellowstone were close to the forest edge when seen.[70] However, as one moves farther north where the grizzly has survived somewhat better, the frequency of observation in open areas increases.[71]

In the Flathead Valley of western Montana, there are rich potential sources of food for grizzlies in the fruits of abandoned and untended orchards. The grizzly utilizes these foods by staying in forest or shrub cover during the day and feeding on fruits during the night.[72]

The European brown bear, which belongs to the same species as our grizzly, is perhaps the ultimate example of how human selection pressure can influence the habitat use and behavior of bears. In Europe brown bears have coexisted with fairly dense populations of people for many centuries. The bears have been extirpated from most of their former range and, where remnant populations survive, the bears are extremely wary of people, even in areas where hunting has been banned for over forty years.

I studied bears in one such area, Abruzzo National Park in the Appenine Mountains of central Italy. Here the bears did not have an aggressive bone in their bodies, at least with regard to human beings.[73] Superficially they looked like little grizzly bears. Our work left me with the impression that the bears seldom left cover and that much of their foraging took place during twilight or nighttime. (Because we did not use radiotelemetry we could not confirm this supposition.) Studies done on an even smaller number of bears in northern Italy did use telemetry and found that there the bears almost never left cover except during darkness or twilight.[74]

So while grizzly bears and their relatives probably evolved to be able to feed in open areas, competition with people selects for bears that hide from human beings rather than forage in the open. The specific areas in which a person might anticipate encountering grizzlies during daytime hours therefore depends on the distribution and abundance of food in the region, as well as the history and current nature of interaction between grizzlies and people.

13

Signs of Bear Activity

WHILE hiking in bear country, there are a number of indications besides seeing bears that will tell you if bears are using an area. Traces of bear activity are called "field sign." Most field sign made by grizzly bear is hard if not impossible to differentiate from that made by black bear. If the area is inhabited by grizzlies, prudence suggests you treat all questionable sign as if it were made by a grizzly. For example, both black and grizzly bears searching for insects will use their claws to turn over surface rocks. Look for such stones. Both species of bears will also dig out insect nests either from the ground or from tree stumps or deadfall. Torn apart, rotten wood is therefore a sign of bear feeding.

One indication of grizzly bear versus black bear activity is evidence of digging for roots, bulbs, corms, tubers, or small mammals. I have pointed out that black bears seldom, if ever, dig for these foods. Such diggings by grizzly bears may either be extensive, covering one hundred square feet or more, or small in size being only a single scoop. Larger ones are easiest for inexperienced people to spot. If you see diggings, try to estimate how old they are. Remove the soil that the bear in digging has thrown on top of nearby plants and grasses. Is the vegetation that you have uncovered still as fresh-looking as nearby vegetation that was not covered? If so, you ought to be looking over your shoulder or making some kind of noise. What has been eaten at the

Biologist examines digging made by grizzly bear for hedysarum roots.

David Hamer

digging site? If it was bulbs or other underground-storage organs of plants, then probably there are some aboveground parts of the plant that have not been consumed. Examine these. Are they wilted, shriveled, or browned, or are they fresh? The estimated age of plant parts gives you an idea of how recently a bear was there.

If clear tracks have been left by a bear, then you have a good chance of being able to identify which species of bear made them. Both black and grizzly bears have short, broad feet with five toes on both front and back feet. The front-paw track of a bear is different from the hind-paw track. Bears walk more on their front toes than on their front heel. Therefore, front-foot tracks seldom show the imprint of the front heel. The hind foot, however, typically shows both toe and heel imprints.

Because bears can't retract their claws, claw marks are often part of a track. A mature grizzly's front claws are longer, 1.5 to 3.9 inches, than are its hind claws, 0.6 to 1.8 inches. A black bear's front claws are more curved and shorter, 1.1 to 2.0 inches.[1] The longer front-claw length of grizzly bears can be useful in differentiating black and grizzly bear tracks. To measure claw length, see top p. 187.

Note the claws on the grizzly bear female in the photograph on page 187. Visual recognition of this characteristic is not very useful for a person whose primary concern is safety. Anyone close enough to be able to clearly see the claws on a female grizzly with cubs, which

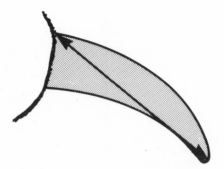

How to measure claw length. Claw length is the straight-line distance between the base and the end of the claw.

is what this bear was, is potentially in trouble. The photograph was taken as part of a population survey of grizzly bears in Banff National Park. The warden who took the picture, Bill Vroom, has more than forty years of field experience with grizzlies and an excellent ability to read their behavior. In case he made a mistake, he was armed and is expert in the use of a firearm.

Within the same region adult grizzly bears, being larger than black

Female grizzly bear with cubs (out of sight) sensing danger from people, Banff National Park. _G.W. Vroom_

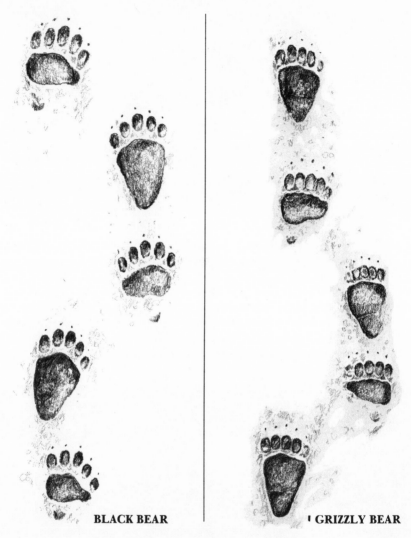

Tracks and gait of grizzly and black bears.

bears of the same sex, also leave larger tracks. Track size is not, however, a good criterion with which to differentiate the species. The size of tracks made by a male black bear and a female grizzly can be the same. Look for claw marks in relationship to the toes as a better indicator of species. Another reason why track size alone is seldom adequate to identify bear species is that the size of the impression left

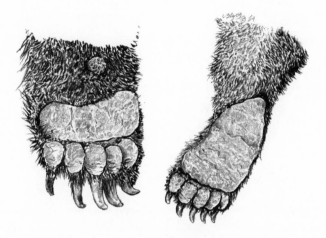

Sketches of right front and rear foot of grizzly bear.

by the same foot will be different in mud, in snow, or on dry ground. Remember this when trying to estimate the size of the foot that left a track.

Four characteristics of tracks are useful in determining whether they have been made by black or grizzly bears. Very large tracks are usually from grizzly bears. I don't give measurements because track size varies so much depending on substratum. If a track seems very large, look at other track characteristics.

Sometimes, claw imprints are left in tracks. If there are claw imprints, then the longer distance between the toes and claw imprint left by a mature grizzly bear contrast with the shorter distance in a black bear track.

The two most accurate characteristics for differentiating black and grizzly bear tracks are the arc of the toes and whether or not the toe imprints are joined.[2] These characteristics are present in juveniles and adults and on front and hind feet. The toes of a black bear arc more, whereas the grizzly's are more in a straight line. This characteristic can be tested on clear tracks by placing a straightedge at the base of the big-toe track and lining the straightedge up along the top of the pad. If the line passes below the middle of the small toe, this indicates a grizzly bear. If the line passes above the middle of the small toe, it is probably the track of a black bear. Also, the toes of a grizzly bear are more joined together than are the toes of a black bear. In reasonably firm substratum, most grizzly bear toe tracks are joined, whereas

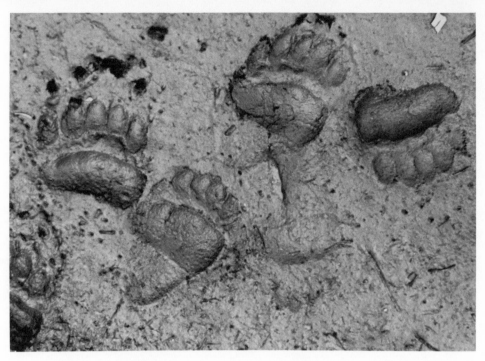

Grizzly bear tracks. Note the arc of the toe tracks, the joined toe tracks, and claw marks.   *Stephen Herrero*

most black bear toe tracks are separate. In mud a black bear's toe separation may not show. Figure on p. 192 illustrates the use of all of the foregoing characteristics for differentiating bear tracks.

When tracks are made in soft, freshly dug ground, they do not last long. A rain is usually enough to obliterate or obscure them. Knowledge of this helps in estimating the age of tracks. Bear tracks in snow can be differentiated from those of other species of large mammals by an observer in an airplane or a helicopter. In a study of the location of grizzly bear dens in Banff Park, we frequently observed tracks in the snow from a helicopter. We used the tracks to find dens and denning areas.[3]

Seeing bear tracks can be better than actually seeing the bear. You can imagine how big it was, whether it was a mother with cubs, which way it was traveling, what gait it was using, and whether it had any foot injuries. Some individual bears leave distinctive tracks. Olaus J. Murie's book, *A Field Guide to Animal Tracks*, contains excellent information about interpreting bear tracks, gaits, and field sign. Sets of tracks can also be sources of aesthetic delight. And track photography is safer than bear photography.

At least one useful differentiation may be made on size of track alone. Mother bear and young groups can be identified, at least when the cubs are a year or less, by the size difference between the "big"

Bear tracks in snow. Abruzzo National Park, Italy. *Franco Zunino*

bear's and young bears' tracks. We have been measuring the size of tracks left by cubs and yearling grizzlies under a variety of conditions. Table 4, p. 193, shows our results and also presents some sizes of measured adult female grizzly tracks for comparison. Because mother grizzlies are potentially dangerous, you should learn to recognize the tracks of family groups.

The scats, or droppings, of bears are one of the more common traces indicating that a bear was or is nearby. Bear scats can be told from those of other large mammals by their composition and to a lesser extent by their shape and volume. Of all the mammalian scats with which a bear's might be confused, those of horses and human

Differentiating black and grizzly bear tracks.

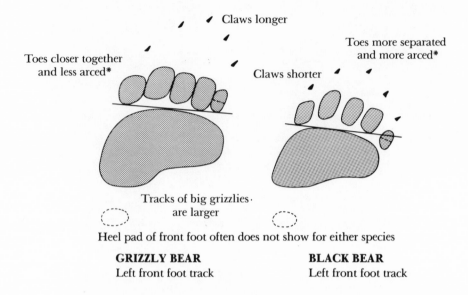

Claws longer

Toes more separated
and more arced*

Toes closer together
and less arced*

Claws shorter

Tracks of big grizzlies·
are larger

Heel pad of front foot often does not show for either species

GRIZZLY BEAR
Left front foot track

BLACK BEAR
Left front foot track

beings are the most similar. Horse scats are, however, usually lighter colored, contain smaller plant fragments, and are usually larger in volume.

Black bear and grizzly bear scats are hard to tell apart in the field or even in the lab. Research biologists have for years used the two-inch rule of thumb. Scats larger than this diameter have been attributed to grizzly bear.[4] David Hamer and I measured the diameters of 104 grizzly bear feces, which we found in our study area in Banff Park. We found that sixty (58 percent) of these had diameters of less than two inches. Obviously if only large scats were attributed to grizzly bears, we would have misidentified the bear species that left the scat more than half the time. What is worse is that large scats seem to be most often deposited by large bears, and so you have a good chance of correctly identifying male grizzly bears, but female grizzlies and young grizzlies might be assumed to be black bears.

Even a superficial examination of the composition of a scat may give you important information. Although bear scats seldom smell

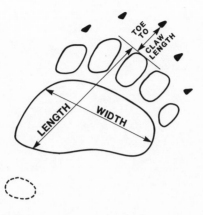

How to measure bear track size.

TABLE 4
Measurements of grizzly bear track size, Banff National Park*

ADULT FEMALE, FRONT FOOT (INCHES)			DATE	CUBS OF ADULT FEMALE, FRONT FOOT (INCHES)		
Width	Length	Toe to Claw		Width	Length	Toe to Claw
				Young of Year		
5.1	5.1	2.0	13 June 76	2.6	3.2	0.6
4.7	5.1	1.4-1.6	16 Oct. 76	3.0-3.3	3.5-3.7	1.2-1.4
4.9	4.7	2.0	19 Aug. 77	3.0	3.0-3.2	0.4
4.3-4.7	4.5-4.9	1.6	7 Oct. 70	3.5-3.7	3.2-4.1	0.8-1.4
				Older offspring		
4.3-4.7	4.9	1.8	23 June 76	4.1	4.7	1.4
5.1-5.5	5.5	1.6-2.0	June 77	3.2-3.5	3.7	1.6
4.3-4.9	4.3-4.7	1.6-2.2	27 Oct. 78	3.7-4.1	3.7-4.1	1.2-1.6
5.5-5.9	5.3-5.9	1.6-2.0	May 79	3.7-4.1	3.9-4.7	1.6-1.8

*Most measurements made by David Hamer.

Grizzly bear summer scat. The bear has been feeding on green vegetation.

Stephen Herrero

bad and probably don't contain parasites transmittable to people,[5] I still don't touch them with my skin or clothing. The remains of roots, bulbs, corms, or tubers suggest grizzlies. Field scat analysis along with a correct estimation of the age of a scat can tell you what bears were feeding on at a given time. If the scat is fresh and you can identify some of its components, then you will have a much better idea of where to expect bears to be. Items such as berries, ants, and digested meat or hair are easy to identify in scats. Few green plants can be readily identified by field examination of scats.

Because of the danger of surprising any grizzly bear at an animal carcass and because a grizzly may remain close by a carcass for up to two or even three weeks,[6] you should learn to recognize the scats of bears that have been eating meat. When feeding on flesh, the bear leaves scats that are typically runny and black. Some hair may be present. Some scats passed after feeding on green vegetation may also be black, however they are fibrous rather than runny. Meat scats stink. Vegetation scats don't.

Some scats such as those left when a bear has been eating a green plant called horsetail (*Equisetum arvense*) disintegrate after about a month with rain; others, as when a grizzly bear has been eating hedysarum roots, may persist for several years. In general, the more moist and soft a scat is, the fresher it is. As a scat grows older, it also becomes dryer and harder unless there is rain or snow. Precipitation can cause confusion by moistening old scats, but you have other clues. As with trying to estimate the age of digging sites, you should examine the condition of the vegetation underneath the scat. Is it yellowed with age or as fresh as the surrounding vegetation? Are there insects, their larvae, or eggs in the scat? If there are, this suggests that the scat is at least several days old.

For the field biologist, a scat collection can become a window into important events in the life of bears. Most people are either too tradition-bound or too squeamish to look through this window.

The number of scats present in an area provides its own clue regarding bear activities. If bear scats are all within about a ten-yard radius and number around three to ten, then you may have discovered a bedding area, because bears often defecate near bedding areas. During the course of their daily cycle, bears have several periods of sleep and rest. Often a few scrapes on the ground or into a rotten log suffice to prepare the bed. Check for bear hairs on trees near beds if in doubt about a given depression in the ground. I have often found bear hair on trees adjacent to beds. This suggests that bears rub on them. A bedding area will normally be used for a few hours and then abandoned. Some bedding areas are reused over a period of days or even year after year.

During the summer heat, it is possible to surprise a bear or bear family while they are bedding if a person is traveling cross-country through shaded and cool microenvironments. I know of no incidents, however, in which this has occurred.

Many scats are also deposited over a larger area than that referred to above when several bears are feeding at a concentrated and somewhat prolonged food source. Examples of this are ripe and productive berry patches, salmon-spawning areas, and extensive patches of certain sedges or horsetails. Bears often bed near these areas. Beware!

The most loathsome scat for me to discover is a grizzly bear dropping with evidence of garbage feeding. Bits of plastic bags or aluminum foil are conclusive. This spoils my perception of what I thought was a wilderness area, and I won't camp there because of the danger of garbage-habituated bears.

I've discussed the dangers of carcasses, but some of the points are worth repeating in the context of field sign. A potential sign of this danger is the presence of crows, ravens or other scavenging or predatory birds. Chances are that the object of their interest is a dead animal, and they may be sharing the carcass with a grizzly. Bears use their acute sense of smell to locate dead animals or "gut piles" in hunted areas. If the wind is right even our second-rate sense of smell will sometimes help us to detect a decaying carcass. When in bear country avoid the temptation to investigate rotten meat odor, groups

Grizzly bear burying the carcass of a bull elk. Scavenging birds often signal the presence of a carcass—and a bear for approaching hikers.

of scavenging birds, or anything that you suspect is a buried carcass. Remember as well that not all rotting meat will attract birds.

Other signs of current bear use of an area are more subtle and less easy to read. Signs of berry feeding are hard to notice even though bears are seldom delicate when feeding on berries. They feed by moving their mouths along branches and manipulating their lips and teeth. Branches are sometimes pulled toward the mouth with paws. The feeding process often results in berries falling to the ground. Bears may also break the branches of berry bushes while feeding. Bears never pick the last berry from a bush as a fussy human picker would do. Instead, they move from one bush to another, abandoning a bush as soon as the quantity wanes.

Signs of grazing on green vegetation are perhaps the most difficult to identify. Sometimes tracks are faintly discernible on vegetation that has been crushed by a bear's foot. One morning, high in the Appenine Mountains of Abruzzo National Park in Italy, Franco Zunino and I saw a perfect set of bear tracks crossing a meadow. The bear had apparently walked on the meadow before the frost melted. We arrived several hours later and saw the tracks left in the previously frosted and now broken grass.

The easiest sign of green-vegetation feeding to recognize occurs when bears are feeding in moist meadows, stream edges, or avalanche slopes. Because these areas have a lush plant growth, when a bear walks through them, it crushes enough plants to leave a more or less distinct trail. Along the trail you may find cropped green plants. The remaining stem of cow parsnip or angelica is particularly noticeable where either exists and has been fed on.

Because bears eat highly nutritious parts of plants, they will sometimes, when feeding on horsetails, just nip off the growing tips of the plants. At other times, particularly during earliest growth stages when the entire plant is more nutritious, it will be eaten closer to the ground. When this occurs, it is hard to differentiate bear grazing on horsetails from that of ungulate grazing. Look for fresh ungulate sign such as tracks and droppings in addition to looking for bear sign. Other traces indicating that bears have been grazing on green vegetation are even more difficult to identify. When bears are grazing on young grass, the cropped grass looks much the same as if an ungulate had fed on it. Look for tracks or droppings as additional clues.

The final bear sign to mention in the context of safety is rub-marking trees on which bears may rub, bite, or claw. Careful examination should reveal fresh bear hairs or sap running from recent wounds made by bear claws or teeth, or shredded bark with signs of cambium feeding.

Marking trees are commonly located on well-used bear trails and serve a poorly understood role in chemical and visual communication between bears.[7] Sometimes these trees are used so often, by many different bears over many years, that holes made by bears placing their feet on the same spot become distinctly visible either leading up to a mark tree or at its base. Sometimes foot marks leading up to mark trees are seen as surface marks, appearing to have been scraped into the ground. Bear hair left on such trees can be identified under the microscope.[8] Superficially bear hair looks thin, like human hair, as opposed to being coarse like elk or moose hair. Grizzly bear hair (in contrast to that of black bear) is often white-tipped at the end. Bears do not rub only on marking trees. They will also rub on sign-posts, outhouses, research equipment left unattended, or on a variety of other man-made artifacts.

As I have mentioned, black bears, especially young ones, readily climb trees. Bear claw marks, usually left on the tree after climbing, are fairly easy to spot on the bark of deciduous trees such as aspen. Claw marks are only obvious on coniferous trees after they have been repeatedly climbed by bears. Such claw marks usually indicate that

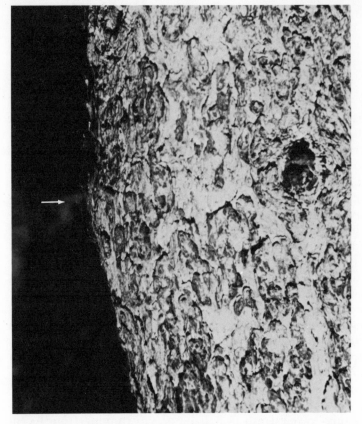

Bear rubbing trees, such as this spruce, sometimes have bear hairs clinging to them. This is another form of bear sign.

Stephen Herrero

bears are in the general area. They are seldom an obvious sign of recent bear use.

Perhaps the most dangerous travel situation of all is when people want to go through dense brush and by far the easiest route is to get down on all fours and crawl like a bear. Remember what I said about looking for moving bushes, which may indicate bears, before entering such an area. On a well-used bear trail individual footprints become discernible as depressions or holes, just as they do near rub-marking trees.

I traveled on hands and knees for over half a mile along such a trail while hiking from the shore to the interior of Katmai National Monument in 1965. I did not know much about bears then, but it did not require much knowledge to realize the danger and, perhaps, foolishness of the situation. This area has a significant population of grizzlies (brown bears). While crawling, my companion and I yodeled and whooped like two characters pursued by demons. That we survived such nonsense without incident was certainly either testimony to the tolerance of the bears or to our good luck.

Black bear claw marks on a fruit tree in an old orchard, Yosemite
National Park.   *David Graber*

Black bear trail used for more than a decade in Minnesota.
                                                 Lynn Rogers

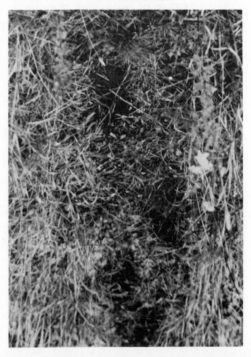

⌒14⌐

Learning
and Instinct

BEARS don't behave like robots. Each bear is an individual with a personality and a specific set of experiences. The outcome of experience is learning. Bears learn where to find things to eat. They learn where people are often encountered. They learn about their environment. Because of learning, each bear is able to tailor its response to a specific situation. Despite this, the range and extent of flexibility of behavior are constrained by genetic influences on behavior. A black bear female with cubs has a somewhat different range of behavioral options in a confrontation than does a grizzly bear mother. Different ranges of behavior have been adaptive for individuals of each species in the different environments in which they evolved.

Learning helps to adapt bears to constantly occurring changes in their present environment. A new food source appears, such as a garbage dump or a berry patch that is just starting to yield a lot of berries twenty-five years after a fire. Bears' exploration and curiosity help them to find the new food source. They learn the extent of the food available and the location of the site. They develop impressions regarding their perceived danger of the site.

Instincts are behaviors whose principal elements are coded in genes. They are behaviors that were successful in the past. For example, successful ancestral bears may have survived and reproduced because of their curiosity, exploration, and many other genetically influenced traits favoring the discovery of new food sources. But the overbold bear, ever since people had rifles, has had increased chances of being shot. Such individuals were seldom ancestors to present-day bears even though, before human predation became intense, boldness was probably an advantageous trait.

Instincts, learning, and other traits of a given bear all interact in a specific environment to produce action. Should a bear feed at a garbage dump? Should a bear explore beyond its home range? The approach-avoidance seesaw goes up and down with a unique balance point for each individual bear.

The variability of bear behavior, even in situations that are superficially similar, can be illustrated by considering the case in which a grizzly bear mother with young cubs is suddenly confronted by a person at close range. She does not invariably charge the person, although there is a certain probability of her doing so. A decision is quickly made by the bear. Probably little thought is involved, but many factors have an influence on the decision. Instincts regarding defense of young interact with instincts related to survival and avoidance of danger. The personality of the bear comes into play. Is she a particularly aggressive mother or is she tolerant? Her personality interacts with her past experience. What outcomes has she experienced when confronted with people or other bears in the past? What is the nature of the environment in which the present encounter is occurring? Are there ready routes of escape for the cubs and herself?

The mother's brain instantly processes and interrelates many pieces of information and reaches a decision. Either she charges the person or she does not. If she charges, then another decision, equally complicated, must be made. Should she contact the person or stop the charge? Although her genes store elements of answers that have worked for her ancestors, these genes have also created flexible behavior that allows her some latitude to adjust these patterns to fit specific situations.

Approach-avoidance conflict may be intense in the bear. She may charge, stop only a couple of yards from a person, then wheel and run off for one hundred feet, only to wheel and run back again toward the person and face the same decision again regarding whether to make contact or not. If the person runs or threatens her, this probably increases the chances of an attack. Not all bears vacillate in such circumstances. Some have made their decision. The closer you are to a grizzly when it senses you, the greater is the chance it may attack rather than flee or threaten you. (Such is the case for elephants[1] and many other dangerous African mammals.)

Bears are not simple stimulus-response machines. They are much more like people than they are like insects. If you approach various people at random on a dark street and suddenly grab them from behind, some will faint, others will scream, and others may punch or shoot you. What women do will be somewhat different from what men do. The same considerations apply to bears in confrontations with people. The outcome of a given confrontation is the result of bringing the variable behavior of a given bear into interaction with the much more variable behavior of a given person. No wonder the outcome is hard to predict!

CURIOSITY AND EXPLORATION

Bears are curious. Their curiosity has been studied by bringing bears into controlled environments such as fenced, outdoor laboratories. As a result of experiments in which young bears and other Carnivores were given novel objects, Ellis Bacon suggested that a black bear's level of attention to such objects "may be greater than that of any other North American Carnivore."[2] Bears, especially young bears, manipulate new objects with their forepaws and bite or grasp them with their teeth. Bears must learn what foods are good to eat in a given area. Many plant species and plant parts are no doubt tested to discover those that "make a bear feel good" and those that are available in adequate quantity and at an acceptable risk to merit feeding. Young bears learn to eat certain foods by watching and mimicking their mothers, but at some time young animals must set off and forage on their own.

Curiosity can lead to the discovery of new food sources, which may be important for the survival of sub-adults. I cannot give a specific example of this for bears, but observations on the Japanese macaques (*Macaca fuscata*), of Koshima Island, Japan, showed that it was a young, two-year-old female who first tried washing dirt from sweet potatos to make them edible. The sweet potato soon became a major food for 90 percent of the troop.[3] Only the old males seldom learned how to treat this food. Mothers usually learned it and taught their infants.

Curiosity by bears around people usually will lead to people's food or garbage, but eventually this leads to the death of the bear. Even though curiosity is part of the essence of a bear, it may not be a good trait around people.

DISCRIMINATION AND GENERALIZATION

Learning to tell the difference between similar situations is called discrimination learning. In Chapter 10 I mentioned that laboratory tests have shown that black bears quickly learn discriminations based on color or form. Discrimination learning also commonly occurs with free-ranging bears. For example, black bears in Great Smoky Mountains National Park were able to learn the difference between tourists and their vehicles at roadsides, and uniformed park rangers and their vehicles. Rangers who chased bears from the roadside had hoped that the message learned would be a general one—avoid all vehicles and people at roadsides. What the bears quickly learned, however, was that tourists gave handouts and that rangers harassed them.

HABITUATION AND AVOIDANCE

I've mentioned how habituation occurs when an animal becomes used to something. Habituation is very important in a bear's life. The salmon near McNeil River Falls, Alaska, attract many bears. When socially subordinate bears visit the falls early in the season, they flee when dominant animals are sensed at long distances. But as the season goes on, the distance at which they will run shortens significantly.[4] Such avoidance is necessary to prevent harm, but running away costs energy, both in running and because it takes a bear away from important foods. Avoidance of potential danger is important, but when that danger repeatedly does not lead to harm, habituation usually occurs. Abundant foods may come to draw bears closer and closer to potential sources of danger.

This same process appears to happen with regard to bears and people. Both black and grizzly bears have some natural wariness—a reluctance to come close to people. Grizzly bears seem to be significantly more wary of people and human environments than are black bears. Black bears appear to habituate faster to people than do grizzlies, though no scientific tests have been done to establish this as fact. The curiosity and drive to get food may cause a bear to enter the edge of a campground under cover of dark and trees. Perhaps a camper startles the bear and it flees. But the bear felt no pain and perhaps, in a few nights, food smells once again come from the direction of the campground. The bear tries again and perhaps again and again until its inborn avoidance of strange situations no longer rules its behavior. The situation has become familiar to the bear. Easily digested foods have been found and nothing bad has happened. The bear is habituated to the campground environment, including people. The bear starts coming to forage in the campground right after the campers have finished their dinners and other bears have not yet raided the garbage cans.

Perhaps a camper almost bumps into the bear while both are

heading for the trash container. The man drops the bag of garbage and walks hurriedly away. The bear runs away too but soon returns and finds a bag of steak bones and potatoes with sour cream on the ground. Soon other campers are accosted. Some of them drop or throw food. Some chase after the bear, rekindling limited avoidance. But people shouting or banging pots together inflict no pain and the bear soon learns this. By this point the bear has not only learned where human garbage and food can be found, but it has also learned how to get them from people.

One day the bear comes during the afternoon while people are picnicking. There are more people than the bear has ever faced before and the bear flees. But it comes again on another afternoon and a smaller group of picnickers quickly abandon their table when the bear persists in coming toward them. It sits on the table and is still eating when a gun sounds, and it feels an instant of pain, then sleeps. The warden has used a Capchur gun to inject drugs that sedate the bear for a while.

When the bear wakes up, it does not recognize where it is. It wanders for a few miles, but then a creek appears that seems familiar. A previous search for food in a bad year brought the bear here before. In three days it is back at the campground. The grasses eaten along the way are less satisfying than the more calorie-rich garbage. The bear sees a camper with an armload of groceries. The bear charges at the camper and again groceries are dropped. The bear is still eating and barely feels the pain of the 30.06 bullet that pierces its chest and collapses both lungs, ending its life.

I am sure that in general this hypothetical scenario has been repeated thousands of times. Everything that this bear learned served only to reinforce the behavior of foraging for human garbage and food at campgrounds. It could not learn by dying. Its major negative experience came too late and too drastically. But imagine that this bear had certain traits that first brought it into the campground. Perhaps it was a very curious bear, and once drawn into camp by its curiosity, maybe it habituated to people more easily than other bears of the same age and sex. Perhaps it was also a bit more aggressive in foraging, a trait given to it by the genes of successful ancestors, but ancestors that seldom encountered people. Regardless of what traits it possessed, they won't be passed on by the dead bear.

When aggressive confrontation behavior develops on human hiking trails, the bear can obtain hikers' packsacks, which it subsequently tears open and feeds on! Such a bear may be called a "mugger bear." As I have mentioned, during the late 1970s this foraging strategy became common among many black bears in Yosemite National Park,

California. Even the more wary grizzly bear can become a mugger, and although this is rare to date, it has been reported in Banff National Park, Alberta, and Glacier National Park, Montana, two places where human-use levels are high in some of the grizzly's habitat.

Whereas "mugger" grizzlies are rare, even in Glacier Park, I have mentioned how large numbers of hikers in some areas have created habituated grizzlies which either do not flee from people or only flee when people are very close.[5] Trails and campgrounds can sometimes be located away from important grizzly bear habitat but, if these facilities occur in bear country, then habituation or food-conditioning may occur.

To help prevent habituation, food conditioning, or both, aversive conditioning techniques could be used as soon as a problem begins. These measures might help to keep most grizzlies from getting used to people. But grizzlies are smart. They may just learn to avoid the rangers who haze them.

Research conducted at the McNeil River Falls, Alaska, campground and along nearby trails has clearly shown that grizzly (brown) bears that do not receive any food rewards learn to stay out of campgrounds.[6] This area is, as I have mentioned, a prime salmon-fishing spot for bears. The campground is about a mile away from the falls, and since 1973 it has been limited to a maximum of ten people during any given period from July 1 to August 15. Bears are never allowed to enter the campground area. If a bear does enter, it is either scared off by shouting or by firing shotgun shells or flares near it; and if this fails, the bear is shot with number 9 birdshot. The campground manager, who is the only person permitted to shoot a bear with the birdshot, is careful to avoid hitting a bear's eyes. Follow-up studies of radio-collared bears have shown that all "shot" bears have learned to stay out of the campground and that no bears have been injured. The birdshot apparently didn't penetrate the bear's hide. Rubber bullets, which are now being tested in Alaska on grizzly (brown) bears, will probably prove more effective.[7]

Why do the bears learn to not enter McNeil River Falls campground? It is very important that bears never get food at the campground. The abundance of natural foods available nearby no doubt helps to establish other foraging patterns. The instant, painful, yet nonlethal and probably noninjurious nature of the shooting with birdshot also has the necessary characteristics for rapid avoidance learning. Another important dimension of the success at McNeil's campground is that no other human-use sites exist nearby to teach bears to forage on human garbage or food.

The bears at McNeil River Falls are clearly habituated to the presence of people. When photographing the bears, people are only about fifty yards away from the main concentration of bears. However, bears are not allowed to approach photographers. Approach is discouraged by using the same adversive techniques employed in campgrounds—birdshot and noisemaking. This demonstrates that in certain situations, such as McNeil River Falls, habituation can be isolated from approach.

Habituation of bears to people is, however, limited. During the sixties and early seventies, more than ten photographers at a time were sometimes at McNeil. Alaska Fish and Game personnel suspected that when more than ten photographers were present, the bears' use of the area began to decrease.[8]

By using research to discover the main feeding areas and other habitats used by bears and trying to regulate human activity in these areas, the process of bear habituation to people can be controlled. This can only occur where bears do not have access to human garbage and food. A few experiences with human foods may make it impossible to teach a bear to stay away from people, no matter what aversive agents are employed. This is because bears are capable of forming discriminations between specific situations that lead to pain and general situations that more often may lead to food. Research has clearly established, however, that bears not conditioned to human foods nor habituated to people avoid sites of human activity.

HUNTING AND AVOIDANCE

Some people have suggested that hunting grizzly bears in national parks is necessary to have grizzlies that avoid people. In this chapter I have shown that there are other means of keeping grizzlies and people reasonably apart.

Hunting is in fact a poor way to teach a bear anything since there is little opportunity to learn. Death isn't an instructor—it is an eliminator. Hunting grizzlies in national parks would eliminate any bear that wasn't elusive and secretive. Human safety might increase, but hunting is incompatible with the wildlife-protection objectives of national parks. Also, hunting records from the Yukon Territory show that about one out of four grizzlies are wounded rather than killed.[9] Overall, hunting might not increase human safety because of the increased danger from wounded bears, and the danger of a hunter shooting a person.

$\smile$ 15 $\diagdown$

Aggression
and Submission

Some people have hoped that learning about bears' language of aggression might enhance human safety, either through a better understanding of a bear's intentions or by enabling people to communicate their own submissiveness or aggression more effectively to a bear. This approach raises two questions. Can we understand some of the black or grizzly bears' language, and if we do will knowledge of it be useful to people interested in safety around bears?

Konrad Lorenz, who shared a Nobel prize in 1973 for his research on geese, suggested that because bears are primarily solitary animals and have thick skin covering the head and face, they do not use the face and ears to communicate intent before attacking.[1] Work by David Henry and myself, which has been confirmed by others, clearly proved that Lorenz was wrong.[2] Bears do use facial features and their ears (along with other gestures) to convey aggressive intent, and therefore a knowledge of the language of aggression may interest anyone concerned about safety. Unfortunately this knowledge does not appear to me to be very useful in avoiding injury. This is because neither sudden attacks nor maraudings during the night often give a person time or opportunity to evaluate a bear's intentions before the bear has attacked. The ability to recognize high- and low-intensity threats by black or grizzly bears may, however, help some people recognize

207

when a bear is sufficiently agitated that attack may follow if you do the wrong thing. In addition, understanding of agonistic* behavior among bears does help to develop a general understanding of bears.

GENERAL CHARACTERISTICS OF AGGRESSION AND SUBMISSION

Black and grizzly bears are solitary for much of their lives. Except during the breeding season and at abundant, concentrated food sources, they usually avoid close proximity with one another. At feeding aggregations, a combination of limited hierarchical organization (the most aggressive bear eats where and when it wants to)[3] and mutual avoidance allows each bear to feed. When feeding on abundant but somewhat dispersed food sources, such as a lush green meadow, they typically space themselves hundreds of yards apart. Avoidance of confrontation appears to be their rule except during the breeding season when adult males may fight more often with one another.

Zoologists believe that much of aggression in animals is threat or bluff because of the possibility of injury even to winners. Losers of contests indicate submission in a variety of ways. Attack seldom follows. Among bears actual combat has most often been observed in situations in which the advantage of the aggressor is major, such as when an adult male bear may kill a sub-adult, or when the rewards of combat are very high, such as when adult males fight during the breeding season. The same general situation holds true with regard to agonistic interactions between bears and people. Threat and bluff prevail; actual contact and injury are rare.

Very few agonistic interactions among bears result in physical injury. At the garbage dump in Jasper National Park, where John Courtney and I studied agonistic interactions between black bears, contact followed by injury only occurred in 2 of 131 (1.5 percent) of all interactions in which I judged that dominance was established.[4] Similar low percentages (1.3% to 4%) of physical contact during agonistic interactions have been observed regarding grizzly (brown) bears

---

*J. P. Scott (1956) defined agonistic behavior as being any behavior associated with fighting or conflict, including escape or passivity. *Agonistic*, therefore, refers to all behaviors associated with aggression and submission. It also refers to other conflict behaviors.

at McNeil River Falls.[5] All of these interactions took place at abundant, concentrated food sources.

Most contact fighting leading to injury between bears takes place between adult males during the breeding season. Wounds and scarring can often be seen on the head, neck, and shoulder region of adult males of both species.[6] In addition to wounding in these areas, Lynn Rogers reported four cases of male black bears ages four to eleven having bone calluses on their penis bone, indicating mended fractures.[7] He also observed a three-year-old male who during breeding season had a raw and swollen penis with the tip missing. In private, but not in print, Lynn speculates that these penis wounds were inflicted in the breeding season during male-to-male combat.

I know of only one incident of human injury caused by an aggressive male bear during breeding season, but a person who suddenly confronts either the winner or loser of a fight could well be injured. In Jasper Park we watched two adult male black bears engaged in a noncontact aggressive interaction. The loser of the encounter ran over to a sub-adult male bear, who was not part of the interaction, and tore a five-square-inch strip out of the young bear's side. Ethologists call this redirected aggression. If close to the action, a person could be the victim of such an attack.

Aggression is important not only among adult male bears during breeding season but is periodically important throughout the lives of all bears. Predation is a form of aggression that is practiced by both black and grizzly bears as the opportunity arises. Aggression may also help adult females to maintain control over areas for their own and their offspring's use. One detailed study of black bears showed that resident adult females used aggression to repel other adult females from the borders of territories.[8] Aggression also serves a very important role for mother bears in the protection of young and, indeed, for all bears in protecting themselves from other bears and animals.

Bears do not treat people like other bears, but black and grizzly bears do direct some of the same threats toward people that they do toward members of their own species. In terms of the outcomes of agonistic interactions between bears and people, bears seem to act as if we are unique. For example, people are very rarely treated as prey, even though when unarmed few of us would be a match for all but the weakest of bears. As I have mentioned, I believe that the primary force shaping this restraint has been the ability of even primitive peoples to sometimes kill bears. In addition, human beings got more and more successful at killing bears as years went by. This message got into the genes of surviving bears, and for the most part it is still with them. This has caused an inborn avoidance of people, although clearly habituation or new combinations of genes can occasionally overcome this tendency.

THE EVOLUTION OF AGGRESSION IN FEMALE BEARS

Andy Russell has described the difference in aggressive behavior between black and grizzly bears: "To compare him [the grizzly] with his lesser cousin, the black bear, is like standing a case of dynamite beside a sack of goose feathers."[9] I have already stressed how these differences result in more serious human injuries being inflicted by grizzly bear mothers as compared to black bear mothers. Why should the two species, which have so many similarities, be so different behaviorally?

My field observations of the two species gave me clues and helped me formulate a hypothetical explanation for the differences.[10] I have observed that young black bears readily climb trees when startled. I have seen a black bear cub climb a tree only a few weeks after it came out of its den.[11] Gordon Burghardt has seen black bear cubs in captivity weighing "only about two lbs." climb trees when startled.[12] Black bear cubs require no signal from their mothers to climb a tree when potential danger appears. Wherever trees are large enough for cubs to climb out of reach from the ground, they have some protection.

Throughout their evolution, and also today, young black bears have had to protect themselves from predators. People, adult grizzly and black bears (especially males), wolves, and coyotes are some of the more recent predators that have been documented to kill young bears.[13] During the early evolution of bears, more predators existed than survive today.

But certainly the black bear mother defends her cubs—or does she? The answer is a qualified yes. The mother's response when threatened with potential danger will be to flee with the offspring, to climb a tree with them, or to stay on the ground and direct aggressive actions toward the intruder while the cubs find shelter up a tree or in dense vegetation. Charges toward a potential source of danger are the aggressive action that would precede physical contact. But for black bear mothers such charges very seldom end in contact. Out of the ninety-one agonistic interactions that John Courtney and I observed in Jasper National Park between black bear mothers and another bear, only two of these (2 percent) ended in physical contact.[14]

How then does the mother black bear protect her cubs? The cubs actually protect themselves either by going into dense cover or more

Only rarely do black bears fall from trees. This young bear fell while sleeping.

commonly by climbing high trees, often going to near the top of trees fifty to one hundred feet tall or higher and then occasionally climbing out onto fairly small limbs. When I first saw this, I used to fear that one of them would slip and fall. But I never saw a fall even though play at these heights (the danger sometimes seemed to be soon forgotten) could result in one cub slipping and its body swinging beneath a limb. At these heights, and on small-diameter limbs, the cubs were protected even if a male bear or unarmed person chose to climb after them.

The mother bear normally either climbs into the tree with the cubs or stays nearby on the ground and directs threats toward the potential source of danger. If the mother climbs the tree she may join the cubs and further shield them from danger. The photo on page 212 shows a cinnamon-colored black bear mother who is using her body to shield her cub from rocks being thrown by a group of ignorant teenagers. If the female remains on the ground, aggressive threats may be directed toward the intruder, whether it be bear or person. Specific components of this language are discussed later in this chapter, but the following example illustrates a mother black bear's aggression in this circumstance.

In spring of 1968, I spent twenty-three days observing a black bear female and her single cub of the year while they were on ground beds outside their den.[15] On April 13 I went to observe the bear family on this bed. John Courtney asked if he could come, and I reluctantly said yes. Before, at this bed, I had made a slow approach to within

Black bear mother stands at base of tree to protect young, Jasper National Park.
Stephen Herrero

Black bear mother shields young from rock-throwing teenagers. Jasper National Park.
Stephen Herrero

seventy-five feet of the bears and then sat down and kept quiet and still. John and I approached to this distance and observed the bears for an hour, but then John became restless and stood up to stretch—instead he slipped and fell forward. The mother bear promptly jumped up from her bed and charged. John, going against everything that I had told him previously, also jumped and ran away. Obeying my intellect and not my instincts, I stayed without moving and photographed her charge. The photos show the mother bear during and at the end of the charge, which stopped thirty-nine feet from me. As she faced me, steam came from her nostrils (the day was cold), and the hair on her back and neck seemed to be erect, making her already formidable appearance even more threatening. The charge left my heart throbbing in my chest and my breathing coming in gasps, but it helped to convince me of the soundness of my data showing that black bear mothers very seldom terminate charges with contact.

But why should this be? Black bear mothers certainly act as if they will attack a potential source of danger. Their action and appearance are important. Black bear mothers are great bluffers. Charges, paw swats, huffing, and snorting are some of the aggressive gestures and sounds that they direct toward intruders. They display weapons such as teeth and claws. Displays, threats, and warning sounds also happen very fast, giving an element of surprise. But contact and injury very seldom follow. I developed the hypothesis that this type of defense evolved because mothers that used it often were able to chase away potential sources of danger without resorting to combat. Because combat could lead to injury of the mother bear and the cubs could be protected without combat, black bear females with cubs evolved a strategy of bluffing. However, the behavior of generations past can only be inferred and not observed. Mine is only one possible explanation of bluffing by female black bears as a form of aggression.

In this context it is easy to see the importance to black bears of trees and other escape terrain such as dense brush. Trees or dense brush are the core of the mother bear's defense of offspring. Even sub-adult black bears usually climb trees to escape perceived danger. Adult males, which normally have little to fear from most other black bears, seldom climb trees. However, when pursued by packs of hunting dogs they too will climb trees. The black bear is primarily a forest-adapted animal with something as fundamental as safety tied to the presence of its primary escape terrain, which is trees. No wonder the black bear ventures from the forest reluctantly.

The grizzly bear mother typically lives in different environments and shows a more aggressive protection of offspring. At feeding aggregations in Alaska, grizzly (brown) bear females with young phys-

Black bear female with young of the year (nursing) on ground nest, Banff National Park.

The bear charged when one of the biologists nearby shifted position.

She stopped the charge about forty feet from us, seeming to expand her chest and raise her hair.
Stephen Herrero

ically contacted other bears during aggressive encounters in a greater percentage (6 percent) of their encounters than did any other class.[16] Even for grizzly bear females with young, however, noncontact forms of aggression, such as charges, are far more common than is physical contact.

But the documented instances of human injury following sudden confrontation with a grizzly bear female with young substantiates my claim that their behavior is different from that of black bear mothers. To understand why requires a journey back in time for several million years, to the age when the grizzly bear line first evolved.[17] A dynamic environment existed then. Great sheets of ice advanced and retreated at least four times over the several million years of the Pleistocene. The retreating glaciers are thought to have left behind extensive tree-less plant communities in highly productive early stages of succession. There was abundant, high-quality vegetation for a bear to eat. In addition, there were many other grazers and browsers utilizing the glacial-edge environments. For a bear this meant occasional prey as well as carcasses of dead animals to scavenge. There was one problem for bears. The black bears that existed in North America and Asia probably needed the forest for reasons of safety.

I suggest that grizzly bears evolved from forest-dwelling ancestors by developing adaptations that allowed them to feed and survive in the open environments created by glacial retreat. I have described how natural selection favored longer claws and greater development of muscles related to digging for food. Natural selection also favored females that could effectively defend their cubs in a treeless environment. Here the cubs could not provide for their own protection by climbing out of harm's way. The female had to repel potential predators, and these certainly existed. Wolves were numerous, and large cats, such as the saber tooth, were present. Other bears were threats as well and the cubs lacked the safety of trees.

I hypothesize that natural selection favored aggressive female grizzly bears. When the cubs were on the ground, predators might have been persistent to the point that the mother bear would resort to attack after threats failed to remove the danger. I suspect that even here contact with animals that represented danger was the exception. This would have been true because of the previously mentioned dangers to mother bears in such circumstances. When, however, potential sources of danger suddenly appeared at close range, the threat may have been a trigger for action. Whatever the circumstances were, the grizzly bear mother evolved as a bear more likely than did the black bear mother to physically attack some potential sources of danger. Human beings seem to fit into this category.

Thus the grizzly bear developed structures and behaviors that allowed it to eat the more abundant foods of open environments, and while in the open to defend itself and its cubs.

HOW GRIZZLY BEARS EXPRESS AGGRESSION

All studies that have examined the social structure of grizzly bears at feeding aggregations have reported that adult males are the most dominant and aggressive age/sex class, followed by adult females with young.[18] At McNeil River Falls, Alaska, Egbert noted that adult male grizzly (brown) bears participated in few encounters that involved overt threat since most other bears avoided them.[19] He characterized the encounters of adult males with other age/sex classes by saying that: "Usually the big males seemed taciturn, outwardly ignoring the other animals. Most walked with a slow lumbering gait and had a relaxed face as they moved to the river to fish."[20] However, their "scars and battered ears . . . belied their apparent lack of aggressiveness. . . ." Aggression among adult males reached a peak during the breeding season. During this period adult males, in contrast to their usual behavior, became extremely aggressive. For example, "Charlie Brown," the top-ranking male observed by Egbert at McNeil River Falls, "attacked and dislodged another (mating) adult male." One sub-adult grizzly (brown) bear (sex not stated) was thought to have been killed by one of four adult males who were pursuing females in estrous.

Scientists[21] and naturalists have observed adult male grizzly bears killing other bears during breeding season. Andy Russell describes an incident that park personnel observed in Mt. McKinley Park.[22] "A three-year-old male grizzly approached an adult male and female which were together during breeding season. The adult male charged the young male and ran after it on a road where the park employees were in a truck. The young male next left the road and tried to escape down a draw. The adult male caught it and with one swipe of his paw the big bear killed and almost disemboweled the other."

In Jasper National Park tourists watched a large, probably male, grizzly bear severely maul and kill a 150-pound smaller male.[23] The date, June 11, 1970, would have been during the end of the breeding season. A Canadian Wildlife Service autopsy of the dead bear revealed eighty-nine puncture wounds, a portion of the spleen protruding from the abdomen, a two-inch hole in the chest, a crushed rib cage, a broken right shoulder, a dislocated neck, a broken nose bridge, and a crushed skull.[24]

Three young grizzly (brown) bears squabble over fish at NcNeil River Falls, Alaska.
Derek Stonorov

Adult female grizzlies may also rarely kill other bears. John Crawford tells of an incident observed by Alaskan pioneers Stan and Edna Price at Pack Creek in southeastern Alaska.[25] A young grizzly (brown) bear mother with one cub was approached by an adult male. The mother bear growled, and the male tried to leave but she ran after and caught him. In less than twenty seconds the female "bit and tore at the bear's head, nearly scalping him, and, with a ripping bite low on the flank, eviscerated him. But the bear, after being mortally injured, still managed to bite her deeply in the back and sever her spinal column." Both bears were dead when Stan Price examined them.

Because adult bears have the power and weapons to kill one another, all successful bears readily communicate with a language of aggression and submission. Threat and appeasement signals have evolved because they reduce the incident of actual combat and the danger of injury to both parties.

If communication stops, death may result. John Craighead told me of an instance in which a five-year-old female grizzly was drugged and hence collapsed on the ground. Before researchers could get to her, an adult male grizzly rushed to her and killed her. Similarly, bear

Grizzly (brown) bear female with young threatens another bear by flattening her ears and lowering her head, McNeil River Falls, Alaska. *Derek Stonorov*

Grizzly (brown) bears engaging in a low-level aggressive display known as jawir McNeil River Falls, Alaska. *Derek Stono*

cubs have been observed eating their mothers several hours after the mother's death. Signals between bears are fundamentally important— a mother bear may become a carcass to be scavenged if she stops signaling "I am functioning as your mother." Bears appear to be more pragmatic than sentimental.

TABLE 5

Behavior components done by bears during encounters
and their relation to social status*

	BEHAVIOR COMPONENT	DOMINANCE	SUBORDINANCE
LOCOMOTION	Approach	70	5
	Charge	55	10
	Run or walk away	0	82
	Back up	0	52
	Stiff-legged walk	31	24
CONTACT	Bite	10	3
	Swipe	17	4
BODY ORIENTATION	Frontal orientation (head typically high)	51	21
	Lateral orientation	3	12
	Sitting	4	10
	Lying down	0	4
	Higher elevation	11	5
HEAD ORIENTATION	Head down	21	21
	Head drop	0	12
	Facing away	0	9
	Neck stretch	32	10
MOUTH	Mouth shut	13	23
	Mouth open	24	23
	Mouth open, canines showing	35	17
	Muzzle twist	13	2
	Jawing	17	11
EARS	Ears up	13	14
	Ears back	57	56
VOCALIZATION	Huffing	—	—
	Woofing	—	—
	Growling	—	—
	Roaring	—	—
	Bawling	—	—

*From Stonorov and Stokes[27], and Egbert[28].

NOTE: Certain components were associated largely with dominance: frontal orientation, approach, showing of canines, muzzle twist, and neck stretch. Other components were shown largely by subordinates: lateral orientation, turning away and dropping of the head, and sitting or lying down.

Many of the grizzly bear's aggressive and submissive behaviors can be recognized by people. Table 5 (p.219) lists the behavioral components observed during agonistic interactions among grizzly (brown) bears at McNeil River Falls in 1970.[26] Any such taxonomy of behavior is artificial in that a graded and variable series of actions are classified into discrete units to help people better recognize and understand what is going on. Still, such a listing of the components of agonistic behavior does much toward characterizing aggression. Note, for example, the apparently important signal value of the head region. The position of the head (high or low) and the orientation of the head (facing away or forward) are important. The mouth and ears have a range of positions that bears seem to recognize. Body orientation and motion, as in charges or running away, appear to be fundamental signals. Sounds such as roaring, growling, and huffing are readily distinguished by human observers if they are close enough to hear. Note that the frequency of the contact behaviors of biting and swiping between bears was relatively low.

These units of agonistic behavior can be sequenced together in many different ways. However, a typical high-intensity encounter has been described by Stonorov and Stokes:[27]

> The two animals directly faced each other with front legs stiffened, heads slightly lowered, and began a dramatic slowdown of movement. Ears of both combatants were back with mouths wide open, exposing the canines. Salivation sometimes occurred. This phase of the overall encounter was called the "confront." If one bear did not back down at this point, a second stage, the "charge," usually ensued. In a charge one or both bears ran at the other with head slightly lowered, ears back, mouth slightly open, and head and body oriented directly toward the opponent. If neither bear turned aside at this point there were swipes, biting, and locking of jaws. As the fight continued one bear eventually slowly backed away while dropping its head to an even lower position than its opponent. The fight usually ended at this point as the subordinate walked or ran away.

One thing that characterizes such encounters but was not mentioned in this account were the "thunderous roars" that typically accompanied actual fighting.[28] According to Egbert, such roars could usually be heard in his camp, which was located 1.2 miles from McNeil River Falls.[29]

What does an understanding of agonistic behavior among grizzly bears tell us about human safety around these bears? In bear-bear interactions the frequency of contact and injury is low. Most components of aggressive behavior relate to bluff and threat. In bear-person interactions, when a bear is trying to move a person away, as when the bear's personal space is being violated, bluff and threat are also typically used. Contact occurs infrequently in grizzly-human encounters, just as it does in bear-bear encounters. McArthur observed many agonistic interactions between grizzly bears and people on trails in Glacier National Park, Montana, but saw no contact.[30]

Bears, like other Carnivores, seem ready to chase anything that runs. In bear-bear encounters, Egbert observed that "few bears which stood their ground initially were physically attacked." This information, combined with my finding that many persons have been injured while trying to run from grizzly bears, further reinforces the idea of standing one's ground if you are hiking and are confronted by an aggressive grizzly bear. Related to this, Egbert noted that:[31]

> Young bears were most likely to attempt harassment of people, whether by refusing to give ground, by following, or with bluff charges. It was an important point among our field personnel to never permit a younger bear to dominate them lest we would be continually harassed by that animal from then on. These young bears apparently tested whatever they encountered. . . .

Running from such young bears might trigger chase and in rare circumstances could lead to contact. While grizzlies don't communicate with people in the same manner as they communicate with other grizzlies, some actions that people can take may be readily recognized by a grizzly in certain contexts: a direct stare with eye contact is an aggressive or dominance signal as is a loud, sharp shout or other loud noise. If a person has decided to try to intimidate a grizzly, then these may be appropriate actions. Conversely, by not staring and not making loud noise, you may be able to calm an agitated female with cubs. I am sorry that my recommendations can't be more black and white—remember, grizzlies aren't machines. At the least, knowledge of the grizzlies' communication system can help us to better understand them and can let people know when a bear is agitated.

HOW BLACK BEARS EXPRESS AGGRESSION

Agonistic behavior serves the same functions for black bears as it does for grizzly bears. Aggression is a means used by individual bears to help them gain resources such as food or mates. Submissive behaviors

Adult male black bears (note different color phases) in intensive interaction before attack...

...followed by an attack.   *Lynn Rogers*

allow a bear to signal to another that the dominant can have the resource in dispute, at least for the moment. As for grizzly bears, most disputes over resources are settled by using threats until one bear backs down and indicates its willingness to let the dominant have the resource. Only rarely is the subordinate physically attacked. As with grizzly bears, occasional cases of adult males killing sub-adults and even adult females with offspring have been recorded.[32] Young bears typically avoid serious confrontations with adult males or adult fe-males with cubs. Adult males engage in confrontations that may lead to physical injury during the breeding season.[33]

Black bears will congregate in a manner very similar to that of grizzlies. When food is abundant, concentrated, and prolonged in availability, as at a dump, they will come together and tolerate mutual spacings ranging from five feet to one hundred feet or more. As with grizzlies, when the food resource is more dispersed but still somewhat concentrated, a separation of typically one hundred yards or more is normally maintained by mutual avoidance.[34]

As has been observed for grizzly (brown) bears, agonistic behavior is made up of relatively stereotyped components and the sequencing of the components can occur in many different ways. However, certain patterns occur frequently. Table 6 summarizes the principal com-ponents of black bear agonistic behavior observed by John Courtney

TABLE 6
Components of black bear agonistic behavior*

	FEMALES WITH YOUNG	ADULT MALES
PHYSICAL ACTIONS		
Entering dump and being sensed	2	4
Slow approach	10	7
Head down, back arched	14	0
Standing broadside	8	0
Standing stiff-legged facing animal	1	0
Mouth open, jaws snapping	2	2
Paw swat or cock	19	6
False charge	111	14
Chase	89	13
Head to head	12	0
Charge with contact	2	2
Inflicting physical injury	0	2
VOCALIZATIONS		
Huffing	6	0
Snorting	30	1
Gurgling	14	5
Loud growling	0	1

*From Herrero[35].

and me at a garbage dump in Jasper National Park.[35] Contact between bears only occurred in six (5 percent) out of 131 dominance-
submission interactions and, as I previously said, only two (1.5 percent)
of these resulted in injury. Four out of six of these contact encounters
involved one adult male, "Blackbeard." He also inflicted the only two
injuries to other bears that we observed. So actual physical injury
appears to be a rare component of agonistic interactions that occur
when black bears interact over food at garbage dumps.

In a manner similar to grizzly (brown) bears, the head, ears, and
mouth assume many different positions that appear to be recognized
as signals by other bears. While most of the agonistic signals used by
black bears are similar to those of grizzly bears, two differences stand
out in my mind: Black bears either cock a forearm, as if to swat the
ground, or actually do this quite often. This behavior is seldom observed with grizzlies. The other striking difference is that grizzly bears
typically growl loudly (roar) when fighting. Black bears do not.

A typical sequence of black bear agonistic behavior has been given
by Robert Jordan,[36] who stated that an offensive threat by an adult
might occur in the following sequence:

1. Sniffing the air or objects with unfamiliar odors.
2. Looking directly at the individual to be threatened. (Heavy panting may
   occur before or during looking directly.)
3. Charging at the individual or veering slightly into bushes or trees (sometimes panting while charging) and stopping suddenly.
4. At the moment of stopping, slapping one or both feet down on the ground
   or to the side against any object such as a tree or bush which would produce
   a sudden surprising sound. Concurrent with the slap, air is expelled from
   the mouth with a startling rush (i.e., huffing). . . .
5. Opening and closing the mouth rapidly to produce a series of loud pops
   (jaw-popping).
6. Turning the head away and averting the eyes, often accompanied by licking
   the lips and panting.
7. Standing, walking, or running away.

Whereas interactions between black bears at feeding aggregations
have not been studied as much as those occurring between grizzlies,
agonistic interactions between black bears and people have been studied more. At the Jasper Dump, John Courtney and I observed more
than a hundred instances in which people aggressively displaced black
bears from where they were feeding or resting. For example, we
recorded fifty-seven instances in which people threw rocks at black
bears, even females with cubs at close range. People also frequently

Adult male black bear, Jasper National Park. Note blond coloring.

Stephen Herrero

advanced close to a black bear, usually causing it to leave, in order that the person could take a picture. In one instance, Blackbeard, the most aggressive adult male bear, had just opened a five-square-inch cut on the side of a sub-adult bear. Within a few minutes tourists

TABLE 7
Types of aggressive acts, ranked by frequency of occurrence*

RANK	TYPE OF AGGRESSION	DESCRIPTION	FREQUENCY	PERCENTAGE OF TOTAL
1	2	Blow vocalization (snort)	257	41.19
2	4	Charge	234	37.50
3	6	Bite–snap	51	8.17
4	5	Quadripedal swat	45	7.21
5	3	Bipedal swat	22	3.53
6	7	Running toward crowd	8	1.28
7	1	Low-moan vocalization	7	1.12

*From Eager and Pelton[38].

Large male black bear, Crater Lake National Park.   *Stephen Herrero*

crowded to within thirty feet of Blackbeard and took his picture. He fed quietly and without response. Despite having been pelted with rocks and otherwise harassed, black bears directed aggressive displays at people only fifteen times. The most common displays directed toward people were snorting (huffing), false charges, and paw swat or paw cock. These same displays were also common in bear-bear interactions.[37]

Other studies of black bear interactions with people have also documented the tolerance that black bears normally show toward people. Jane Tate Eager and Mike Pelton, working in Great Smoky Mountains National Park, observed 392 panhandling sessions in which people either fed black bears or black bears approached people for food.[38] Here the relationship was different than at the dump in Jasper where food was readily available to bears. In the Smokies the bears wanted food from people, and most of the bears were accustomed to getting it. Out of the 392 panhandling sessions, 220 (56 percent) contained no aggression by bears, whereas 172 (44 percent) involved at least one aggressive act. All together 624 aggressive acts were observed. Table 7, p. 225, lists which acts were classified as being aggressive and their frequency of occurrence. Most of these were committed by bears that were regular panhandlers and had seemingly learned that aggression could yield food, or at least that it did not lead to bad results.

As previously mentioned, only thirty-seven (6 percent) aggressive acts out of 624 resulted in contact between black bears and people. No serious injuries were observed. Overall, black bears exhibited significant restraint when dealing with people. Eager and Pelton give an interesting example of this reluctance to injure people:[39]

> Three young boys had been pursuing Phoenix periodically throughout the session, frequently standing within one metre of her. She "warned" them on three occasions not to approach so closely; these warnings included twirling around rapidly to face them and jaw popping. One of the boys later tantalized her by attempting to hold food out of her reach (perhaps emulating the man who had done so earlier); yet this was an impossible task since she was taller when standing bipedally than he. She grabbed the cookie in her mouth, and then literally pushed the boy away with her front limbs. Still, not to be deterred, the boys persisted in aggravating her. Shortly thereafter while they were standing very closely behind her, Phoenix turned and from a bipedal position knocked one of the boys to the ground. . . . she first bit him on the neck and then on the lower back. This was not so gruesome as it sounds. She did not even puncture the skin, and there were no superficial wounds visible immediately thereafter.

The factors that precipitated the bears' acts of aggression toward people in the Great Smoky Mountains National Park are listed in Table 8, p. 228. Crowding, either by itself or in combination with other acts, was the most frequent human action preceding aggression. Crowding or petting, by themselves or in combination, preceded twenty-nine (78 percent) of the thirty-seven aggressive actions that terminated in contact.

Black bears in Yosemite National Park, despite extensive camp and car raiding, were shown by Barrie Gilbert and Bruce Hastings to have been almost incredibly reluctant to injure people.[40] These researchers observed 992 interactions between black bears and people. Both bears and people most often acted neutrally toward each other. Bears were rarely aggressive toward people (1.3% of all responses, 70 out of 5,785 responses), but people were more frequently aggressive toward bears (16.3% of all responses, 960 out of 5,885 responses). No instances of injury or even of physical contact were observed.

TABLE 8
Apparent precipitating factors for aggressive acts,
ranked by frequency of occurrence*

RANK	PRECIPITATING FACTOR	FREQUENCY	PERCENTAGE OF TOTAL
1	Crowding	244	39.10
2	Photographing–Crowding	67	10.74
3	Other[a]	49	7.85
4	Another Bear	40	6.41
5	Harassing–Crowding	30	4.81
6	NPS Personnel	29	4.65
7	Petting	27	4.33
8	Photograph kneeling–Crowding	23	3.69
9	Petting–Crowding	19	3.04
10.5	Harassing	16	2.56
10.5	No apparent reason	16	2.56
12	Three factors[b]	14	2.24
13	Handfeeding–Crowding	13	2.08
14.5	Handfeeding	11	1.76
14.5	Photographing (kneeling)	11	1.76
16	Photographing	6	0.96
17.5	Cessation of feeding	3	0.48
17.5	Toss feeding	3	0.48
19	Toss feeding–Crowding	2	0.32
20	Photographing with flash–Crowding	1	0.16

[a]All factors considered peculiar to a certain panhandling session (e.g., feet dangling over the wall, motorcycle engine revving, etc.), and not likely to occur in other sessions, were included in this category.

[b]Since combinations of three factors were fairly infrequent, they were all included in one category.

*From Eager and Pelton[38].

As mentioned earlier, most black bear-inflicted injuries are minor. But I must again stress that black bears may become predators on man, although rarely, and in other cases may inflict serious injury. Anyone interested in safety around bears should remember that the power to seriously injure or even kill is always there.

16

Bears and People in Rural and Remote Areas

RURAL dwellings and agricultural operations have many tempting foods that entice bears. Beehives, gardens, fruit trees, garbage cans, compost piles, and livestock can become a bear's banquet.

During the summers, when I am not involved in field research, I usually base myself with my family at our small rural farmstead at the north end of the Slocan Valley of British Columbia. Our retreat is a two-acre speck of cleared land surrounded by forest, which here and there is dotted with other small farmsteads. Black bears are common; grizzlies still roam the high country and, on rare occasions, descend to near our home.

All of our "problems" have been with black bears. "Problems" don't occur every year. However, if green-up is late on the mountain slopes, or if the huckleberry crop fails, then we can count on bears visiting. In particular, we prepare to do battle for our garden or our tree fruits. Our dog and the neighbor's dog work overtime barking to announce the arrival of hungry bears and trying to chase these bears from the farmsteads.

Once while I was roofing, in a year so dry that the huckleberries were little more than dried shrouds, I heard my dog in a frenzy of barking. From the roof, I could see three different black bears simultaneously approaching the apples and plums, each bear entering from a different side of the clearing. Like many a farmer, I hurried down from the roof and I grabbed the nearest weapon, which happened to be a pitchfork. I charged and yelled at the bears. They ran off but, of course, they were soon back.

Over the years, I have learned how to better prevent such problems. I have also studied and investigated the difficulties that other people living in rural and remote areas have had with bears. Because bears occasionally cause significant economic damage to human endeavors such as beekeeping or sheep raising, scientists have been paid to study such situations and to develop ways to outfox bears. In this chapter I try to synthesize what is known.

LIVING IN BEAR COUNTRY

Garbage and Garbage Dumps

If you have chosen to live surrounded by forest and bears, the outside garbage can should not be used except for nonfood items. Any foods or cans or bottles containing traces of food should be temporarily stored in the basement, root cellar, or elsewhere where bears can't get access. Bear-proof garbage cans, concrete bunkers, or "dumpster" types of containers such as are used in parks are all fairly bear-proof but they are normally too expensive for home use. If bears become used to visiting your home for garbage, you increase the danger of a bear breaking into your kitchen or harvesting some of your garden.

In North America, food wastes, and hence edible garbage, are a part of our lifestyle. Garbage dumps will attract bears unless special precautions are taken. In some rural communities bears at the dump are a fact of life. The scale of operation makes it impractical to adopt garbage processing systems such as landfill or complete incineration, each of which, if properly carried out, leaves no edible waste for bears.

A landfill operation that doesn't allow bears to feed must meet strict design standards and operation procedures.[1] The bear-proof landfill needs to be surrounded by electrical cyclone fencing that has sufficient concrete footing so that bears can't dig under. Edible garbage must be deeply buried regularly so that food odors do not tempt bears to try and tear fences down despite the strength or electrification of the fence.

High-temperature incineration is another technique that can be very effective in converting edible food waste into inedible and un-attractive ash.[2] Incomplete low-temperature combustion, however, leaves you with bears foraging through ashes to pick out edible bits. In some areas air-quality standards will not permit incineration.

The costs of designing, building, and maintaining either type of operation make such solutions impractical for the small, rural community. However, cooperation of all communities within a regional district may support either bear-proof landfill or complete-combustion incineration. Without such bear-proofing, "dump" bears are as inevitable as winter in Canada. They not only cause nuisance problems for homes near a dump, but most often such bears are shot and killed.

Perhaps we should try to mimic the peasants who lived in the Appennine Mountains of the Abruzzi region of Italy where I worked in 1971. Nearly ten thousand people and about a hundred bears lived in or nearby Abruzzo National Park. I mentioned how, along with park naturalist Franco Zunino, I studied these bears and presented a plan for their survival.[3]

Because there were several small garbage dumps in the park, I expected to find bears at them, just as one does in similar situations in North America. Zunino told me that bears did not visit the dumps. I could not believe it, and so I went to see for myself. It was true—not a bear, nor a scat, nor even a track. I looked more carefully at these dumps. There were no discarded foods. Such items were either eaten or composted in town where the bears never ventured. These Italians did not throw food away the way we did back home. Such a strange and wonderful discovery.

One of the many things to investigate before buying a piece of rural property is its proximity to garbage-disposal sites. We were once offered a parcel of riverfront land in the Columbia Valley of British Columbia that actually surrounded the local dump. While I like bears, we did not wish to have them visiting our home whenever they tired of the food selection available at the dump.

If you insist on living near a dump in bear country, then at least be prepared for the occasional break-in or marauding bear. Bear trails to and from garbage become distinct after a few years. Start at the dump and cautiously look for any trails leading near your property. If these trails exist, chances are that you can occasionally watch the parade and sometimes it will come to your home.

A strategy for protection against bears that most people are unaware of is locating dumps or homes so that they are surrounded by cleared areas. This type of location takes advantage of black bears' reluctance to venture more than several hundred yards from forest or dense bush cover.

Fiberglass shelter destroyed by grizzly bear, Banff National Park, 1968.

David Shakleton

Break-ins

Just because there are bears around does not preordain that they will break into your home or kitchen. Immaculate sanitation and garbage handling are the tricks that can lead to compatibility. Bears are smart enough to quickly learn where they do and do not get food. Break-ins can be minimized through sanitary handling of garbage and food, such as I have described. You may also try to build your house sturdily enough to repel all bear invaders.

Two of my personal experiences further illustrate how break-ins by bears can be minimized.

The first experience concerned the cabin in Banff National Park where our grizzly bear study team lived for six months during each of five years from 1976 to 1980. This cabin had a unique reminder for us that we were in grizzly country. One of the first things we noticed when we moved in was that, just above one of the handmade chairs at the kitchen table, the log walls had a deep raking made by the claws of a grizzly bear, which had, no doubt, been intent on getting food. A repaired spot in the roof suggested that the grizzly had entered by tearing a hole in the roof. We shared every meal with that reminder of the past and the thought that, if the past were repeated, we could end up with a grizzly on our table. Our cabin was in the middle of the densest concentration of grizzly bears in Banff Park, and so there was little room for sloppiness on our part. We had come to study bears, not to do battle with them in our home! So we usually did not eat fresh meats, especially odorous varieties such as bacon, and we burned all edible garbage in our wood stove. Bears seldom came to investigate our cabin although we were only half a mile from the junction of two major bear travel routes, and natural foods were eaten by bears within a few hundred yards of the cabin.

Our only encounter with grizzlies at the cabin came when Dick Russell from the Canadian Wildlife Service came to visit. We then had a pair of two-and-one-half-year-old cubs around that had recently been weaned by their mother. They were exploring their way into young adulthood. Although previously their mother had always led them to things to eat, now they had to discover food on their own. One afternoon their explorations brought them onto our porch while everyone was away. They didn't find anything to eat, but they did find Dick's rubber boots. These they chewed and shredded as if they were the tastiest bone, except that they did not eat them. Over the summer these curious young bears visited us several more times. Since we offered nothing more than rubber boots for them to chew on, they stopped coming around.

The second experience further shows how bear break-ins can be controlled. The nearest neighbors to our farm, John and Bay Herrmann, have lived in the midst of bear country for more than ten years. Their kitchen is a post-and-beam structure with a roof and walls that are boarded in for only five feet. Most of the rest of their kitchen is open to the air. There is no front door, and the back door, which is seldom closed, is made of small, single glass panes—French door style.

Our friends live on a beautiful hilly ridge with a view that sweeps down along a thirty-mile-long, fiordlike lake rimmed with mountains. Black bears regularly check near and even in their home to see what is available. Normally there is nothing left around for them. But more aggressive bears eventually will pry the door off the icebox (the home is not electrified) or break a jar or two. When this happens, all foods go into storage in cellars or automobiles. A few warning shots may eventually be fired at overbold bears and the amazing thing, even to me, is that bears soon stop coming around, apparently when they realize there is nothing to eat.

In years of food-crop failure for bears, problems increase. When natural foods are abundant, my neighbors may go a whole year without being visited by a bear. There is a dynamic, but acceptable, tension between these neighbors and the bears. In over ten years they have shot only one bear, not for kitchen break-in problems but because it repeatedly ravaged fruit trees.

Cabins or houses located in bear country that are left unoccupied for more than a day or two might need tight-fitting wooden shutters and strong doors. Any gap large enough for a bear claw is probably large enough for a bear to pull a shutter off or to rip a door open. Bears may also tear holes in walls or roofs to gain entry.

Safety for Children

Children (especially those 12 and under) should be carefully tended when bears are around. In rural areas, black bears and children may end up sharing berry patches or children's play areas and, while such situations seldom lead to injury because black bears will normally move or flee, they have at least four times led to children being killed. Most rural dwellers know the woods well enough not to panic over black bears' danger to children. Our four children all grew up playing in bear country. I have always watched them carefully, however, and have kept them close when I knew that black bears were nearby.

Bears and Bees

Folklore tells us that bears like honey, but it does not mention their liking for larval forms of bees. Black bears are a significant economic problem for beekeepers wherever hives are introduced into bear country. In Alberta, honey production in the Peace River District is an important industry, with 75,000 hives maintained annually.[4] Between 1973 and 1977 the estimated total damage by bears ranged from $70,000 to $200,000. Between 1972 and 1979 a minimum of 818 black bears were removed. Most of them were shot. Alberta's Fish and Wildlife Division and Department of Agriculture investigated the value of adversive conditioning resulting from vomit-inducing chemicals placed on honeycomb bait and the use of electroconvulsive shock.[5] Neither technique was consistent in keeping bears away from beehives.

A third alternative, protective electric fencing, has brought the problem under control. One effective design for protecting bee yards is portable. It can be constructed by two men in two hours and can be dismantled in half an hour.[6] Electrical circuits and fencing designs for repelling black bears have continually improved over the years[7] to the point where I now regard properly installed and maintained electric fencing to be a highly effective black or grizzly bear deterrent.

The amateur beekeeper experimenting with a few hives may not wish to invest in electric fencing to keep bears away. Alternatives include placing hives on top of roofs (some shading is, however, highly desirable) or placing bees on elevated platforms such as metal-sheathed poles, which black bears can't climb. The platform method is said to be used by some small-scale beekeepers in the southern United States.[8] I have successfully kept bees on a roof but I haven't used a platform.

Bears and Fruits and Vegetables

Tree and bush fruits are always attractive to bears, but in years when natural foods are relatively poor, problems of orchard depredation increase.[9] As in protecting beehives, electric fencing is the most effective solution for keeping bears away from your fruit. In the well-planned orchard, trees are grouped and this permits efficient fencing. Other fruit crops, such as strawberries and raspberries, might as well be located nearby so as to be included inside the same fence. The rural dweller with only a few trees or bushes or whose fruits are scattered about a farmstead may not be able to fence. An alert and somewhat aggressive dog, which will locate, bark at, and chase bears approaching your fruits, is invaluable.

Failure to protect fruit-bearing trees from bears almost certainly means damage to fruit trees. Bears will not bother the trees until the fruit is ripe (their food habits have much in common with people's), but then watch out! I once picked almost the entire crop from our favorite prune-plum tree. The fruit that was left was located at the ends of the highest branches and was the hardest to pick. We put boards with nails sticking outward all around the trunk of the tree and on the major limbs and left for a few days. When we returned, the twenty-year-old prune-plum lay on the ground as a heap of broken branches and limbs. Apparently, the bear had not been able to reach the fruit without knocking the tree down. There was no blood on my ineffective nails, and so I figured that the bear must have grabbed a limb while standing on its hind legs and pulled itself up into the tree. Since then I have tried to pick all ripe fruit before leaving. Somewhat unlike human beings, black bears will also eat fruit that has begun to wilt on trees or even fruit that has fallen to the ground.

Bears may also be a problem with certain vegetables such as corn[10] and carrots or with grain crops like oats.[11] As much, or more, damage may be caused by bears trampling crops as is caused by bears eating crops. Here again, electric fencing, a dog, and the location of the garden as far as possible from trees or cover for bears are effective in preventing excessive problems.

Livestock

Domestic animals are not as adept at escape from bears as are wild ungulates. Sheep are particularly easy prey and must be closely herded, watched, and, preferably, penned at night in bear country. In both Virginia[12] and in Minnesota,[13] black bear predation on sheep has been a significant economic problem. Davenport[14] claimed that proportionately few black bears became sheep killers, but that the trait persisted once acquired.

On the other hand, many people run sheep in areas where black bears are prevalent. The disposal of individual, sheep-killing black bears is normally an acceptable management action. The extent of sheep losses typically depends on how well managed the flock is.

The Yellowstone ecosystem contains one of the last of two remaining significant populations of grizzly bears in the contiguous United States. Researchers there have concluded that sheep raising is incompatible with maintaining this "threatened" population of grizzly bears, since sheep ranching operations have been heavily involved in poaching or otherwise disposing of predaceous bears.[15]

In the summer of 1970, the year before I arrived to work on bears in Italy, a bear climbed onto the roof of an Italian shepherd's shed in Abruzzo National Park during the night. The roof collapsed, and about 220 pounds of excited bear came face to face with a penned flock of panicked sheep. In the morning, the shepherd found about eighty dead sheep and a still-excited bear.[16] Normally, however, bears will kill only one or two sheep at a time. Unless they are disturbed, they will consume the dead sheep.

The record for sheep kills by a single bear in one attack probably goes to a black bear in Idaho that killed 235 sheep by running them off a cliff during the summer of 1980.[17]

Cattle are less subject to predation than are sheep. As with predation on sheep, it is individual bears that become problems when they learn to kill domestic animals. There is evidence from New Hampshire that a single 450-pound male black bear killed at least twenty-seven cows over a two-year period.[18]

Some predation exists almost everywhere both cattle and grizzly bears are found. Some grizzlies may come to include predation on cattle as an important component of their individual strategy for survival.[19] Depending on the population status of grizzlies in the general area where the problem is occurring, the grizzly preying on cattle may have to be trapped and relocated or be disposed of. Without careful field examination, it is easy to confuse scavenging of carcasses by bears with killing by bears. A scavenging bear is not necessarily a livestock killer as well.

Both sheep and cattle attract a variety of predators during lambing or calving. Where possible they should be penned during birthing. Dead domestic animals also attract scavenging bears. Whenever a dead animal is suspected to be nearby, the site should be approached with caution, and then only while you are armed or on horseback. Despite the potential danger of such situations, a study of numerous sheep

"The record for sheep kills by a single bear in one attack probably goes to a black bear in Idaho that killed 235 sheep by running them off a cliff during the summer of 1980."

kills in Idaho reported no human injury despite several instances when grizzly bears were approached at sheep kills.[20]

Both pigs and foods typically fed to pigs may attract bears. When pigs and other animals are slaughtered, bears may be drawn from a distance by the odor. The only grizzly bear seen near our farm was apparently attracted when pigs were being slaughtered.

Years of Food-Crop Failure for Bears

When natural foods, such as berries, are relatively unavailable for bears, then people can expect the omnivorous food habits of bears to drive them to seek any human foods, crops, or domestic animals that are available. In years when natural food crops fail, bears become bolder than during normal years and the challenge of repelling them from orchards and camps can take on a new magnitude.

During such years certain black bears may undertake long-range movements in search of food[21] and may become more dangerous to people. I've mentioned that in Alaska during one berry failure year, 1963, five black bear inflicted injuries, including one death, occurred.[22] Data from Minnesota support the view that a causal relationship exists between berry-crop failure and an increase in property damage by black bears.[23]

Grizzly bears may respond differently to major berry-crop failure. I have found no evidence that grizzly bear attacks on people increase with food-crop failure. This lack of an increase in injuries may be because grizzlies in many areas include roots as an important component of their diet during fattening. Where root crops are found, they never fail and they may buffer the grizzly somewhat from berry failures.

During David Hamer's and my work in the Cascade Valley of Banff National Park, 1976 was a year in which buffaloberry (soapberry) production was estimated to have been only 2 to 15 percent of that counted during abundant years. Despite this, the number of grizzly bear cubs born—the ultimate test of nutritional success—was high the next year.[24]

In the Yukon, Pearson[25] was studying grizzlies during a year of major failure of their principal berry crop, the soapberry. The bears were able to fatten sufficiently on roots to be able to successfully hibernate. However, Pearson thought that they lost weight compared to years when berries were abundant.

Bark Stripping and Sapwood Ingestion

During the spring when there is relatively little for bears to eat, black bears, especially in the Pacific Northwest, may cause serious economic damage to managed second-growth forest. I have mentioned how they can strip bark from trees and eat the sapwood. This problem does not seem to increase danger to people. Management responses to bark stripping and sapwood ingestion have included sport hunting and killing by paid damage-control agents.[26]

Predator Control Specialists

Most rural residents can only legally shoot problem bears in self-defense or during hunting season. If the problem can't be solved by removing the attractant for bears, by electric fencing, dogs, or some other such means, then professional help may be called. Predator-control specialists usually are employed either by fish and wildlife agencies or by departments of agriculture. They are trained in the art of capturing specific problem bears. Their tools typically include snares and portable culvert traps, as well as drugs to sedate captured animals as necessary. Predator control specialists may also evaluate damage claims if your area has a loss-compensation program. In years of food-crop failure for black bears, many complaints tend to come in at the same time. If your complaint involves a very aggressive black bear, and children regularly play in the area where the problem is occurring, then stress the urgency of your particular case. Children may have to be kept inside until the bear is captured, shot, or moves on.

REMOTE CAMPS IN BEAR COUNTRY

Resource exploration or guided hunting or fishing operations often make use of "remote base camps," which are located some distance from other human settlements. Such camps may be occupied for a few days or for months. A number of people usually use such a camp. Remote base camps are usually more complexly organized and are bigger than backpacking camps.

The first rule of bear safety in remote camps is once again proper sanitation and bear-proof food storage. No edible garbage should be left around for bears to discover. However, since sanitary landfill operations and, often, high-temperature combustion are not possible, then alternate means of food-waste disposal must be found. While solutions will vary depending on whether food wastes can be eventually flown out by helicopter or packed out by horse or person, most situations involve some storage of such wastes.

I recommend storing food wastes and food inside one specific area protected from bear depredations by electric fencing.[27] To reduce the quantity of wastes stored, burning may be desirable. But remember that without high temperatures and complete combustion of wastes, charred residues are likely to attract bears. Therefore, such a burning site should be inside the area protected by electric fencing. If the scale of operation is too small or too transient to merit installing a portable electric fence, then the remote camp operation takes on some characteristics similar to those in a recreational backpacking camp.

Once a bear gets food from your camp, chances are good that it will be back again sometime. If initial probes yield nothing to eat, then bears will stop coming around unless they are successful at raiding similar camps nearby. Because bears are quick learners, the remote camp crew soon establishes a relationship with the local bears. Seasonal changes in the availability of natural foods may alter this established rhythm if, for example, there is a failure of the fall berry crop. If this happens, a few problems can turn to many, but a camp that has experienced no problems will probably continue that way. Good sanitation and food storage will eliminate most of the difficulties that people in remote camps might have with bears.

Andy Russell tells a story about a camp that became a regular dining hall for bears.[28] The bears became so bold that they visited the cook tent, which was also the storage place for all of the camp's food. The frustrated cook had waited up several nights in a row to shoot a robbing bear but had instead fallen asleep. The cook decided to perk up his flagging alertness by tying one end of a cord around a slab of bacon and the other around his own ankle. His alarm system sort of worked. He awoke to a gentle tug on his ankle and the bear eating bacon at the other end. But when the cook startled and grabbed for his rifle, the bear bolted for the door, bacon in mouth. The cook flew behind the bear until the cord broke.

Camp layout can help to reduce problems. Place tents in a line rather than a circle so as to avoid cornering a bear and to allow safe shooting if the only option is to shoot the bear. The eating tent should not be located near the sleeping tents unless everything is protected by electric fencing. Most food storage must be near the eating and cooking area for convenience. Without electric fencing food should be stored in bear-resistant, odor-trapping containers such as metal drums with tight-fitting lids. Camp in the open, away from cover for bears if possible.

People in every remote camp located in bear country should have rehearsed what they will do when a bear appears. As I have stressed, loud noises, many people, repellents, and noisy, aggressive dogs may all help to put the run on a bear. If the bear continues to be aggressive, firearms backup and training are important. A firearm should be stored in a location known to all with shells in the magazine but not in the chamber. The camp cook has a special responsibility regarding bears as he or she may often be alone during the day.

People operating out of remote camps also have to think about possible bear encounters while engaged in field work. The field camp may be able to afford one very important safety element that recreational backpackers cannot. This is radio communication either by VHF or Single Side Band. Radio communication can give a field party quick contact with help after many different types of injuries. Prompt radio contact with support personnel can mean life or death after a bear mauling. Barrie Gilbert and Cynthia Dussel-Bacon are both alive today because of their VHF radios.

Early-warning detection systems may be desirable around camps in grizzly bear habitat because it is useful to know whenever this potentially dangerous species is nearby. Polar bears, which are the most predaceous of all bears, have spurred the development of technologies to detect bears when they are near remote camps.[29]

Dogs have previously been mentioned for their value in detecting and, if properly trained, in repelling bears around rural dwellings.

The same is true in remote camps where in addition to sensing bears they also provide food-scrap cleanup and companionship.

FIREARMS

Because national and most other parks are wildlife sanctuaries, the art of being safe around bears in these jurisdictions does not include carrying or using firearms. Outside such sanctuaries, however, one can often carry firearms for personal protection. This opportunity does not extend to side arms without special permit.

Since the repeating rifle is the firearm with which western people extirpated the grizzly bear from much of its former range, perhaps it ought to follow that properly armed people would be reasonably safe from bears. Yes and no, maybe and sometimes, for some people and not for others, is my answer. Remember that our ancestors who settled the West were often out to shoot grizzly bears whenever they got a chance. Western settlers picked their shots and certainly did not wait until an enraged grizzly bear was charging unless they unexpectedly surprised a grizzly. Even with the odds dramatically on the side of the settlers, grizzlies still injured enough people badly enough that several books of fact and lore exist depicting encounters between grizzlies and settlers, hunters, and trappers.[30]

In addition to hunting, firearms are useful in several situations around bears. The first such situation involves a bear approaching a person considering him as prey. Such incidents, whether they involve black or grizzly bear, seldom begin with a charge by the bear. It is not the bear but the person who feels threatened. I have stressed that this is a very rare situation but clearly one in which a firearm could save your life.

A firearm is also useful when a very aggressive bear shows up around camp and cannot be persuaded to leave. Such bears normally have a history of feeding on people's food or garbage and may have to be killed. Of course, if an aggressive bear actually attacks you or a companion, a firearm may be a lifesaver, or it may cause a wounded bear to intensify its attack. The risk of shooting a companion who is being mauled must also be considered.

Finally, a firearm might be useful if you suddenly encounter a grizzly bear, especially a female with cubs, and you are charged by the grizzly. If you have a firearm, you may choose to shoot a charging grizzly bear, but remember that a wounded grizzly is almost always highly dangerous and may try to attack the person who has wounded it. Since black bears almost never charge at and contact people in incidents preceded by sudden surprise, the discussion that follows primarily concerns the grizzly.

For protection against a suddenly encountered and charging grizzly, many people will be safer without any firearms, despite the legality of carrying them in most nonpark and remote areas. I think that for some people, carrying a firearm tends to turn off the alertness to signs of bears and to situations in which bear danger might develop. With the perceived security of a firearm, people become bolder, which can be bad for several reasons. If you are expert with firearms under "combat" conditions, you are more likely to provoke grizzlies and hence to have to use your expert ability. In this case the unnecessary killing of a grizzly bear may occur. On the other hand, if you are not expert with firearms in tense situations, you run the risk of wounding and further enraging a grizzly. To kill a charging grizzly bear in order to defend yourself, you must be capable of shooting to kill an object hurtling at you, perhaps through dense brush, at speeds of up to forty-four feet per second. If you aren't expert enough to do this, then you may be better off without a firearm or at least keeping the firearm for use only in very few situations.

Let's assume that the days of shooting grizzlies on sight are over and that you carry a firearm only for protection. Prior to going into the bush, you have reviewed in your mind the situations under which you would shoot to kill a grizzly. The most likely situation would be when a grizzly is charging at you. When to shoot is not an easy decision. Part of the grizzly bear's language of aggression includes "false charges." The charges are called false because the bear stops short of contact, either with a person or another bear. Most grizzly bear charges at people do not end in contact, even though such charges may seem to be full out. False charges are also often repeated before the bear leaves. No doubt many grizzlies have been shot unnecessarily during charges that would not have ended in contact. Unfortunately grizzlies do not indicate whether their charges are "false" or real. Without a weapon you sweat and wait and see what will happen next. You might climb a tree depending on how close the bear and the tree are.

With a firearm you have more options but even more difficult decisions. If a tree is nearby and the charge begins from far enough away, you might choose to climb taking your firearm with you. If there are no trees, or there is not enough time to climb, then chances are that you have already decided whether or not and at what range you will shoot. By not shooting you still keep open the option of playing dead if the attacking grizzly is a female with cubs. If you wound her, then you should try to kill her.

"Warning" shots before an attack occurs will in some cases send a grizzly fleeing and in other cases precipitate a charge. Bears might also respond neutrally to shots. A warden I was with shot in front of a sub-adult grizzly, close enough to it to splash dirt in its face. The bear showed little response. Later the same day a shot in the air caused a large, adult male grizzly to flee.

If a grizzly is charging and you have decided to shoot to kill, shooting distance will depend upon the type of firearm you have, your proficiency as a marksman, and the nature of the specific situation. To give the bear a reasonable chance to stop and to give yourself reasonable safety, the person expert with firearms should perhaps wait until a charging grizzly is from fifty to one hundred feet away or even closer. This is far too close for anyone not expert with firearms, but only experts increase their margin of safety by considering shooting. At these distances a charging grizzly bear, not shot, will reach a person in one-and-one-half to two seconds. The right shot will stop a charging grizzly before it reaches you even at close range.

If you feel that you must kill a grizzly bear in self-defense, then there is a best place to shoot and several firearms to choose from. If you shoot at close range, you want not only to kill the charging bear but also to stop its charge before it reaches you. At very close range

Where to shoot a bear (cross-hatched area).

a good first shot is through the shoulder and into the body. This is aimed at breaking a shoulder blade and crippling the bear, thus slowing the charge. A second shot then can quickly be placed anywhere in the vital zone to kill the bear. Head and neck shots should not, as a rule, be attempted with a charging grizzly bear because these targets are too small.

Choice of proper firearms for safety depends upon many factors. An adequate and popular defensive weapon is a twelve-gauge, short-barrel, repeating shotgun with at least a five-shot capacity. The ability to shoot fast is essential. Pump actions and semiautomatics have this capability. Dependability must be thoroughly established prior to carrying such a weapon in bear country. The shotgun is a weapon of last resort to be used at close range only. Many persons doing field work with grizzly bears carry shotguns some of the time. Choice of ammunition varies. Large-diameter buckshot (00 gauge—"SSGs") gives a person the advantage of nine to eleven pellets, which, depending upon the barrel, will disperse about one inch for every 3.3 feet. I personally know of one charging female grizzly that was shot and killed at about fifty feet with large-diameter buckshot. I do not know of any failures. Some experts, however, are suspicious regarding the ability of large-diameter buckshot to kill grizzlies, believing that penetration is inadequate except at about fifty to sixty-five feet or less. Buckshot also could be dangerous if you try to shoot a grizzly bear that is attacking someone else. Your chances of hitting both the bear and the person are too great with buckshot. The alternate choice of ammunition for shotguns is the rifled slug. At close range these have adequate killing power and the ability to shatter a shoulder bone. Rifled slugs have the disadvantage of requiring more careful aim than does the large-diameter buckshot.

High-powered hunting rifles are clearly established to be the most effective firearm for killing grizzlies. They have the same disadvantage as the rifled slug for the person facing a charging bear. One must be able to hit a rapidly charging, hurtling object. Bolt actions are much slower than pump actions or semiautomatics. Rifles have an added disadvantage for bears in that some persons with high-powered rifles will be tempted to shoot noncharging bears at long distances. They also have limitations in dense brush since woody stems are more likely to deflect rifle bullets than shotgun slugs. Telescopic sights may interfere with the "instinctive" shooting that may be necessary at close range. Open sights should be installed if a person is designing a "bear" gun.

Despite the limitations of high-powered rifles, tests prove they are the most effective bear-killing firearm.[31] The "best" firearm depends on ballistic performance and a person's ability to tolerate firearm recoil. United States Forest Service researchers in Alaska concluded that four cartridge-bullet combinations were superior for protection against bears.[32] The .458 Winchester Magnum with 510-gr soft-point bullets was the "surest" combination for shooters who could handle the recoil. The .375 H & H Magnum with 300-gr soft-point bullets had less recoil than the .458 Magnum, but for many people recoil was still severe. The .338 Winchester Magnum with 300-gr bullets had less recoil than the .375 Magnum but only slightly less effectiveness. The .30-06 with 220-gr bullets had mild recoil with adequate ballistics.

Side arms have a more limited role for protection against charging grizzly bears. My reason for saying this is mainly because of the superior marksmanship required to hit a charging bear in the right places. Most experts agree that a .44 Magnum with 240-gr bullets has adequate close-range killing power in the hands of a well-practiced person who can handle its recoil.

Regardless of what firearm you choose, you must be thoroughly familiar with its mechanism and you must protect it from the effects of water, dirt, and twigs. When traveling in an area where bear hazard is anticipated, you should make sure the magazine of a rifle or shotgun is loaded. Normally a shell in the chamber is dangerous because of possible accidental discharge; however, imminent danger may justify putting a shell into the chamber, except perhaps with a side arm.

If you plan to travel armed and seriously consider trying to kill a charging grizzly bear, then you must be expert with your chosen firearm. The type of shooting that I have described is not hunting. It is self-defense shooting under extremely demanding conditions. Training should include shooting hundreds of rounds with the chosen firearm under a variety of conditions chosen to simulate field conditions. Accurate shooting should become something that you do almost without thinking. If possible, moving targets should be used. Accurate shooting under such conditions has been called "instinctive," because of the frequent lack of precise aim that is possible when hunting with telescopic sights and high-powered rifles. In the extreme, shotguns or rifles may be discharged while still at the hip rather than at shoulder level. The psychological impact of a charging grizzly is something difficult to simulate in training. In choosing whether and when to carry a firearm, each person must try to predict how he would behave if charged.

During the fall of 1979, Monte Adams, an experienced big-game hunter, was looking for mountain sheep in the mountains of southern Alberta. He entered a subalpine meadow where there was fresh sign of bears feeding on berries. What happened next is conjecture, because he was hunting alone, but it appeared that he was charged by a female grizzly who had cubs. It also appeared that he already had ammunition in the chamber of his rifle and that he jammed the rifle by trying to put another round into the chamber. He was badly mauled by the female grizzly, which, combined with a delayed rescue operation, caused his death.[33]

Three biologist colleagues of mine as well as myself have been involved in incidents in which charging grizzlies were shot, all at exceedingly close range. The first incident involved Dick Knight and Steve Judd, who were two of the principal researchers for the Yellowstone Regional Interagency grizzly bear study team. Dick and Steve led a party of four that had to pursue a radio-collared female grizzly with cubs, believed to be wounded, into dense bush. One could not imagine a more potentially dangerous situation. The biologists knew approximately where the bear was because she was wearing a radio-collar. Despite this, she charged them unexpectedly through the bush. She was first shot at about twelve feet using a twelve-gauge shotgun loaded with large-diameter buckshot. This slowed her charge enough that she was then killed with another shot.

The second situation occurred when Brian Pelchat, a biologist working for Alberta Fish and Wildlife, had sedated a female grizzly without cubs by using a new drug with which his party had little experience. The bear suddenly came out of the sedation, alert and aggressive. Brian, who was working with the bear, ran (the right reaction in this situation) and the bear pursued. A ranger who was at the site with a twelve-gauge shotgun (in case anything went wrong), shot and killed the bear with rifled slugs when the bear was only a few yards behind Brian.

I previously described an incident that I was involved in where Keith Brady, a park warden, shot and killed a charging female grizzly bear with a .338 Winchester when she was only eight or nine paces from us.

Firearms are sometimes essential for safety when doing research on grizzly bears and may increase the margin of safety for certain people working or recreating in grizzly bear habitat. However, without careful attempts to avoid confrontation, and without proper choice of firearm and training in its use, a firearm might endanger the user more than its absence would.

‾17‾

Bear Management

EFFECTIVE management of bears has to be guided by a clear concept of what the desired relationship between bears and people should be in a given area. An excellent example comes from Glacier National Park, Montana, in a brief policy statement in which the joint goals of conservation of bears and provision for human safety are recognized.[1]

Bear management policy is to maintain natural population dynamics, foster pristine habitat relationships, and encourage shyness as the characteristic behavior of bears in the presence of humans. Policy further recognizes that shyness may not be a completely natural behavior, but an artifact of selective pressures against undesirable traits over the past century. Selective pressures are considered to be removals of individual animals with inherent tendency toward aggressive conflict with humans.

Policy is implemented using behavioral science as the basis for management decisions. Behaviors classified as defensive will be considered natural with management response directed toward human use control. Behaviors classified as aggressive will be considered undesirable with management response directed toward bear removal. Opportunity for expression of either behavior will be minimized through park wide human use management. Tolerance of any behavior which leads to use of defined human use areas will be limited.

This is a clear statement that the park wants to maintain its bear populations so that bears exist as much as possible apart from direct

247

human influences. It is a tough policy because it recognizes that all sources of human food and garbage must be controlled, that particularly aggressive bears will be killed, and that the type of behavior evidenced by bears depends partly on managing the distribution and levels of human use. Most people would agree that natural bear populations are desirable in national parks, but some might hesitate at managing bear populations for certain traits, claiming that such bears are no longer wild. This may be a valid criticism, but selection by people against aggressive bears has been going on ever since people have had the weapons with which to kill bears. Experiments have shown that aggressive strains of mice can be selectively bred,[2] and anyone who has met a Doberman Pinscher under the wrong circumstances knows that some dog strains are more aggressive than others. We can and are selecting against particularly aggressive bears.

I have mentioned that the European brown bear is regarded as a member of the same species as is the grizzly bear. However, thousands of years of isolation in a somewhat different environment and with different selection pressures have created quite a different bear. In Europe the brown bear is smaller, shy of people, and much less aggressive toward people than its North American counterpart, the grizzly.[3] There are also very few brown bears left in Europe. Thousands of years of coexistence between Europeans and brown bears have left behind a race of bears that excel at avoiding people.

I am not suggesting that this is what we want in our wilderness parks in North America—bears molded to be able to adapt to large numbers of people. But even if the wilderness stays wild and the number of visitors is regulated, the unusual grizzly bear that cannot tolerate people closer than five hundred feet without attacking has been and will continue to be a doomed animal. Whether we like to admit it or not, we have been managing bear populations for certain behavioral traits and we will continue to do this in the future. The Glacier Park policy, which tries to allow a bear to defend itself when it feels threatened in the backcountry, represents an attempt to maintain wilderness and most of the characteristics of grizzly bears without encouraging bears that might be particularly dangerous to people.

Glacier Park officials also realize that not only are certain grizzlies inherently more aggressive than others but that all grizzlies habituated to people are dangerous to campers. Glacier has chosen to manage its bears both in regard to genetic predispositions and learned traits. This is a sophisticated and necessary approach to maintain "natural populations" of bears in wilderness areas.

UNRESOLVED MANAGEMENT QUESTIONS

Good management of bears and people prevents trouble rather than reacting to problems as they come. Some of the major issues and decisions related to human safety that face agencies and individuals responsible for managing bears and people are:

1. Where to locate trails and campgrounds and what use levels and types of use should be permitted.

Trails that pass through important habitat for bears increase the chances of encounters. Research on both black and grizzly bears has documented that as visitor trail use increases so do reported bear incidents.[4] The rate of injuries may not increase, however, even though the total number of injuries does.[5] Many of the trails and campsites in national park areas evolved at a time when park visitation and trail use were low. I have previously stressed that if we are to accommodate more and more people, and camping as well as hiking, this will require relocation and selective closure of certain trails to avoid large numbers of people using a trail at the same time that bears are frequenting the area through which the trail passes. New trails and relocated trail segments should avoid important bear habitat and, if it is necessary to route a trail through a bear area, trails should be designed so that people can see at least fifty-five yards ahead. These design criteria were followed in locating and building many of the trails in Alberta's new Kananaskis Country recreation area.[6]

The way people use trails is also important. In grizzly country the danger of a sudden encounter decreases if people are alert and cautious and if grizzlies know where to expect people. But modern back-country recreationalists are going further and faster. Cross-country travel is becoming increasingly popular, thus making people's activities less predictable to grizzlies and sudden encounters more probable. Also, in many areas people are now running or are riding mountain bikes in grizzly country. As well, cross-country skiers are out during a portion of the year when all grizzlies aren't in their dens. These activities, which are characterized by speed, not cautious attention to the possibility of encountering a bear, will probably soon be associated with grizzly bear inflicted injuries.

Campgrounds should be located away from seasonally important bear habitat to avoid habituation, the opportunity for feeding on human foods or garbage, and to decrease the chance of bears, especially grizzlies, entering camp at night, and in the worst cases preying on people. If separation is not desirable for other reasons, then protective sleeping compounds may have to be provided for tent campers, especially in grizzly bear habitat. This is now being done for backpackers whose route has them spending a night in grizzly country at Many Glacier, in Glacier National Park, Montana. There backpackers sleep inside a stockade made secure against all large mammals except human beings.

Detailed research into how bears use their environment will be required to achieve whatever is the desired degree of separation between bears and people. This knowledge is particularly important regarding grizzly bears that coexist with significant numbers of human recreationalists. Regulating the behavior of people may be the greatest challenge of all.

2. How to keep human foods and garbage away from bears.

I raise this question so often because of the clear relationship between human injury and both black and grizzly bears that have become accustomed to foraging for people's food. Somewhere in the process of doing this most bears also seem to lose much of their wariness of people. Aggressive tendencies are more likely to be shown.

The solution of making human foods unavailable to bears sounds simple, but it has proved to be one of the most difficult wildlife management challenges ever faced in North America. The problem is persistent because bears regularly find holes in the system. If all of the dumps are closed inside a park, then dumps outside a park, perhaps previously not so desirable because of low volumes of garbage, become primary targets. Most campers may learn how to foil bears by properly storing their foods, but a few careless people can create a bear that is dangerous to both careless and careful people alike. Also, bears may live for twenty to thirty years and they remember previous experience with food for a long time.

In some places small towns exist near bear habitat. This is the case with the Banff townsite in Banff National Park, where the garbage and bear problem has been recognized for over twenty years. However, the problems of garbage management in this town of about five thousand permanent residents, which serves millions of visitors a year, have led to many problem bears. I mentioned how in August of 1980 the availability of garbage attracted a large male grizzly that fatally mauled a visitor.[7] That year, in the vicinity of Banff, there were forty-eight black and fifteen grizzly bear relocations and eleven black and nine grizzly bears destroyed. This far exceeds acceptable levels. Yet the solution to this type of problem is clear: Store all human food and garbage so that bears cannot get at them. To achieve this, however, requires the cooperation and support of park managers, concessionaires, residents, and visitors.

A variety of bear-proof garbage-storage containers are now available, as is valuable information on how to keep camp food away from bears.[8] Much has also been learned about the timing and implementation of effective garbage-management systems. Glacier and Yellowstone Parks in the United States both now have very successful systems. The need to trap only a few bears each year is concrete evidence of their success. Given a high enough priority, backed with adequate funding, the food and garbage problem can be solved.

Food and garbage storage in bear country outside parks will be a problem for many years to come. Hunters, fishermen, trappers, rural residents, and people living in remote camps all have the potential to attract bears. Concern, education, assistance, and enforcement of regulations can all help to upgrade food and garbage storage in these situations.

3. What to do with problem bears.

No system is without fault. As long as we have people and bears, some bears will become dangerous nuisances and violate even the best-managed food- and garbage-storage systems. Over the past thirty years, an elaborate technology has evolved in North America in response to problem bears. Trap and transplant operations are as much a part of our campground culture as Coleman stoves and sleeping bags. Yet for the most part, the trapping and transplanting of bears should become a thing of the past as it becomes harder and harder for bears to find human foods or garbage.

Campgrounds should become places for people. Bears should not be attracted by food or garbage. Without these attractions they will soon stop coming. Those few bears who do end up in campgrounds should either be chased away or otherwise deterred by management personnel or be trapped and transplanted before becoming accustomed to feeding there.

Some problem black bears can be successfully relocated, depending on relocation distance, terrain and habitat factors, and the age, sex, and experience of the bear.[9] Relocation of black bears is difficult in small parks or areas. The grizzly is considerably harder to relocate. Because of its larger home range and the difficulty of finding suitable areas to take them to, transplanting grizzly bears is usually not much more than a holding action.[10]

Many a wildlife manager has wished that there were some way to re-educate a bear that has become used to feeding on human foods and to convince it to do otherwise. The idea of "negative conditioning" is popular today. Using this technique the bear is supposed to suffer somewhat whenever it tries to get at food or garbage. I've mentioned the use of techniques ranging from shooting bears with noninjurious but painful rubber bullets to spraying bears with repellents containing cayenne pepper. Experiments to date all point in the same direction. A variety of negative treatments will help to repel a bear if it never has had any experience with getting human food or garbage, but once a habit of feeding on garbage (or beehives, orchard fruit, or back-packers' food) has developed, then it is exceedingly hard to break. Bears learn to avoid specific situations, such as wardens or rangers in uniform who might administer a deterrent,[11] but they do not avoid the general situation of roadside feeding, for example, because overall it leads to food rewards.

Unfortunately I think that negative conditioning of bears can only be an important management technique for bears that have not yet developed habits that involve people and our food. I mentioned that grizzly (brown) bears in the campground near McNeil River Falls in Alaska are either chased out or if they persist they may be shot non-injuriously but painfully in the hindquarters with birdshot. This is one of the few situations in which negative conditioning has been demonstrated to work in keeping bears away from places designed strictly for people. It works because the campground is small and the manager is strict in never letting a bear into camp and in enforcing garbage- and food-storage rules.

For a long while campground-foraging bears were trapped and in some instances two, three, or even four attempts were made to relocate them. Today conditions are hardening. Parks are for the most part trying to be more successful in making food and garbage unavailable to bears. At the same time bears that become accustomed to feeding on these sources and also act aggressively toward people are dealt with less tolerantly. Often they are killed rather than being transplanted. This can be seen as part of the overall idea of managing bear populations with selection against aggression toward people.

A related issue is the prevalent view among some people that just trapping and drugging a bear can turn it into a more aggressive individual even in the absence of problems with human foods. How-ever, bears must be trapped, drugged, and marked in order to carry out biological research, which is necessary for management. There is no evidence that this makes either grizzlies or black bears more dan-gerous to people, and there is some evidence that it doesn't.[12] One exception is the brief period when a bear, especially a grizzly, is recovering from having been drugged.[13]

4. How to communicate essential information about bears effectively to people.

"You are in bear country," "Bear facts,"—today there are few parks in bear country that do not provide visitors with a pamphlet describing the basics of safety around bears. However, a study carried out in Yosemite National Park found that 92 percent of the backcountry users stated that they stored their food properly, whereas only 3 percent actually did so.[14] This disparity suggests that park managers and interpreters will have to develop better communication systems to educate and motivate the people who visit bear country. Pamphlets, books, films, personal contact and instruction, closed-circuit audio, interpretive lectures and shows—all of these techniques and more should be used to inform people about bears.

Enforcement of regulations must accompany attempts to educate people about what is right in bear country. Communicating essential information about bears will not solve all problems. Some people choose to ignore or purposely act contrary to what others tell them is the right way to do things. Such people's actions can lead to injury to themselves and others and can also lead to bears having to be killed.

5. Is hunting of bears necessary or desirable to make bears reasonably safe for people?

This question has been raised particularly regarding grizzly bears. Hunting most species results in animals that avoid people, at least during the hunting season. Unhunted populations usually accept people at closer distances before fleeing. Hunting is one potential means of changing grizzly bear behavior so that surviving bears avoid people. This may or may not increase overall safety because of the obvious danger to hunters and the possible danger from wounded bears and from the hunters themselves.

One purpose of most national parks and similar reserves in North America is to maintain all animal populations without hunting. Accepting this objective as related to the potentially dangerous grizzly bear implies intensive management of people and grizzly bears. Katherine McArthur Jope's research on grizzly bears in Glacier Park, Montana, implies that grizzlies habituated to people and thus fairly often close to them aren't necessarily more dangerous to hikers.[15] Such bears, after an initial period of confrontation when first experiencing hikers, may come to ignore the predictable disturbance of hikers on trails. Such bears, having lost their fear of man, may, however, be the kind of bear that is more likely to enter a quiet backcountry camp and once there attack someone. More research is needed to convince me that such habituated bears are acceptably safe for hikers. I'm convinced they are dangerous for campers.

If we want to have both grizzly bears that regularly flee from people and also have high levels of human recreational use but no hunting, then we might try to mimic some of the effects of hunting. Repellents might be applied to bears when they first experience people. The question is, do we want to condition grizzly bears to avoid people? Is this to be the grizzly's fate in its last sanctuaries in the contiguous United States? If we were successful we might drive grizzlies away from important habitat, causing possible population decline. Since the grizzly is classified as a threatened species in the lower forty-eight states under the terms of the Endangered Species Act, it is questionable whether using deterrents that decreased grizzly populations would be legal. A combination of research to tell us what is

Large male grizzly bear killed by a bus near Lake Louise, 1978, Banff National Park. *Stephen Herrero*

possible and a lot of soul-searching to help us decide what is desirable will be needed to resolve these issues.

SAFETY FOR BEARS TOO

If a book titled *People Attacks* were written for bears, it could only depict our species as being typically bloodthirsty killers—aggressive, dangerous, often inflicting fatal injury to bears. Since the arrival of Europeans in North America, the grizzly bear has been shot, trapped, poisoned, and had extensive portions of its habitat converted into ranch land, housing, highways, and recreational playgrounds. The grizzly's population has dwindled from an estimated one hundred thousand to probably fewer than one thousand in the contiguous United States.[16]

Even grizzlies that spend much of their time in sanctuaries free from hunting are eventually killed by people. For grizzlies trapped, marked, and studied in Jasper National Park, Dick Russell and his colleagues found that seven out of eight cases of known mortality were directly caused by wardens, poachers, or hunters inside or outside the park. The total known mortality was 25 percent of the marked population.[17]

In Yellowstone National Park, in order to wean grizzly bears from garbage feeding and campground foraging, it was necessary to kill five grizzlies during 1968, ten in 1969, twelve in 1970, and six in 1971.[18] The total mortality in the Yellowstone ecosystem during this period may have been much higher. The Craigheads and Joel Varney believe that twenty-one grizzlies died in 1968, twenty-three in 1969, and fifty-three in 1970.[19] Almost all mortalities were caused by man. The Craighead research team thought that if population trends set in motion by these actions continued, the grizzly could possibly become extinct in Yellowstone. The grizzlies in the Yellowstone ecosystem apparently recovered from this population low in the early 1970s. Today, however, they may be threatened again. The current Yellowstone research team, headed by Dick Knight, estimated in 1981 that a minimum of 197 grizzlies survived in the Yellowstone ecosystem. Despite protection under the Endangered Species Act, as many as fifteen grizzlies died during 1981 and as many as seventeen died in 1982.[20] Through 1982, of ninety-seven radio-collared grizzlies, thirty-seven were known or suspected to be dead; thirty-one deaths (84%) were man-caused.[21]

With the development of most of North America, the grizzly bear did not flee to the mountains, as some people believe, but stayed and was killed in most places where it lived, surviving only in those portions of North America that are most remote and difficult to develop.

Grizzly bear populations cannot sustain high mortality rates and survive. Species that during the course of their evolution were frequently preyed on by other species or that were frequently decimated by environmental conditions generally evolved high reproductive rates if they survived. The grizzly was and still is another kind of animal. It has one of the lowest reproductive rates of any land mammal in North America.[22] It has few young and generally takes good care of them. Adult grizzlies, free from human influences, may live twenty to thirty years. Another reason why grizzly bears can't sustain high mortality is that they occur in low population densities compared to most other species. Typically a large area of land is needed to support one grizzly bear. The actual size depends on how productive the land is. In the Yukon, research suggests that an annual hunting kill of 2 to 3 percent is all that can be sustained without probable population decline.[23] This has often been exceeded even in some of the supposed sanctuaries of national parks where grizzlies are found.[24]

Since we have had difficulty in regulating the kill of grizzly bears in strictly protected areas, it should not be surprising that sustained yield hunting outside of parks and reserves has been an even more difficult objective to achieve. The grizzly is a highly valued trophy animal, the hunting of which can generate expenditures of many thousands of dollars. Yet opportunities to hunt grizzlies are limited by the bear's inability to survive with more than modest levels of killing. Very few grizzly populations have ever been substantially hunted without population decline. An exception to this may be the grizzly (brown) bear population on Admiralty, Baranof, and Chichagof Islands in southeastern Alaska.[25] New management strategies, such as late fall hunts that select for killing male bears (since females enter dens earlier), may help to achieve the goal of hunting without population decline.[26]

One of the greatest difficulties we face in attempting to maintain grizzly bear populations and monitor their mortality is our inability to estimate how many grizzly bears there are in a given area. Since the early 1970s Dick Knight and his colleagues have tried to estimate the grizzly bear population in the Yellowstone ecosystem. They want to determine how much mortality this population can stand from all sources and maintain itself. Despite the expenditure of about $200,000 a year to answer these and related questions, a point estimate of the population couldn't be made until 1981.

Somehow we have to learn not only how to count grizzly bears, given sufficient money to capture and mark many animals, but also how to estimate numbers when lesser funds and no marked animals are available. Clearly we will be dealing with crude estimates. If they are too crude, then the grizzly could vanish from the contiguous United States while the bear biologists are still debating how to count them.

If mortality is not excessive, then all the grizzly needs to survive is adequate habitat to support a population big enough to withstand year-to-year fluctuations. A computer simulation of grizzly bear population dynamics indicated that populations of fewer than fifty to ninety (depending on age and sex of bears) occupying less than 391 to 5,270 square miles (depending on habitat quality) have less than a 95 percent chance of surviving one hundred years.[27]

Any population depends on adequate habitat. Almost everywhere, grizzly bear habitat is threatened because it is subject to multiple use of one kind or another. In national parks, grizzly country is also used for recreational activities, roads, and facility development. These developments usually require fire suppression. The self-regeneration of the habitat is altered wherever natural fire regimes are significantly changed by fire suppression.[28] Good grizzly bear habitat is often related to diverse vegetation mosaics caused by a combination of natural fire regimes and mountainous terrain.[29]

Outside national parks the grizzly has to compete with livestock, forestry, fire suppression, mineral-, oil-, and gas-related activities, road building, hunting, housing, and recreation. For the grizzly to survive outside national parks will require well-researched and clearly articulated management plans that attempt to spell out what the effects will be on grizzly bear populations as a result of different logging strategies, different hunting regulations, and various other types of developments. Such a set of guidelines has been developed for the National Forest Lands, which surround Yellowstone National Park and support grizzly bears.[30]

We may choose not to try to maintain the grizzly bear everywhere it still exists. My hope is that further restrictions in the grizzly's range will be the result of rational decisions made by considering the value of having grizzly bears versus the value of other land-use options. To let them die out through carelessness and lack of concern would be a sad loss of a species that has fired human imagination for thousands of years and that today has come to symbolize wilderness, the challenge of the frontier that shaped our culture, and the challenge of maintaining wildlife in the future.

We have been more successful in learning to live with the black bear than with the grizzly. Although the same history of hunting, poisoning, trapping, and habitat alteration has occurred for the black bear, it has survived in most places. At least three factors are responsible for this: The black bear typically occurs at higher population densities than the grizzly; the black bear usually has a higher reproductive rate than the grizzly; and the black bear is more tolerant and better able to coexist with people. Despite fairly high mortality rates, the black bear normally survives provided that its primary habitat, the forest, exists. Most studies of black bear mortality suggest that they have maximum sustainable mortality rates ranging from approximately 12 to 18 percent.[31] The black bear's future looks reasonably bright.

WHAT IS A BEAR WORTH?

The decisions we make about how we will manage bears depend on our attitudes and values related to bears. Because black and grizzly bears did and will continue to inflict occasional serious injury to people, they must create benefits for other people to counterbalance the trauma that they bring to a few.

In all of the more populated areas where either black or grizzly bears are found, their survival rests on a conscious decision to let them live. If, for example, we decided to extirpate the grizzly bear from the Yellowstone ecosystem, we clearly have the technological ability to kill them, although it might take a few years and a lot of hunting, trapping, or poisoning. Whether we can maintain them in places such as Yellowstone is less certain because it means giving up opportunities for trail and facility development in some places and regulating the amount of human recreational use of others. Currently, however, the situation is modestly hopeful.

For some people the idea of saving anything as potentially dangerous as the grizzly bear is wrong. Biologists like Gardiner Moment have written articles urging that grizzly bears be extirpated from heavily used national parks such as Yellowstone and Glacier.[32] An old-timer in Banff Park, who likes to bait conservationists, is fond of saying, "We've gotten along fine without dinosaurs for millions of years and we could do just fine without the grizzly." And I think that he is right, for we are an adaptable species, and our future does not rest directly on that of the grizzly or any other bear.

Neither the grizzly nor the black bear plays a critical role in ecosystem functioning. The grizzly and black bear are ecological generalists much like we are. They may function as a grazer, browser, scavenger, or predator. Occasionally bear predation may influence the population dynamics of other species such as elk or moose.³³ But, if we killed all bears there would be no ecosystem collapse.

But for many of us the world would be a poorer place without bears. We keep bears not because they are an essential part of nature but because of what they do for the human mind, body, and soul. We track them through wood and swamp in search of a black bear rug to rest before a fireplace. We curse the same species when it eats all of our delicious, ripe garden strawberries, but we also seize the challenge and plan how to have both strawberries and bears the next year. Our feelings are shattered when we find out that a bear has killed or seriously maimed someone, and for me there is always the knowledge that this would not have happened if there were no bears. So why do we keep them, especially the grizzly, which is now so close to extirpation from the contiguous United States that it would not take much to reduce them to only memories of a wilder, less controlled past?

We maintain grizzly bears because there is no other animal in North America that drives our imagination as does the great bear. Anyone who chooses to travel on foot unarmed in grizzly country has accepted a potentially dangerous challenge. True, the chances of injury from a grizzly are very low, but still few people travel on foot in the grizzly's home without thinking about what they will do if they see one. All bear tracks, droppings, scratchings, even a few hairs, become clues that a grizzly may be around. You ask yourself, how old is the sign? What does it mean? Was it made by a grizzly or a black bear? Suddenly the wilderness comes alive, and you may discover that the essence of wilderness is the challenge it gives us to use our common sense to look after ourselves and our friends in an environment where the supports of civilization are few.

If you see a grizzly you instantly become one of the few who have shared moments with the species that cannot adapt to the domestication of North America, the species that defines one of the few types of wilderness we have left. Feelings of fear, inspiration, and awe may generate images of pristine North America when it was complete with bison and wolves and when man was still a pioneer treading on the edge of something big and rich beyond definition. But images of mauled and mutilated people may also enter your mind, for this too is a part of the grizzly.

Most people, I believe, are willing to accept the slight chance of injury in order to maintain both species of bears. Several public opinion polls have shown that only a few people out of a hundred want the grizzly destroyed.³⁴ A survey of 119 people who suffered either property damage (105) or injury (16) from black bears in Great Smoky Mountains National Park revealed only one person who thought black bears shouldn't be in the park.[35]

We shall probably choose to coexist with the black bear, and even the grizzly bear, in many of the areas where these bears are still found. Natural populations of grizzly bears, unhabituated to people and feeding as they have for thousands of years on products of their natural environment, will become a sign that at least somewhere there is still genuine wilderness. Where the black bear survives, people will know that there is a forest with room enough not only for some tree harvesting and clearing for home and farm but also for wild things.

In learning to coexist with black and grizzly bears, we will need to develop not only more efficient resource and people management but we shall also have to change some of our attitudes and expectations. Wild bears should not be regarded as our friends. They are too dangerous and too powerful to semi-tame. They exist in a world of their own where biological evolution has left them adapted to survive the vicissitudes of nature but not some of the ways of man. Neither black nor grizzly bear should be a part of our campground environment, nor should they be fed along roadsides. The days of the bear-feeding shows in national parks are gone, but some people still expect bears to perform for them in exchange for scraps and tidbits.

Coexistence should come to mean that bears and people jointly use some of the same environments but, to the greatest possible extent, that bears live without exploitation of our foods. Mutual avoidance, which in human terms means mutual respect, is a desirable end state. We need a sort of standoff between bears and people rather than the petting, feeding, and garbage eating that have characterized the past in some of our parks.

If we can learn to live with bears, especially the grizzly, and if we can learn to accommodate the needs of bears in their natural environment, then maybe we can also find ways to use the finite resources of our continent and still maintain some of the diversity and natural beauty that were here when Columbus arrived.

Notes

Introduction

1. Herrero, Stephen. 1970. Human injury inflicted by grizzly bears. Science 170: 593–598.
2. The circumstances regarding the grizzly bear-inflicted death of Wilf Etherington are documented in reports prepared for Parks Canada by A. S. Anderson, then Chief Warden for Banff National Park, and M. Rose, Acting Area Resource Manager.
3. My sources of information regarding Barrie Gilbert's mauling were reports prepared for Yellowstone Park by Bruce Hastings and Mary Meagher, and a report by and conversations with Barrie Gilbert.
4. Herrero, Stephen. 1983. Social behavior of black bears at a garbage dump in Jasper National Park. Pages 54–70 in E. Charles Meslow, ed. 5th International Conference on bear research and management. International Association for Bear Research and Management, publisher.
5. Hamer, David and Stephen Herrero (eds.). 1983. Ecological studies of the grizzly bear in Banff National Park. Final report. Report prepared for Parks Canada, Western Regional Office, Calgary, Alberta, 303pp.
6. Herrero, Stephen, Wayne McCrory, and Brian Pelchat. In press. The application of grizzly bear habitat evaluation to trail and campsite locations in Kananaskis Provincial Park, Alberta. To be published in: Proceedings, 6th International Conference on bear research and management, 1983.
7. The final report on this work is being prepared for 1985 for the Western Regional Office of Parks Canada, Calgary, Alberta. It will be titled: Studies of grizzly bears, Waterton Lakes National Park by David Hamer, Stephen Herrero and Keith Brady.

Chapter 1 | GRIZZLY BEAR ATTACKS

1. Kelsey, Henry. 1929. The Kelsey Papers. Public Archives of Canada and The Public Record Office of Northern Ireland. Ottawa, 128pp.
2. Twaites, Reuben Gold. (ed.). 1959. Original journals of the Lewis and Clark Expedition 1804–1806. Antiquarian Press Ltd. New York. 7 Volumes and atlas.
3. Ibid. p.303, Vol. I.
4. Ewers, John C. 1958. The Blackfeet-Raiders on the northwestern plains, Univ. of Oklahoma Press, Norman, p.85.
5. Twaites, R.G. Op. cit. p.29, Vol.III.
6. Ibid. p.351, Vol.I.
7. Ibid. p.25, Vol.II.
8. Storer, Tracy I. and Lloyd P. Tevis, Jr. 1955. California grizzly. Univ. of Calif. Press, Berkeley and Los Angeles, p.216.
9. Ibid. p.26.
10. Ibid. pp.29–30.
11. Macey, Anne. 1979. The status of the grizzly bear (*Ursus arctos horribilis*) in Canada. Nat'l Museum of Sciences, Ottawa, 54pp. and appendices.
12. This point is hard to study and document. See, however: Knight, Richard. 1981. Notes on some behavior patterns in radio-instrumented grizzly bears. Interagency Grizzly Bear Research Team, Bozeman, Montana, 10pp. Unpublished.
13. Singer, Francis J. 1982. Problem analysis—Grizzly bear management in Denali National Park. National Park Service, Anchorage, 41pp. unpublished. In this paper Singer showed that between 1972 and 1981 parties of one or two formed 29% and

261

47% of all backcountry parties. Parties of one were particularly vulnerable to injury, receiving 57% of all injuries. Parties of two received 29%.

14. Brown, Robert and Larry Kaniut. Undated. Mauling victims. Alaska Dept. of Public Safety, Anchorage. 7pps. Unpublished.
15. Martinka, C.J. 1982. Rationale and options for management in grizzly bear sanctuaries. Paper presented to: 47th North American Wildlife and Natural Resources Conference, Portland. 15pp.
16. Kaniut, Larry. 1983. Alaska bear tales. Alaska Northwest Publishing Company, Anchorage. p.251.
17. Ibid. pp.71–72.
18. Martinka, C.J. Op. cit.
19. Meagher, Mary and Jerry R. Phillips. 1983. Restoration of natural populations of grizzly and black bears in Yellowstone Park. Yellowstone Nat'l. Park, Mammoth, 17pp. + figures. Unpublished.
20. Herrero, Stephen. 1976. Conflicts between Man and grizzly bears in the national parks of North America. Pages 121–145 *in* M. Pelton, J.W. Lentfer, and G.E. Folk (eds.). Third International Conference on bear research and management. I.U.C.N. New Series No. 40, Morges, Switzerland.

21. Ibid. pp.140–141.

Chapter 2 | SUDDEN ENCOUNTERS WITH GRIZZLIES

1. My source of information for the death of Barbara Chapman and the mauling of Andrew Stepniewski was the files of Glacier/Revelstoke National Parks, Canada.
2. Kaniut, Larry. 1983. Alaska bear tales. Alaska Northwest Publishing Company, Anchorage. p.91.
3. My sources regarding Bruce Gilbert's mauling were reports prepared for Yellowstone Park by Bruce Hastings and Mary Meagher, and a report by and conversations with Bruce Gilbert.
4. Ibid.
5. The point is hard to study and document. See, however: Knight, Richard. 1981. Notes on some behavior patterns in radio-instrumented grizzly bears. Interagency Grizzly Bear Research Team, Bozeman, Montana, 10pp. Unpublished.
6. Clifford J. Martinka, Chief Research Biologist, Glacier National Park, Montana, was the first to use the term "defense reaction." It is a good description of the situation.
7. Egbert, Allen L. 1978. The social behavior of brown bears at McNeil River, Alaska. Ph.D. thesis, Utah State University, Logan. 117pp.
8. My source of information for this incident comes from a letter which Judy Donaldson, one of the people mauled, wrote to me. Ms. Donaldson was a graduate student in Zoology at the Univ. of British Columbia, Vancouver, when this incident occurred.
9. My source of information for this incident comes from a detailed letter which Dr. Ian Stirling sent me. Dr. Stirling is a research biologist with the Canadian Wildlife Service, Edmonton, Alta.
10. Kaniut, L. Op. cit.
11. Lamb, W. Kaye (ed.). 1960. *Simon Fraser* Letters and journals, 1806–1808. MacMillan Co. of Canada Ltd., Toronto, pp.225–226.
12. J.S. Hittel. 1863. The resources of California. . . San Francisco, 464pp. As cited in: Storer, Tracey I. and Lloyd P. Tevis, Jr. 1955. California grizzly. Univ. of Calif. Press, Berkeley and Los Angeles, p.213.
13. This point is hard to study and document. See, however: Knight, Richard. 1981. Notes on some behavior patterns in radio-instrumented grizzly bears. Interagency Grizzly Bear Research Team, Bozeman, Montana, 10pp. Unpublished.
14. Hamer, David, Stephen Herrero and Keith Brady. 1981. The grizzly bear in Wa-

terton Lakes National Park. Report prepared for: Western Regional Office, Parks Canada, Calgary, Alberta. 51pp.
15. My source of information for this incident comes from a hospital interview which Martha McCallum and I conducted with the Janz's. I subsequently wrote up and submitted this interview to Waterton Park.
16. My source of information for this incident comes from a hospital interview which I conducted with Kelly Joakim.
17. Kaniut, L. Op. cit.
18. This information was given to me by John Craighead during July, 1968. Dr. Craighead is currently director of the Wildlife and Wildlands Institute, Missoula, Mont.
19. My source of information was the files of Glacier National Park, Montana.
20. United States Department of Health and Human Services. Public Health Service. Office of Health Research, Statistics and Technology. National Centre for Health Statistics. "Vital Statistics," Vol. 2—Mortality Part B. Hyattsville, Maryland.

Chapter 3 | PROVOKED ATTACKS

1. Kaniut, Larry. 1983. Alaska bear tales. Alaska Northwest Publishing Company, Anchorage. 318pp.
2. Ibid.
3. Ibid. pp.68–70.
4. Hahn, Robert. 1968. As quoted in the *Lethbridge Herald*, Alberta, Canada, 3 June.
5. Letter from Cliff Martinka to me dated 17 July 1970. Mr. Martinka is currently the supervisory research biologist in Glacier National Park, Montana.
6. Russell, Andy. 1967. Grizzly Country. Alfred A. Knopf, New York. 302pp.

   Crawford, John. 1980. Wolves, bears and bighorns. Alaska Northwest Publishing Company, Anchorage. 175pp.
7. My source of information for this incident was the Mt. McKinley (now Denali) National Park files.
8. Kaniut, L. Op. cit. pp.58–61.
9. The circumstances regarding the grizzly bear-inflicted death of Wilf Etherington are documented in reports prepared for Parks Canada by A. S. Anderson, then Chief Warden for Banff National Park, and M. Rose, Acting Area Resource Manager.
10. This point is hard to study and document. See, however: Knight, Richard. 1981. Notes on some behavior patterns in radio-instrumented grizzly bears. Interagency Grizzly Bear Research Team, Bozeman, Montana, 10pp. Unpublished.

    Also Dick Russell, Canadian Wildlife Service, Edmonton, Alberta, has drugged several hundred grizzly, black and polar bears, primarily with Sernylan. He reports that bears after drugging are more wary of people.

Chapter 4 | THE DANGERS OF GARBAGE AND HABITATION

1. Herrero, Stephen. 1970. Human injury inflicted by grizzly bears. Science 170: 593–598.

   Herrero, Stephen. 1976. Conflicts between man and grizzly bears in the national parks of North America. Pages 121–145 *in* M. Pelton, J.W. Lentfer, and G.E. Folk, eds. Third International Conference on bear research and management, I.U.C.N. New Series No. 40, Morges, Switzerland.

2. Scientific study of this idea has not been done. I consider it to be a reasonable inference from talking to and reading the reports of persons using radiotelemetry to study grizzly bears.

3. Herrero, Stephen. Op. cit.
4. Ibid.
5. Schullery, Paul. 1980. The bears on Yellowstone. Yellowstone Library and Museum Association, Wyoming. 176pp.
6. This work is headed by Dr. Richard Knight, who is leader of the Interagency Grizzly Bear Research Team, Bozeman, Montana.
7. My source of information for this incident was the files of Yellowstone National Park, Wyoming.
8. Personal communication from Mr. Cliff Martinka, Supervisory Research Biologist, Glacier National Park, Montana.
9. Glacier National Park. Undated. Grizzly bear attacks at Granite Park and Trout Lake in Glacier National Park, August 13, 1967. U.S. Dept. of Interior, National Park Service, 22pp.
10. Correspondence found in files of Glacier National Park, Montana.
11. Moving a person's body from the scene of an attack is typically what occurs in attacks that I believe were motivated by predation.
12. Olsen, Jack. 1969. Night of the grizzlies. Signet Books, New American Library Inc., New York, 175pp.
13. Glacier National Park. Op. cit.
14. Ashley, Kenneth. Chairman, Board of Inquiry. Undated. Findings of Board of Inquiry regarding death of Mary Patricia Mahoney, Glacier National Park, September 23, 1976. United States Dept. of Interior, National Park Service, 7pp.
15. My source of information for this incident was the files of Banff National Park, Alberta.
16. Ashley, Kenneth. Chairman, Board of Inquiry. Undated. Fatal grizzly bear maulings of Kim Eberly and Jane Ammerman, July 24, 1980. United States Dept. of Interior, National Parks Service, 10pp.
17. Ibid.
18. Russell, R.H., J.W. Nolan, N.G. Woody, and G.H. Anderson. 1979. A study of the grizzly bear in Jasper National Park 1975 to 1978. Final report. Prepared for Parks Canada by the Canadian Wildlife Service, Edmonton, Alta. 136pp.
19. Jope, Katherine Louise McArthur. 1982. Interactions between grizzly bears and hikers in Glacier National Park, Montana. M.Sc. thesis, Oregon State Univ., 100pp.
20. Jope, Katherine Louise McArthur. Ibid.
21. Ashley, Kenneth. Chairman, Board of Review. Undated. Probable fatal grizzly bear mauling of Lawrence Byron Gordon, September 26 or 27, 1980. United States Dept. of Interior, National Parks Service, 7pp.
22. Letter from Katherine McArthur-Jope to myself. Ms. McArthur is currently a research biologist at Katmai National Park, Alaska.
23. Hubbard, George, Richard Knight, Christopher Serveen, Gary Brown, and Ken Gallik. Undated. Final report, Grizzly bear—Roger May Incident, June 25, 1983. United States Dept. of Interior. 6pp. + appendices.
24. Telephone conversation with Dr. Mary Meagher, Research Biologist, Yellowstone National Park, Wyoming.
25. Yellowstone National Park. Draft report on case incident number 842913, Brigitta Fredenhagen, July 30, 1984. United States Dept. of Interior, unpaginated.
26. Telephone conversation with Dr. Mary Meagher, Research Biologist, Yellowstone National Park, Wyoming.
27. Yellowstone National Park. Op. cit.
28. Ibid.

Chapter 5 | OTHER ATTACKS

1. One of the first things a scientist learns is that just because two events are correlated doesn't mean that one causes the other. To see if causality exists scientists conduct

experiments where they systematically change one or a few situations and note responses. We can't do this regarding bear attacks. Instead we have to look at records of attacks and try to infer causal circumstances. The problem is further complicated because a circumstance, such as habituation, may only lead to attack in a grizzly bear having a certain personality and a specific opportunity.

2. Norm Woodie sent a copy of his daily log to me. Mr. Woodie is currently a warden in Jasper National Park, Alberta.

3. Cramond, Mike. 1981. Killer bears. Outdoor Life Books, New York, Charles Scribner's Sons, New York. 301pp. + appendix.

4. Ibid.

5. My source of information for this incident was the files of Kluane National Park, Yukon Territory.

6. Glacier Bay National Monument. 1976. Case incident record number 760016. United States Dept. of Interior. 1p. + 2 supplementary pp.

Kaniut, Larry. 1983. Alaska bear tales. Alaska Northwest Publishing Co., Anchorage. 318pp.

7. Glacier Bay National Monument. Op cit.

8. Kaniut, Larry. Op. cit.

Chapter 6 | AGGRESSION WITHOUT INJURY

1. In the remainder of the 135 non-injurious encounters the person's preceding activity was either unknown (19%, 26 out of 135 cases) or was classified as "other" (19%, 25 of 135 cases).

2. My source of information for this incident was a letter to me from Chris Dunkley. Mr. Dunkley is currently retired and lives in Calgary, Alberta.

3. My source of information for this incident was one of my "Bear–human aggressive encounter questionnaires" filled out by Jenny Clark. At the time this incident occurred Ms. Clark was a naturalist in Jasper National Park, Alberta.

Chapter 7 | THE TOLERANT BLACK BEAR

1. Jonkel, C.J. and F.L. Miller. 1970. Recent records of black bears (*Ursus americanus*) on the barren grounds of Canada. J. Mamm. 51 (4): 826–828.

Graber, David Murray. 1982. Ecology and management of black bears in Yosemite National Park. Coop. National Park Resources Studies Unit, Univ. Calif., Davis 202pp. + appendices.

2. Seton, Ernest Thompson as referenced in Ben East. 1977. Bears. Book Division, Times Mirror Magazines, Inc. p.53.

3. Seton's figure was based on no concrete information regarding the large numbers of black bears in western North America.

4. Rob-and-run tactics were particularly prevalent in the back-country of Yosemite National Park during the 1970s.

5. My source of information for this incident was the files of Yellowstone National Park, Wyoming.

6. Eager, Jane Tate and Michael R. Pelton. 1979. Panhandler black bears in the Great Smoky Mountains National Park. Report presented to: United States Park Service, Southeast Region. 176pp. + appendix.

7. Singer, Francis J. and Susan Power Bratton. 1980. Black bear/human conflicts in the Great Smoky Mountains National Park. Pages 137–140 *in* C.J. Martinka and K.L. McArthur, eds. Fourth International Conference on bear research and management. Bear Biology Association, publishers.

8. Harms, Dale R. 1980. Black bear management in Yosemite. Pages 205–212 *in* C.J. Martinka and K.L. McArthur, eds. Fourth International Conference on, bear research and management. Bear Biology Association, publishers.

9. Ibid.
10. Ibid.
11. My source of information for this incident came from the files of Yellowstone National Park, Wyoming.
12. East, Ben. 1977. Bears. Book Division, Times-Mirror Magazines, Inc. p.53.
13. Erickson, Albert W., John Nellor, and George A. Petrides. 1964. The black bear in Michigan. Research Bulletin 4, Michigan State University, Agric. Experimental Station, East Lansing, Michigan. 102pp.
14. Harger, E.M. 1970. A study of homing behavior of black bears. M.Sc. thesis, Northern Michigan University, Marquette. 81pp.
15. I received this information in a letter from Dr. Lynn Rogers, a research biologist with the U.S. Forest Service, Ely, Minnesota.
16. Singer, Francis J. and Susan Power Bratton. Op. cit.
17. Cardoza, James E. 1976. The history and status of the black bear in Massachusetts and adjacent New England States. Research Bull. No. 18, Mass. Div. of Fisheries and Wildlife, Westborough. pp.69–70.
18. East, Ben. Op. cit.
19. Ibid.

Chapter 8 | THE PREDACEOUS BLACK BEAR

1. Whitlock, S.C. 1950. The black bear as a predator of man. J. Mammal: 31(2): 135–138.

2. Hurn, D.R. Sept. 2nd, 1976. Memorandum to the Honorable the Minister. Subject: Black bear attack on child. British Columbia Fish and Wildlife. 1p.

3. My source of information regarding this incident was the files of Jasper National Park, Alberta.

   In addition to the death that occurred in Jasper National Park, another death occurred in Glacier Bay National Monument, Alaska. In early August, 1980, Thomas Schulz, age 27, was attacked and killed by a black bear at Sandy Cove in an apparent act of predation.

4. Anon. Aug. 30, 1971. Special incident report—Bear slaying and hunt. Nat'l Park Service, Rocky Mountain Nat'l. Park, and Shadow Mountain National Recreation Area, unpaginated.

5. Kaniut, Larry. 1983. Alaska bear tales. Alaska Northwest Publishing Company, Anchorage. 318pp.

6. Bechard, R.J. July 4, 1979. Girl attacked by bear (Karen Austrom). Occurrence report, No. 79-0738, Royal Canadian Mounted Police, British Columbia, unpaginated + appendices.

7. Ellis, Martin Dwight. August 15, 1980. Statement to Royal Canadian Mounted Police, British Columbia.

8. Kruuk, Hans. 1972. The spotted hyena: A study of predation and social behavior. Univ. of Chicago Press, Chicago and London, 335pp.

9. One source of information for this incident was a letter to me dated July 6, 1978 from Mr. J.A. Simpson, Park Superintendent and District Manager, Algonquin Park District, Ontario.

   Crammond, Mike. 1981. Killer bears. Outdoor Life Books, New York, Charles Scribner's Sons, New York. 301pp. + appendix.
10. Crammond, Mike. Ibid.
11. Ibid.
12. My source of information for these incidents was a letter to me dated October 26, 1983 from Mr. Hugh H. Hunt, Wildlife Branch, Saskatchewan Parks and Renewable Resources.
13. Rogers, Lynn. 1976. Effects of mast and berry crop failures on survival, growth,

and reproductive success of black bears. Trans. N. Amer. Wildl. and Nat. Resources Conf. 41: 431–438.

14. Hatler, David Francis. 1967. Some aspects in the ecology of the black bear (*Ursus americanus*) in interior Alaska. Master's thesis, Univ. of Alaska, Fairbanks. 111pp.

15. Worley, David E., Kenneth R. Greer, and Dan Palmisciano. 1983. Possible relationships between trichinellosis and abnormal behavior in bears. Pages 280–283 *in* E. Charles Meslow, ed. Fifth International Conference on bear research and management. International Association for Bear Research and Management, publishers.

16. My source of information for data was a letter to me dated June 30, 1981, from Mr. John O'Pezio, black bear specialist, New York State Dept. of Environmental Conservation.

17. Larry Reimer, as described in chapter 8, was one person who knifed and killed an attacking black bear. Larry Kaniut. Op. cit. p.220 describes another knife killing as well as the use of a small boulder to kill a black bear.

Chapter 9 | AVOIDING ENCOUNTERS

1. This film is available on loan from National Film Board outlets across Canada.

2. Harms, Dale R. 1980. Black bear management in Yosemite. Pages 205–212 *in* C.J. Martinka and K.L. McArthur, eds. Fourth International Conference on, Bears— Their biology and management. Bear Biology Associaton, publishers.

3. My source of information for this incident was a conversation with Mr. Keith Brady, Warden Service, Waterton Lakes National Park, Alberta. Mr. Brady did some of the on-site investigation of the attack.

4. Under laboratory conditions grizzly bears often did not respond to sounds made by small bells. See, Miller, Gary D. 1980. Behavioral and physiological characteristics of grizzly and polar bears, and their relation to bear repellents. Master's thesis, Univ. Montana, Missoula, 106pp.

5. Hardy, Dave. Date unknown—about 1981. How to avoid bears while fishing. Alaska Fishing Guide, Volume unknown. pp.92–94.

6. Kaniut, Larry. 1983. Alaska bear tales. Alaska Northwest Publishing Company, Anchorage. pp.266–267.

7. I was one of the people who investigated this incident. The height which the bear climbed was independently measured by warden G.W. Vroom and me.

8. Kaniut, Larry. Op. cit. pp.244–245.

9. Murie, Adolph. 1963 (originally published 1961). A naturalist in Alaska. The natural history library, Anchor Books, Doubleday and Co., Inc. Garden City, New York. 302pp.

10. Several studies have documented this, especially in areas where food is dispersed. See for example: Russell, R.H., J.W. Nolan, N.G. Woody, and G.H. Anderson. 1979. A study of the grizzly bear in Jasper National Park 1975 to 1978. Final report. Prepared for Parks Canada by the Canadian Wildlife Service, Edmonton, Alta. 136pp.

11. See for example. Dalle-Molle. 1984. Field tests and users' opinions of bear-resistant backpack food containers in Denali National Park, Alaska, 1982 and 1983. United States Dept. of Interior, Denali National Park. 22pp. + appendices.

12. The trunk is the most difficult part of a car for a bear to break into.

13. Doty, R.L., M. Ford, G. Preti, and G.R. Huggins. 1975. Changes in the intensity and pleasantness of human vaginal odors during the menstrual cycle. Science 190: 1316–1317.

14. Cushing, Bruce. 1983. Responses of polar bears to human menstrual odors. Pages 275–280 *in* E. Charles Meslow, ed. Fifth International Conference on bear research and management. International Association for Bear Research and Management, publishers.

15. Herrero, Stephen, Wayne McCrory, and Brian Pelchat. In press. The application of grizzly bear habitat evaluation to trail and campsite locations in Kananaskis Provincial Park, Alberta. To be published in: Proceedings, 6th International Conference on bear research and management, 1983.
16. Wooldridge, Donald R. 1983. Polar bear electronic deterrent and detection systems. Pages 264–269, *in* E. Charles Meslow, ed. Fifth International Conference on, Bears— Their biology and management. International Association for Bear Research and Management, publishers.
17. Stenhouse, Gordon. 1983. Bear detection and deterrent study, Cape Churchill, Manitoba, 1982. N.W.T. Wildlife Service, Yellowknife. pp.45–47.
18. Several persons who have worked in the north and used trained dogs for polar bear detection told me that the dogs sometimes slept even when people could see polar bears approaching.
19. Miller, Gary D. 1980. Behavioral and physiological characteristics of grizzly and polar bears, and their relation to bear repellents. Master's thesis, Univ. of Montana, Missoula, 98pp. + appendices.
20. Stenhouse, Gordon. Op. cit.
21. Hastings, Bruce C., Barrie K. Gilbert, and David L. Turner. 1981. Black bear behavior and human-bear relationships in Yosemite National Park. Technical Report No. 2. Final report to the National Park Service, Western Region for Contract CX-1200-9-B051. 42pp.
22. Miller, Gary D. Op. cit.

Rogers, Lynn. 1984. Reactions of free-ranging black bears to capsaicin spray repellent. Wildl. Soc. Bull. 12: 59–61.
23. Jenkins, J.H. and F.A. Hayes. 1962. Studies on a useful method for repelling dogs and other animals. Animal biol. file: dog repellents. U.S. Dept. Agric., Washington, D.C. 5pp. As cited in Rogers, Lynn. Op. cit.
24. Rogers, Lynn. Op. cit.
25. Ibid. Rogers summarizes the results of several studies.
26. Smith, Martin E. undated. Repellents and deterrents for black and grizzly bears. Progress report 1983. School of Forestry, Univ. of Montana, Missoula. 20pp. + appendix. Unpublished.

"Phaser" is available from: Tom Bongard, Bongard Protection Systems, 10850 S.W. 113th Place, Miami, Florida 33126.
27. Rogers, Lynn. Op. cit.

Smith, Martin. Op. cit.

"Halt is available from: Animal Repellents, Inc., Griffin, Georgia 30223.
28. Smith, Martin. Op. cit.

"Skunker" is available from: Bear Country Products, 144 Commercial Street, Sunnyvale, Calif. 94086.
29. Stenhouse, Gordon. Op. cit.

The "Schermuly" flaring/scaring cartridge is made in England. It is available in Canada from: Marine Equipment Ltd., Halifax, Nova Scotia.
30. Stenhouse, Gordon. 1984. Summary report: 1983 bear detection and deterrent research program, Cape Churchill, Manitoba. Dept. of Renewable Resources, Govt. of the N.W.T. 6pp. Unpublished.

Chapter 10 | CHARACTERISTICS OF BEARS

1. Hill, C.A. 1973. Blue bear . . . glacier bear. Zoo Nooz 46(1): 4–18.
2. Allen, J.A. 1909. The white bear of southwestern British Columbia. Bull. Amer. Mus. Nat. Hist. 26: 233–238.

Cowan, I.M. 1938. Geographic distribution of color phases of the red fox and black bear in the Pacific Northwest. J. Mammal. 19: 202–206.

3. Standley, P.C. 1921. Albinism in the black bear. Science 54: 74.

4. Graber, David Murray. 1982. Ecology and management of black bears in Yosemite National Park. Technical Report No. 5. Final report to National Park Service, Cooperative National Park Resources Study Unit, Univ. of Calif. at Davis. 202pp. + appendices.

5. Rogers, Lynn. 1980. Inheritance of coat color and changes in pelage coloration in black bears in northeastern Minnesota. J. Mammal. 61: 324–327.

6. Poelker, Richard J. and Harry D. Hartwell. 1973. Black Bear of Washington. Washington State Game Department Biological Bulletin No. 14. 149pp. + appendices.

7. Cowan, I.M. Op. cit.

8. Graber, David Murray. Op. cit.

9. Ibid.

10. Rausch, Robert L. 1963. Geographic variation in size in North American brown bears, Ursus arctos L., as indicated by condylo basal length. Can. J. Zool. 41: 33–45pp.

11. Ibid.

12. Merriam, C.H. 1918. Review of grizzly and big brown bears of North America. North Am. Fauna, No. 41. U.S. Govt. Printing Office, Washington. 133pp.

13. Little, C.C. 1958. Coat color genes in rodents and carnivores. Quant. Rev. Biol. 33: 103–137.

14. David Hamer and I periodically observed this in the Cascade Valley of Banff National Park, Alberta.

15. Graber, David Murray. Op. cit.

Kingsley, M.C.S., J.A. Nagy, and R.H. Russell. 1983. Patterns of weight gain and loss for grizzly bears in northern Canada. Pages 174–178 in E. Charles Meslow, ed. Fifth International Conference on bear research and management. International Association for Bear Research and Management, publishers.

16. Herrero, S. 1978. A comparison of some features of the evolution, ecology and behavior of black and grizzly/brown bears. Carnivore 1(1): 7–17.

17. Pearson, Art. 1975. The northern interior grizzly bear (Ursus arctos L.). Can. Wildl. Service, Rep't. Series #34. 84pp.

18. Glenn, Leland P. 1980. Morphometric characteristics of brown bears on the central Alaska Peninsula. Pages 313–319 in Clifford J. Martinka and Katherine L. McArthur, eds. Fourth International Conference on bear research and management. Bear Biology Assoc., publishers.

19. Erickson, A.W. 1965. The brown-grizzly bear in Alaska, its ecology and management. Alaska Dept. Fish and Game. Fed. Aid in Wildl. Restor. Proj. W-6-R-5, Rep. 5. 42pp.

20. Glenn, Leland P. Op. cit.

21. Simpson, George G. 1945. The principles of classification and a classification of mammals. Bull. Amer. Mus. Nat. Hist., 85: 350pp.

22. Evidence for this is largely anecdotal. David Hamer and I have one observation which could be interpreted as indicating a female grizzly bear located a carcass by odor when she was several miles away from the carcass. Dick Russell, Canadian Wildlife Service, Edmonton, told me of another instance which likely indicates that a caribou carcass was smelled by a grizzly bear when several miles away.

23. Rogers, L.L. 1977. Social relationships, movements, and population dynamics of black bears in northeastern Minnesota. Ph.D. thesis, Univ. of Minnesota. 194pp.

24. Bacon, Ellis Sutton. 1973. Investigation on perception and behavior of the American black bear (Ursus americanus). Ph.D. thesis, Univ. of Tennessee, Knoxville. 161pp.

25. Ibid.

26. Ibid.
27. Kuckuk, E. 1936. Tierpsychologische beobach tungen on zwei jungen braunbaren. Zeitschrift fur Vergleichende Physiologie. 24: 14–41. As cited in Bacon, Ellis. Op. cit.
28. David Hamer observed this in Banff National Park, Alberta.
29. Kuckuk, E. Op. cit. As cited in Bacon, Ellis. Op. cit.
30. Rogers, Lynn. Personal communication. Dr. Rogers is currently a research biologist with the U.S. Forest Service, Ely, Minnesota.
31. Stonorov, Derek. 1972. Protocol at the annual brown bear feast. Natural History, LXXXI, No. 9, Nov. 72. pp.66–73; 90–94.

Chapter 11 | THE EVOLUTION OF BEARS

1. Kurten, Bjorn. 1976. The cave bear story: Life and death of a vanished animal. Columbia Univ. Press, N.Y. 163pp.
2. Ibid.
3. Ibid.
4. Davis, D.D. 1964. The giant panda, a morphological study of evolutionary mechanisms. Fieldiana Zool. Mem., Vol. 3., Chicago Nat. Hist. Mus. 339pp.
5. Mealey, Stephen P. 1975. The natural food habits of free-ranging grizzly bears in Yellowstone National Park, 1973–1974. M.Sc. thesis, Montana State Univ., Bozeman. 158pp.

Bunnell, Fred L. and Tony Hamilton. 1983. Forage digestibility and fitness in grizzly bears. Pages 179–185 in E. Charles Meslow, ed. Fifth International Conference on bear research and management. International Association for Bear Research and Management, publishers.
6. Mealey, Stephen P. Op. cit.

Hamer, David and Stephen Herrero (eds.). 1983. Ecological studies of the grizzly bear in Banff National Park. Final report. Report prepared for Parks Canada, Western Regional Office, Calgary, Alberta, 303pp.
7. Rogers, Lynn. 1976. Effects of mast and berry crop failures on survival, growth, and reproductive success of black bears. Trans. 41st North Amer. Wildl. and Nat. Resources Conf. pp. 431–438.
8. Alt, Gary. Personal communication. Mr. Alt was a research biologist with the Pennsylvania Game Commission, Harrisburg, Pennsylvania.
9. Herrero, S. 1978. A comparison of some features of the evolution, ecology and behavior of black and grizzly/brown bears. Carnivore 1(1): 7–17.
10. Rogers, Lynn. Personal communication. Dr. Rogers is currently a research biologist with the U.S. Forest Service in Ely, Minnesota.
11. Hornocker, Maurice G. 1962. Population characteristics and social and reproductive behavior of the grizzly bear in Yellowstone National Park. M.Sc. thesis, Univ. of Mont., Missoula. 94pp. Hornocker also mentions that some particularly aggressive males could dominate larger individuals.

Chapter 12 | BEAR FOODS AND LOCATION

1. Folk, G. Edgar, Anna Larson and Mary A. Folk. 1976. Physiology of hibernating bears. Pages 373–380 in M. Pelton, J.W. Lentfer, and G.E. Folk, eds. 3rd International Conference on bear research and management. I.U.C.N., New Series No. 40, Morges, Switzerland.
Pearson, Art. 1975. The northern interior grizzly bear (Ursus arctos L.) Can. Wildl. Service, Rep't Series #34. 84pp.
2. Nelson, Ralph A. 1980. Protein and fat metabolism in hibernating bears. Fed. Proc. 39: 2955–2958.

3. Jonkel, Charles J. and Ian McTaggart-Cowan. 1971. The black bear in the spruce-fir forest. Wildlife Monographs, No. 27: 57pp.
4. Hamer, David and Stephen Herrero (eds.) 1983. Ecological studies of the grizzly bear in Banff National Park. Final report. Report prepared for Parks Canada, Western Regional Office, Calgary, Alberta, 303pp.
5. Davis, D.D. 1964. The giant panda, a morphological study of evolutionary mechanisms. Fieldiana Zool. Mem., Vol. 3., Chicago Nat. Hist. Mus. 339pp.

   Mealey, Stephen P. 1975. The natural food habits of free ranging grizzly bears in Yellowstone National Park, 1973–1974. M.Sc. thesis, Montana State Univ., Bozeman. 158pp.
6. Johnston, A., L.M. Bezeau, and S. Smolick. 1968. Chemical composition and *in vitro* digestibility of alpine tundra plants. Journal of Wildlf. Manage. 32: 773–777.
7. Hamer, David and Stephen Herrero (eds.) Op. cit.
8. Graber, David Murray. 1982. Ecology and management of black bears in Yosemite National Park. Technical Report No. 5. Final report to National Park Service, Cooperative National Park Resources Study Unit, Univ. of Calif. at Davis. 202pp. + appendices.
9. Mealey, Stephen P. Op. cit.
10. Russell, R.H., J.W. Nolan, N.G. Woody, and G.H. Anderson. 1979. A study of the grizzly bear in Jasper National Park 1975 to 1978. Final report. Prepared for Parks Canada by the Canadian Wildlife Service, Edmonton, Alta. 136pp.
11. Atwell, Gerry, Daniel L. Boone, Jack Gustafson, and Vernon D. Berns. 1980. Brown bear summer alpine habitat requirements on the Kodiak National Wildlife Refuge. Pages 297–305 *in* C.J. Martinka and Katherine L. McArthur, eds. Fourth International Conference on bear research and management. Bear Biology Association, publishers.
12. Pearson, Art. Op. cit.
13. Poelker, Richard J. and Harry D. Hartwell. 1973. Black bear of Washington. Washington State Game Department Biological Bulletin No. 14. 149pp. + appendices.

   Taylor, Robert A. 1964. Columbian ground squirrel and cambium found in grizzly bear stomachs taken in the fall. J. Mammal. 45(3): 476–477. This reference shows that grizzly bears will feed on cambium in fall. I assume they will also do this in spring.
14. Hamer, David and Stephen Herrero (eds.) Op. cit.
15. Ibid.
16. Smith, Barney. Personal communication. Mr. Smith is currently the bear research biologist with the Yukon Territorial Government, Whitehorse.
17. Sumner, Jay and John J. Craighead. 1973. Grizzly bear habitat survey in the Scapegoat Wilderness, Montana. Mont. Coop. Wildlf. Rsch. Unit, Missoula. 49pp. + appendices.
18. Rogers, Lynn. Personal communication. Ms. Rogers is currently a research biologist with the U.S. Forest Service, Ely, Minnesota.
19. Murie, Adolph. 1937. Some food habits of the black bear. J. Mammmal. 18 (2): 238–240.
20. Schlegel, M. 1976. Factors affecting calf elk survival in north central Idaho: A progress report. Proc. Ann. Conf. W. Assoc. State Fish and Game Comm. 56: 342–355.
21. Schwartz, Charles C. and Albert W. Franzmann. 1983. Effects of tree crushing on black bear predation of moose calves. Pages 40–44 *in* E. Charles Meslow, ed. Fifth International Conference on bear research and management. International Association for Bear Research and Management, publishers.
22. Personal communication from Mr. Doug Larson, Management Biologist, Yukon Territorial Government, Whitehorse.
23. Brown, Gary. Letter to me dated December 11, 1980. Mr. Brown was then Chief

Ranger for Mt. McKinley National Park.

24. Mahoney, Shane. Personal communication. Mr. Mahoney is currently a research biologist working for Fish and Wildlife in St. Johns, Newfoundland. Mr. Mahoney's ongoing research on the island of Newfoundland has discovered that some black bears are successful, regular predators on adult caribou. There are no wolves on Newfoundland.

25. Henry, David. Personal communication. Dr. Henry is a research biologist currently living in Waskesiu, Saskatchewan.

26. Ibid.

27. Stelmock, Jim S. 1981. Seasonal activities and habitat use patterns of brown bears in Denali National Park—1980. M.Sc. thesis, Univ. of Alaska, 118pp.

28. Smith, Paul A. 1984. Kenai black bears and cranberries: Bear food habits and densities. M.Sc. thesis, Univ. of Alaska, Fairbanks. 144pp.

29. Craighead, John J. and Frank C. Craighead. Grizzly bear-man relationships in Yellowstone National Park. Pages 304–332 in Stephen Herrero, ed. Bears—Their biology and management, I.U.C.N., New Series, No. 23.

30. Herrero, S. 1978. A comparison of some features of the evolution, ecology and behavior of black and grizzly/brown bears. Carnivore 1 (1): 7–17. In this article I review some of the evidence showing that adult male grizzlies may kill cubs and will sometimes eat them.

31. Black bears in Banff National Park, Alberta, are reported to have been seen feeding at Banff's sewage lagoon.

32. Pearson, Art. Op. cit.

33. Ibid.

34. Martinka, C.J. 1973. Interim report on grizzly bear research. U.S. Dept. Interior, Nat'l. Park Service, Glacier National Park. Unpublished, 12pp.

35. Rogers, Lynn. 1976. Effects of mast and berry crop failures on survival, growth and reproductive success of black bears. Trans. 41st North Amer. Wildl. and Nat. Resources Conf. pp.431–438. In this article Rogers briefly reviews responses of black bears to major natural food failure.

36. Alt, Gary. 1980. Hunting vulnerability of bears. (Pennsylvania) Game News (July) 7–10.

37. Pelton, Michael R. and Gordon M. Burghardt. 1976. Black bears of the Smokies. Nat. Hist. 85 (1): 54–63.

38. Storer, Tracy I. and Lloyd P. Tevis, Jr. 1955. California grizzly. Univ. of Calif. Press, Berkeley and Los Angeles, 335pp.

39. Kendall, Katherine C. 1983. Use of pine nuts by grizzly and black bears in the Yellowstone area. Pages 166–173 in E. Charles Meslow, ed. Fifth International Conference on bear research and management. International Association for Bear Research and Management, publishers.

40. Black, Hugh C. 1958. Black bear research in New York. Trans. N. Amer. Wildl. Conf. 23: 443–461.

41. Alt, Gary. 1980. Rate of growth and size of Pennsylvania black bears. (Pennsylvania) Game News (December) pp.7–17.

42. Ibid.

43. Hamer, David and Stephen Herrero (eds.). Op. cit.

44. Mahoney, Shane. Personal communication. Mr. Mahoney is currently a research biologist working for Fish and Wildlife in St. Johns, Newfoundland.

45. The Yosemite National Park data are from: Graber, David M. Op. cit.

The Banff National Park data are from: Hamer, David and Stephen Herrero (eds.) Op. cit.

46. Rogers, Lynn. Op. cit.

47. Hamer, David and Stephen Herrero (eds.) Op. cit. observed this for grizzly bears as have many other scientists. It has also been frequently seen with black bears.

48. Hamer, David and Stephen Herrero. Unpublished observations.

Knight, Richard and Bonnie M. Blanchard. 1983. Yellowstone grizzly bear investigations. Annual report of the Interagency Study Team, 1982. U.S. Dept. of Interior, Nat'l. Park Service. 45 pp.

49. Schleyer, Bart Otis. 1983. Activity patterns of grizzly bears in the Yellowstone ecosystem and their reproductive behavior, predation and the use of carrion. M.Sc. thesis, Montana State Univ., Bozeman. 78pp. + appendices.

50. McDaniel, Jimmie. 1979. Report from Florida. Pages 34–37 in Dale Burk, ed. The black bear in modern North America. Boone and Crockett Club and Amwell Press, Clinton, New Jersey.

51. Folk, G. Edgar Jr., Jill M. Hunt, and Mary A. Folk. 1980. Further evidence for hibernation of black bears. Pages 43–47 in Clifford J. Martinka and Katherine L. McArthur, eds. Fourth International conference on bear research and management. Bear Biology Association, publishers.

52. Nelson, Ralph A., Heinz W. Wahner, James D. Jones, Ralph D. Ellefson and Paul E. Zollman. 1973. Metabolism of bears before, during and after winter sleep. Amer. J. Physiol. 224 (2): 491–496.

Matson, J.R. 1946. Notes on dormancy in the black bear. J. Mammal. 27 (3): 203–212.

53. Nelson, Ralph A. *et al*. Op. cit.

54. G. William Vroom, Stephen Herrero and R.T. Ogilvie. 1980. The ecology of winter den sites of grizzly bears in Banff National Park, Alberta. Pages 321–330 in Clifford J. Martinka and Katherine L. McArthur (eds.) Fourth International Conference on bear research and management. Bear Biology Association, publishers.

55. Ibid.

56. Ibid.

Erickson, Albert W., John Nellor and George A. Petrides. 1964. The black bear in Michigan. Research Bull. 4, Agric. Expt. Sta., Michigan State Univ., East Lansing. 102pp.

57. Erickson, Albert W., John Nellor and George A. Petrides. Op. cit.

58. Ibid.

59. Herrero, Stephen. 1970. A black bear and her cub. Animals 12 (10): 444–447.

60. Pelton, Michael R., Larry E. Beeman and Daniel C. Eager. 1980. Den selection by black bears in the Great Smoky Mountains National Park. Pages 149–151 in Clifford J. Martinka and Katherine L. McArthur, eds. Fourth International Conference on bear research and management. Bear Biology Association, publishers.

61. Herrero, Stephen and David Hamer. 1977. Courtship and copulation of a pair of grizzly bears—with comments on reproductive plasticity and strategy. J. Mamm. 58 (3): 441–444.

62. Alt, Gary. 1978. 14½ miles of bear tracks. (Pennsylvania) Game News (June) 24–29.

63. Nagy, J.A. and R.H. Russell. 1978. Ecological studies of the boreal forest grizzly bear (*Ursus arctos* L.)—Annual report for 1977. Can. Wildlf. Service, Edmonton. 72pp.

64. Alt, Gary Lee. 1977. Home range annual activity patterns and movements of black bears in northeastern Pennsylvania. M.Sc. thesis, Pennsylvania State Univ. 67pp.

Schleyer, Bart Otis. Op. cit.

65. Hamer, D., S. Herrero, R.T. Ogilvie and Tim Toth. 1979. Ecological studies of grizzly bears in Banff National Park, 1978. Parks Canada, Western Regional Office, Calgary. 106pp.

66. Herrero, Stephen. 1972. Aspects of evolution and adaptation in American black bears (*Ursus americanus* Pallas) and brown and grizzly bears (*U. arctos* Linne) of North America. Pages 221–231 in Stephen Herrero (ed.). Bears—Their biology and management. I.U.C.N., New Series No. 23, Morges, Switzerland.

67. Jonkel, C.J. and F.L. Miller. 1970. Recent records of black bears (*Ursus americanus*)

on the barren grounds of Canada. J. Mamm. *51* (4): 826–828.
68. Graber, David Murray. 1981. Ecology and management of black bears in Yosemite National Park. Coop. National Park Resources Studies Unit, Univ. of Calif., Davis. 202pp. + appendices.
69. Alt, Gary L. and James S. Lindsey. 1980. Management of Pennsylvania's black bear: past, present, and future. Paper presented at 36th N.E. Fish and Wildl. Conf., Ellenville, New York, unpaginated.
70. Graham, Dean Chalmus. 1978. Grizzly bear distribution, use of habitats, food habits and habitat characterization in Pelican and Hayden valleys, Yellowstone National Park. M.Sc. thesis, Mont. State Univ., Bozeman. 88pp.
71. Hamer, David and Stephen Herrero, eds. Op. cit.
72. Servheen, Christopher. 1981. Grizzly bear ecology and management in the Mission Mountains, Montana, M.Sc. thesis, Univ. Montana. 138pp.
73. Zunino, Franco and Stephen Herrero. 1972. The status of the brown bear (*Ursus arctos*) in Abruzzo National Park, Italy, 1971. Biol. Consv. 4 (4): 263–272.
74. Roth, Hans U., 1983. Diel activity of a remnant population of European brown bears. Pages 223–229 *in* E. Charles Meslow, ed. Fifth International Conference on bear research and management. International Association for bear research and management, publisher.

Chapter 13 | SIGNS OF BEAR ACTIVITY

1. Anonymous. Undated. Draft Identification manual for Ursidae. Nat'l. Museum of Canada. 30pp. + appendices.
2. Lloyd, Kevin Alexander. 1979. Aspects of the ecology of black and grizzly bears in coastal British Columbia. M.Sc. thesis. Univ. of British Columbia, Vancouver, B.C. 125pp. + appendices. This thesis discusses both the toe arc and the toes joined or not joined as techniques for differenciating black and grizzly bear tracks. The toe arc method was also developed and tested by Dan Palmisciano, of the Montana State Wildlife Lab, Bozeman.
3. Vroom, G. William, Stephen Herrero and R.T. Ogilvie. 1980. The ecology of winter den sites of grizzly bears in Banff National Park, Alberta. Pages 321–330 *in* Clifford J. Martinka and Katherine L. McArthur, eds. Fourth International Conference on bear research and management. Bear Biology Association, publishers.
4. Hamer, David, Stephen Herrero and Lynn Rogers. 1981. Differentiating black and grizzly bear feces. Wildl. Soc. Bull. 9 (3): 210–212.
5. Rogers, Lynn. Personal communication. Dr. Rogers is currently a research biologist with the U.S. Forest Service, Ely, Minnesota.
6. Hamer, David, Stephen Herrero and Keith Brady. 1981. The grizzly bear in Waterton Lakes National Park. Report prepared for: Western Regional Office, Parks Canada, Calgary, Alberta. 51pp.
7. Tschanz, V.B., M. Meyer-Holzapfel and S. Bachmann. 1970. Das informations system bei Braunbaren. Z. Tierpsychol. 27: 47–72.

Rogers, Lynn L. 1977. Social relationships, movements, and population dynamics of black bears in northeastern Minnesota. Ph.D. thesis. Univ. of Minnesota, Minneapolis. 203pp.

Burst, Tom L. and Michael R. Pelton. 1983. Black bear mark trees in the Smoky Mountains. Pages 45–53 *in* E. Charles Meslow, ed. Fifth International Conference on bear research and management. International Association for Bear Research and Management, publishers.
8. Moore, Tommy D., Liter E. Spence and Charles E. Dugnolle. 1974. Identification of some dorsal guard hairs of some mammals of Wyoming. Wyoming Game and Fish Department. 177pp.

Chapter 14 | LEARNING AND INSTINCT

1. Douglas-Hamilton, I. 1972. On the ecology and behavior of the African elephant: the elephants of Lake Manyara. Ph.D. thesis. Oriel College, Oxford Univ., Oxford. 268pp.
2. Bacon, E.S. 1973. Investigation on perception and behavior of the American black bear (*Ursus americanus*). Ph.D. thesis. Univ. of Tennessee, Knoxville. 160pp.
3. Kawai, M. 1965. Newly acquired pre-cultural behavior of the natural troop of Japanese monkeys on Koshima Islet. Primates 6 (1): 1–30.
4. Egbert, Allan L. 1978. The social behavior of brown bears at McNeil River, Alaska. Ph.D. thesis. Utah State University, Logan. 117pp.
5. Jope, Katherine Louise McArthur. 1982. Interactions between grizzly bears and hikers in Glacier National Park, Montana. M.Sc. thesis. Oregon State Univ. 81pp. + appendices.
6. Faro, James B. Letter to me dated February 27, 1981. Mr. Faro is currently a research biologist working for Alaska Fish and Game, Anchorage.
7. Stenhouse, Gordon. Personal communication. Mr. Stenhouse is currently a research biologist working for the Northwest Territorial Government, Yellowknife.
8. Faro, James B. Op. cit.
9. Smith, Barney, Personal communication. Mr. Smith is currently a bear research biologist working for the Yukon Territorial Government, Whitehorse.

Chapter 15 | AGGRESSION AND SUBMISSION

1. Lorenz, Konrad. 1955. Man meets dog. Houghton Mifflin Co., Boston, Mass. 211 pp.
2. Henry, J.D. and S. Herrero. 1974. Social play in the American black bear: Its similarity to canid social play and an examination of its identifying characteristics. Amer. Zool. 14: 371–389.
3. Hornocker, Maurice G. 1962. Population characteristics and social and reproductive behavior of the grizzly bear in Yellowstone National Park. M.Sc. thesis. Montana State Univ., Missoula. 94pp.
4. Herrero, Stephen. 1983. Social behavior of black bears at a garbage dump in Jasper National Park. Pages 54–70 *in* E. Charles Meslow, ed. Fifth International Conference on bear research and management. International Association for Bear Research and Management, publishers.
5. Egbert, A.L. 1978. The social behavior of brown bears at McNeil River, Alaska. Ph.D. thesis. Utah State Univ., Logan. 117pp.
6. I have observed this on adult male black and grizzly bears.
7. Rogers, Lynn. 1977. Social relationships, movements and population dynamics of black bears in northeastern Minnesota. Ph.D. thesis. Univ. of Minnesota, St. Paul. pp.164–165.
8. Ibid.
9. Russell, Andy. 1967. Grizzly country. Alfred A. Knopf. New York. p.81.
10. Herrero, Stephen. 1972. Aspects of evolution and adaptation in American black bears (*Ursus americanus* Pallas) and brown and grizzly bears (*U. arctos* Linne) of North America. Pages 221–231 *in* Stephen Herrero, ed. Bears—Their biology and management, I.U.C.N., New Series No. 23, Morges, Switzerland.
11. Herrero, Stephen. 1970. A black bear and her cub. Animals 12 (10): 444–447.
12. Burghardt, Gordon. 1972. Panel 4: Bear behavior. Page 243 *in* Stephen Herrero, ed. Bears—Their biology and management. I.U.C.N., New Series No. 23, Morges, Switzerland.
13. For a brief review of this see: Herrero, Stephen. 1978. A comparison of some features of the evolution, ecology and behavior of black and grizzly/brown bears. Carnivore 1 (1): 7–17.

14. Herrero, Stephen. 1983. Op. cit.
15. Herrero, Stephen. 1970. Op. cit.
16. Egbert, A.L. Op. cit.
17. Herrero, Stephen. 1972. Op. cit.
18. Hornocker, Maurice G. Op. cit.

    Egbert, A.L. Op. cit.
19. Egbert, A.L. Op. cit.
20. Ibid. p. 50.
21. Dean, Frederick C., Laura M. Darling and Alison G. Lierhaus. In press. An observation of intra-specific predation by Ursus arctos. Can. Field Nat.
22. Russell, Andy. Op. cit. p.39.
23. Woodie, Norm. Letter to me. Mr. Woodie is currently a warden working in Jasper National Park, Alberta.
24. Canadian Wildlife Service autopsy report which is located in the files of Jasper National Park.
25. Crawford, John S. 1980. Wolves, bears, and bighorns. Alaska Northwest Publishing Company. Anchorage, Alaska. p.101.
26. In this table I have synthesized information from two sources:

    Stonorov, Derek and Allen W. Stokes. 1972. Social behavior of the Alaska brown bear. Pages 232–242 in Stephen Herrero, ed. Bears—Their biology and management. I.U.C.N., New Series No. 23, Morges, Switzerland.

    Egbert, A.L. Op. cit.
27. Stonorov, Derek and Allen W. Stokes. Op. cit. p.239.
28. Egbert, A.L. Op. cit.
29. Ibid.
30. Jope, Katherine Louise McArthur. 1982. Interactions between grizzly bears and hikers in Glacier National Park, Montana. M.Sc. thesis. Oregon State Univ. 81pp. + appendices.
31. Egbert, A.L. Op. cit.
32. The rare cases of adult male black bears killing other black bears are reviewed in: Rogers, Lynn. Op. cit. pp.160–163.
33. Ibid. p.89 and p.164.
34. Herrero, Stephen. Unpublished observations.
35. Herrero, Stephen. 1983. Op. cit.
36. Jordan, Robert. 1976. Threat behavior of the black bear (Ursus americanus). Page 61 in Michael R. Pelton, Jack W. Lentfer and G. Edgar Folk, eds. 3rd International Conference on bear research and management. I.U.C.N., New series No. 40, Morges, Switzerland.
37. Herrero, Stephen. 1983. Op. cit.
38. Eager, Jane Tate and Michael R. Pelton. 1979. Panhandler black bears in the Great Smoky Mountains National Park. Report presented to: United States National Park Service, Southeast Region. 176pp. + appendix.
39. Ibid. p.89.
40. Hastings, Bruce C. and Barrie K. Gilbert. 1981. Black bear behavior and bear-human relationships in Yosemite National Park. Wildlife Science Dept., Utah State Univ., Logan. 17pp. + appendix.

Chapter 16 | BEARS AND PEOPLE IN RURAL AND REMOTE AREAS

1. Follman, Erich H., Robert A. Dieterich and John L. Hechtel. 1980. Recommended carnivore control program for the northwest Alaskan pipeline project including a review of human-carnivore encounter problems and animal deterrent methodology. Prepared for Northwest Alaskan Pipeline Company. 113pp. Unpublished.

   Herrero, Stephen. 1982. Bears and proposed Canadian Pacific Railway construction camps in Glacier National Park, British Columbia. Prepared for MacLaren Plansearch Corp., Vancouver, B.C. 42pp. + appendices. Unpublished.

2. Anonymous. 1983. Guidelines for design and operation of refuse incinerators in Alberta. Air Quality Branch, Alberta Environment, Edmonton. 25pp.

3. Zunino, Franco and Stephen Herrero. 1972. The status of the brown bear (*Ursus arctos*) in Abruzzo National Park, Italy, 1971. Biol. Consv. 4 (4): 263–272.

4. Gunson, John R. 1980. Black bear–beeyard management in Alberta. Paper presented at Vertebrate Pest Management Seminar, Canadian Pest Management Society, Edmonton. 10pp.

5. Ibid.

6. Wynnyk, W.P. and J.R. Gunson. 1977. Design and effectiveness of a portable electric fence for apiaries. Alberta Recreation, Parks and Wildlife, Fish and Wildlife Division. 11pp.

7. For reviews see:
Follman, Erich H. *et al.* Op. cit.
Herrero, Stephen. Op. cit.

8. Alt, Gary L. 1980. How do you handle a hungry bear? (Pennsylvania) Game News (February) pp.15–17.

9. I observed and had to deal with this over a ten-year period on my farm in British Columbia.

10. Davenport, Leslie B. Jr. 1953. Agricultural depredation by the black bear in Virginia. J. Wildl. Manage. 17 (3): 331–340.

11. Spencer, Howard E. Jr. 1966 (reprinted). The black bear and its status in Maine. Game Division Bull. No. 4., State of Maine, Dept. of Inland Fisheries and Game, Augusta. 55pp.

12. Davenport, Leslie B. Jr. Op. cit.

13. Jordan, R.M. 1943. Northern Minnesota's biggest problem. Sheep Breeder 63 (12): 52. As cited *in*: Cardoza, James B. 1976. The history and status of the black bear in Massachusetts and adjacent New England states.

14. Davenport, Leslie B. Jr. Op. cit.

15. Knight, Richard R. 1983. Grizzly bears that kill livestock. Pages 186–190 *in* E. Charles Meslow, ed. Fifth International Conference on bear research and management, International Association for Bear Research and Management, publishers.

16. Zunino, Franco. Personal communication. Mr. Zunino is currently a naturalist living in Gioia Vecchio, Abruzzi District, Italy.

17. Beecham, John. Personal communication. Dr. Beecham is currently a research biologist with Idaho Fish and Game, Boise.

18. Silver, H. 1957. A history of New Hampshire game and fur bearers. Survey Rept. 6, N.H. Fish and Game Dept., Concord. 466pp.

19. Murie, Adolph. 1948. Cattle on grizzly bear range. J. Wildl. Manage. 12 (1): 57–72.

20. Johnson, S.J. and D.E. Griffel. 1982. Sheep losses on grizzly bear range. J. Wildl. Manage. 46 (3): 786–790.

21. Rogers, Lynn. 1976. Effects of mast and berry crop failures on survival, growth and reproductive success of black bears. Trans. 41st North Amer. Wildl. and Nat. Resources Conf. pp.431–438. In this article Rogers briefly reviews responses of black bears to major natural food failure.

22. Hatler, David F. 1967. Some aspects in the ecology of the black bear (*Ursus americanus*) in interior Alaska. M.Sc. thesis. Univ. of Alaska, Fairbanks. 111pp.

23. Rogers, Lynn. Op. cit.

24. Hamer, David. In press. The ecology of the grizzly bear, Banff National Park. Ph.D. thesis. Univ. of Calgary, Alberta.

25. Pearson, Art. 1975. The northern interior grizzly bear (*Ursus arctos* L.). Can. Wildl. Serv., Report Series No. 34, Ottawa. 86pp.

26. Poelker, R.J. and H.D. Hartwell. 1973. Black bear of Washington: Its biology,

natural history and relationship to forest regeneration. Biol. Bull. No. 14, Wash. State Game Dept., Olympia. 180pp.
27. Wynnyk, W.P. and J.R. Gunson. Op. cit.
28. Russell, Andy. 1967. Grizzly country. Alfred A. Knopf, New York. 302pp.
29. Wooldridge, Donald R. 1983. Polar bear electronic deterrent and detection systems. Pages 264–269 in E. Charles Meslow, ed. Fifth International Conference on Bear Research and Management. International Association for Bear Research and Management, publishers.
30. Haynes, Bessie Doak and Edgar Haynes, eds. 1966. The grizzly bear: Portraits from life. Univ. of Oklahoma Press, Norman. 386pp.

Storer, Tracy I. and Lloyd P. Tevis. 1955. California grizzly. Univ. of California press, Berkeley and Los Angeles. 335pp.
31. Meehan, William R. and John F. Thilenius. 1983. Safety in bear country: Protective measures and bullet performance at short range. General technical report PNW—152, United States Dept. Agriculture, Forest Service, Pacific Northwest Forest and Range Experiment Station, Portland. 16pp.
32. Ibid.
33. My source of information for this incident was a conversation with Mr. Keith Brady, Warden Service, Waterton Lakes National Park, Alberta. Mr. Brady did some of the on-site investigation of the attack.

Chapter 17 | BEAR MANAGEMENT

1. Anonymous. 1981. Bear management plan. United States Department of the Interior, National Park Service, Glacier National Park, West Glacier, Montana. p.2.
2. McClearn, G.E. and J.C. DeFries. 1973. Introduction to behavioral genetics. W.H. Freeman, San Francisco. 349pp.
3. Zunino, Franco and Stephen Herrero. 1972. The status of the brown bear (Ursus arctos) in Abruzzo National Park, Italy, 1971. Biol. Conserv. 4 (4): 263–272.
4. Jope, Katherine Louise McArthur. 1982. Interactions between grizzly bears and hikers in Glacier National Park, Montana. M.Sc. thesis. Oregon State Univ. 81pp. + appendices.
5. Ibid.
6. Herrero, Stephen, Wayne McCrory and Brian Pelchat. In press. The application of grizzly bear habitat evaluation to trail and campsite locations in Kananaskis Provincial Park, Alberta. To be published in: Proceeding, 6th International Conference on bear research and management, 1983.
7. Anonymous, 1980. Whiskey Creek area bear incidents. Warden Service, Banff National Park, Alberta. unpaginated.
8. A successful, hydraulically powered, self-emptying garbage container is in widespread use in the Rocky Mountain parks of Canada. The units are manufactured by Neufeldt Industries of Lethbridge, Alberta.
9. McArthur (Jope), Katherine L. 1981. Factors contributing to effectiveness of black bear transplants. J. Wildl. Manage. 45 (1): 102–110.
10. Miller, Sterling D. and Warren B. Ballard. 1982. Homing of transplanted Alaskan brown bears. J. Wildl. Manage. 46 (4): 869–876.
11. Pelton, Mike. Personal communication. Dr. Pelton is currently a professor of wildlife management at the Univ. of Tennessee, Knoxville.
12. This point is hard to study and document. See, however: Knight, Richard. 1981. Notes on some behavior patterns in radio-instrumented grizzly bears. Interagency Grizzly Bear Research Team, Bozeman, Montana, 10pp. Unpublished.
13. Wilf Etherington's death is one piece of evidence which supports, but doesn't prove, this contention.
14. Cella, William B. and Jeffery A. Keay. 1980. Annual bear management and incident

report Yosemite National Park. U.S. National Park Service, Yosemite. 13pp. + appendices.

15. Jope, Katherine Louise McArthur. Op. cit.
16. Schneider, Bill. 1977. Where the grizzly walks. Mountain Press Publishing Co., Missoula, Montana. 191pp.
17. Russell, R.H., J.W. Nolan, N.G. Woody, and G.H. Anderson. 1979. A study of the grizzly bear in Jasper National Park 1975 to 1978. Final report. Prepared for Parks Canada by the Canadian Wildlife Service, Edmonton, Alta. 136pp.
18. Cole, Glen. 1971. Interim progress on 1971 bear management program. Memorandum to the Superintendent, Yellowstone National Park, Mammoth, Wyo. unpaginated (see Table 3).
19. Craighead, John J., Joel R. Varney and Frank C. Craighead, Jr. 1974. A population analysis of the Yellowstone grizzly bears. Bull. 40, Montana Forest and Conservation Experiment Station, School of Forestry, Univ. of Montana, Missoula. 20pp.
20. Knight, Richard R. and Bonnie M. Blanchard. 1983. Yellowstone grizzly bear investigations: Report of the Interagency Study Team. U.S. Dept. of Interior, National Park Service. 45pp.
21. Knight, Richard R. and Bonnie M. Blanchard. 1984. Yellowstone grizzly bear investigations: Report of the Interagency Study Team. U.S. Dept. of Interior, National Park Service.
22. For a review of grizzly bear reproductive rates see: Herrero, Stephen. 1978. A comparison of some features of the evolution, ecology and behavior of black and grizzly/brown bears. Carnivore. 1 (1): 7–17.
23. Sidorowicz, George A. and Frederick F. Gilbert. 1981. The management of grizzly bears in the Yukon, Canada. Wildl. Soc. Bull. 9 (2): 125–135.
24. Russell, Richard et al. Op. cit.

Knight, Richard R. and Bonnie M. Blanchard. 1984. Op. cit.
25. Johnson, Loyal. 1980. Brown bear management in southeastern Alaska. Pages 263–270 in Clifford J. Martinka and Katherine L. McArthur, eds. Fourth International Conference on bear research and management. Bear Biology Association, publishers.
26. For partial substantiation see: Alt, Gary. 1980. Hunting vulnerability of bears (Pennsylvania) Game News (July) pp.7–10.
27. Shaffer, Mark L. 1983. Determining minimum viable population sizes for the grizzly bear. Pages 133–139 in E. Charles Meslow, ed. Fifth International Conference on Bear Research and Management, International, Association for bear research and management, publishers. (See note at end of paper.)
28. Hamer, David and Stephen Herrero (eds.) 1983. Ecological studies of the grizzly bear in Banff National Park. Final report. Prepared for: Parks Canada, Western Regional Office, Calgary. 244pp. + appendices.

Martin, P. 1983. Factors influencing globe huckleberry fruit production in northwestern Montana. Pages 159–165 in E. Charles Meslow, ed. Fifth International Conference on Bear Research and Management International Association for Bear Research and Management, publishers.

29. Ibid. (both).
30. Anonymous. 1979. Guidelines for management involving grizzly bears in the greater Yellowstone area. Bridger-Teton, Shoshone, Custer, Gallatin, Targhee National Forests, Grand Teton, Yellowstone National Parks. 117pp. + appendix.
31. Bunnell, F.L. and D.E.N. Tait. 1980. Bears in models and in reality—implications to management. Pages 15–23 in Clifford J. Martinka and Katherine L. McArthur, eds. Fourth International Conference on bear research and management, Bear Biology Association, publishers.
32. Moment, Gardiner B. 1968. Bears: The need for a new sanity in wildlife conservation. BioScience. 18 (12): 1105–1108.

33. Anonymous. 1984. Current management of ungulates and their predators in the Yukon Territory. Yukon Dept. of Renewable Resources, Wildlife Mgte. Branch, Whitehorse. 31pp.
34. Herrero, Stephen. 1976. Conflicts between man and grizzly bears in the national parks of North America. Pages 121–145 *in* M. Pelton. J.W. Lentfer, and G.E. Folk (eds.). Third International Conference on bear research and management. I.U.C.N. Publications, New Series No. 40, Morges, Switzerland.
35. Pelton, Michael R., Charles D. Scott and Gordon M. Burghardt. 1976. Attitudes and opinions of persons experiencing property damage and/or injury by black bears in the Great Smoky Mountains National Park. Pages 157–167 *in* Michael R. Pelton, Jack W. Lentler and G. Edgar Folk, eds. Third International Conference on bear research and management. I.U.C.N. Publications, New Series No. 40, Morges, Switzerland.

Index